The Kind of S

The Kind of Schools We Need
Personal Essays

Elliot W. Eisner

HEINEMANN • Portsmouth, NH

Heinemann
A division of Reed Elsevier Inc.
361 Hanover Street
Portsmouth, NH 03801–3912
http://www.heinemann.com

Offices and agents throughout the world

The author and publisher wish to thank those who have generously given permission to reprint borrowed material:

"Aesthetic Modes of Knowing," in *Learning and Teaching the Ways of Knowing,* Eighty-fourth Yearbook of the National Society for the Study of Education, Part 2, ed. Elliot Eisner (Chicago: University of Chicago Press, 1985), pp. 23–26.

"The Meaning of Alternative Paradigms for Practice" originally printed in *The Paradigm Dialog,* edited by Egon G. Guba, pp. 88–102. © 1990. Reprinted by permission of Sage Publications.

"Forms of Understanding and the Future of Educational Research" originally printed in *Educational Researcher* 22 (7), October 1993. Copyright 1993 by the American Educational Research Association. Reprinted by permission of the publisher.

"What a Professor Learned in the Third Grade" is reprinted with permission from F. K. Oser, A. Dick, J. L. Patry (eds.), *Effective and Responsible Teaching: The New Synthesis.* Copyright © 1992 Jossey-Bass Inc., Publishers. All rights reserved.

Acknowledgments for borrowed material continue on p. 234.

Library of Congress Cataloging-in-Publication Data
Eisner, Elliot W.
    The kind of schools we need : personal essays / Elliot W. Eisner.
      p.   cm.
    Includes bibliographical references and index.
    ISBN 0-325-00029-8 (alk. paper)
      1. Education—Philosophy. 2. Cognition. 3. Education—Research—
United States. 4. Arts—Study and teaching—United States.
5. Educational change—United States. I. Title.
    LB885.E37A3 1998
    370'.973—dc21   98-24114
                           CIP

Editor: Lois Bridges
Production: Vicki Kasabian
Cover design: Jenny Jensen Greenleaf
Cover photograph: Eric Hausman
Manufacturing: Louise Richardson

Printed in the United States of America on acid-free paper
02 01 00 99 98 EB 1 2 3 4 5

Contents

INTRODUCTION   1

COGNITION AND REPRESENTATION

1   Rethinking Literacy   9

2   The Celebration of Thinking   21

3   Aesthetic Modes of Knowing   32

4   Cognition and Representation:
A Way to Pursue the American Dream?   44

THE ARTS AND THEIR ROLE IN EDUCATION

5   What the Arts Taught Me About Education   57

6   The Education of Vision   70

7   The Misunderstood Role of the Arts in Human Development   77

8   Does Experience in the Arts Boost Academic Achievement?   87

RETHINKING EDUCATIONAL RESEARCH

9   The Meaning of Alternative Paradigms for Practice   103

10   Forms of Understanding and the Future of Educational Research   116

11   Reshaping Assessment in Education   132

12   What Artistically Crafted Research Can Help Us Understand
About Schools   149

THE PRACTICE AND REFORM OF SCHOOLS

13   Educational Reform and the Ecology of Schools   157

14   Standards for American Schools: Help or Hindrance?   175

15   What a Professor Learned in the Third Grade   188

16   Preparing Teachers for the Twenty-first Century   206

WORKS CITED   219
INDEX   225

Introduction

The essays that appear in this volume reflect four major areas of my work: arts education, the relationship of cognition and representation, qualitative research methods, and school reform. When I started my journey in the field of education an interest in research methodology was not on my horizon; *arts education* was more narrowly conceptualized as *art education;* cognition and representation were an undercurrent of my thinking, but they were not fully conscious; and school reform was conceived of as curriculum improvement. Furthermore these areas were neatly separated.

I suppose one of the gifts of maturity is an appreciation of the interrelatedness of the processes of the world. That, of course, includes the world of education. School reform depends upon some conception of what reform entails and the direction toward which it is to move. Research methods define the conditions of knowledge and, hence, what will count as evidence. The research methods considered legitimate have a profound bearing as to what will be regarded as successful reform. And as for arts education, the arts represent, at least as I see them, one of our most important means for symbolizing and sharing with others the contents of our consciousness and this surely pertains to how we represent what we have come to know. Education without attention to the arts would be an impoverished enterprise.

Some of the articles I have included in this volume explain the grounds for that conviction and why they ought to be on the reform agenda. Relationships and interactions abound, and so what was once tidy and separate has become complex and interrelated and I hope more complete. The denial of complexity leads to the use of palliatives that fail. We have had enough of them over the past two decades.

In some ways I have treated each of these interrelated areas iconoclastically. For example, the arts have long been viewed as so-called affective areas of activity. The arts, some believe, are activities you *do*, not activities you *think* much about. The arts, others believe, lead their lives in the lower part of the body: not much in the way of cognition there. I argue just the opposite. Certainly the arts appeal to human feeling, sure they traffic in the emotions, but to experience the arts the mind must be engaged and in subtle and sophisticated ways.

The arts also teach us something about the impact of the form of representation we choose to use on what we can convey. Less appreciated is the fact that what we choose to use to represent what we think also influences what we pay attention to. As E. H. Gombrich once quipped, "Artists don't paint what they can see, they see what they can paint."

As for research methods, those working within a traditional scientific paradigm have a shared conception of the meaning of warrant, objectivity, generalization, reliability, and the like. Certainly there are differences among some who share the same paradigm, but the differences tend not to be fundamental. My work has explored alternative domains. It has explored the arts and humanities as resources with which to think about and conduct educational research. In these domains the distinctions between fact and fiction, for example, is not as clear as it once was. After all, science too is a construction, and the novel as well as the survey informs us about the world. I have been interested in such matters and how they might play out as research strategies in education. At one time I thought I was pretty much alone in this interest but I have discovered that others have similar interests in other fields. In anthropology one thinks of Clifford Geertz; in psychology, Jerome Bruner; in philosophy Nelson Goodman; in aesthetics, Susanne Langer—the list could go on. It's in the air and it's reflected in the content of research journals and in the programs of national research meetings.

As for school reform, it was once viewed as essentially curriculum reform; school reform in the post-Sputnik era, to consider one instance, *was* curriculum reform, one subject at a time from the top down—high school before middle school, middle school before elementary school. We did not think of school reform organically, or as I like to think about it, ecologically. We didn't fully realize that more often than not the school would change the message before the message would change the school. I credit my training as a painter to my interest in looking at schools organically, as biological forms, really. Organicism has had a long history in aesthetic theory and the perception of relationships is part of the stock-in-trade of being a painter.

The style these essays take are reflective in character and, I hope, literary in feel. They emanate from my experience in schools as a student, a teacher, and a researcher. In that sense they are empirical: their empiricism is the empiricism of direct experience, which, after all, is the root meaning of the term empirical, but they are not quantitative; language suits my style better and so I use it—or try to craft it—to say what often cannot be reduced to literal language or displayed in coefficients. There is no rule and certainly no logical necessity for empirical work to be quantitative or statistical. Precisely because the worlds we care about can be represented in different ways and because each form of representation we use imposes its own constraints and provides its own affordances, each has its own unique contribution to make to the enlargement of human understanding. One of my aims is to explore the potential new research forms have for the study and improvement of schools. I also hope to encourage others to do so as well.

Related to the iconoclastic character of these essays is another aim, that of problematizing some of the traditional and unexamined assumptions upon which educational practice rests. Acculturation not only enables us to adapt successfully to the culture in which we are situated, it also binds us to the forms that pervade that culture. The taken for granted is seldom seen. The best of the sciences and the arts affords us a fresh view and awakens us to new possibilities. These new possibilities are the children of the imagination. But to bring about productive change also requires an ability to problematize the given, to question existing and often comfortable forms of practice, forms that sustain the status quo. When the status quo works quite well for some groups, it can be hard to change for others. One place to begin is by examining assumptions.

Why, for example, do we group children by age rather than by interest? Why do children shift teachers each year? Why do high school students move from class to class every fifty minutes rather than having the teacher move? Why do we assume that the mark of excellence in teaching is getting all the students to the same place at about the same point in time? Why do we assume the public display of the measured performance of students will improve the quality of education?

Whether or not there is a better way than the ways we now use to organize and conduct schooling is beside the point. It might be the "best" way, but that cannot be determined until we examine the assumptions upon which current practices rest and consider alternatives. I believe we ought to be asking such questions and dreaming up other visions and considering other versions of what schools might be like—or, as they say, what's a heaven for?

All of one's writing is rooted in one's own biography. My biography has been fed by three streams. The first stream grew out of my experience as a child overhearing and later participating in discussions at the dinner table with my parents on questions of social justice, economic equity issues, and matters of civil rights. There was little talk about the arts or education as such, but there was a passionate display of the pleasures of debate and discussion and although I didn't know it at the time, these discussions have had a profound effect upon me for they demonstrated how much fun you could have when you were engaged in the critical examination of ideas. Since neither of my parents finished high school, it was clear that this process did not require certification by diploma or degree. It was there if you wanted it—and it was free.

A second stream developed through my participation in the visual arts as a painter and now as an avid collector of art. The arts taught me that the rush that comes from contemplating a well-crafted work or the feeling that flows from attention to nuance in, say, a Song vessel were not qualities of experience that could be reduced to number or mechanical routine. There is more to life than what is describable by the literal. The arts taught me that form, craft, and imagination mattered; and that surprise could be a friend, not an inconvenient intruder. Art, like the debates in my home when I was growing up, helped shape my attitude toward the life of the mind and made possible the satisfactions I receive from well-crafted form.

The third stream that influenced my thinking about education resided in my experience as a graduate student at the University of Chicago. I did not do well in either elementary or secondary school; I graduated in the 32nd percentile of my high school graduation class and even to achieve this rank I needed the A grades I received from four years of art classes I took in the high school I attended. But Chicago was another story. At the University of Chicago I found a place that felt like home. Many of the issues we debated at Chicago—class, race, equity—were those we debated at home. They were very familiar to me. Chicago felt like a pair of old slippers; in this talmudic institution ideas mattered. At Chicago I found not only an array of impressive intellects, but to my surprise, I found a career. Becoming a professor seemed quite nice. So much for career planning!

Another lesson the University of Chicago taught me was that institutions have their effects by virtue of the milieu they create as well as by the personalities and intellects of those who teach. And there were memorable personalities and intellect there. In education it was my good fortune to study with Benjamin Bloom, Philip Jackson, Bruno Bettelheim, John Goodlad, Jack Getzels, Robert Havighurst, and Joseph Schwab. It was a mighty impressive lot. At Chicago the intellectual atmosphere was palpable. As I said, ideas were taken seriously and you had better be prepared to defend the ideas you advanced. It was an intellectually tough place.

It became clear to me that our schools needed also to provide a milieu that reflected the values we claimed to care about. Put more broadly, schools were in the business of creating a culture in the two senses in which the term *culture* can be used—as a way of life and as a medium for growing things. The creation of that culture has something to do not only with developing the student's cognitive skills but with creating dispositional outcomes as well. Call it conation or call it will, desire provides the wind to fill the sails to move the boat and intellect the rudder to determine direction. With no wind in the sails there will be no movement forward, and with no rudder there will be no direction. The lesson is obvious.

There is another lesson I learned over the years and this one can be regarded as depressing or as exciting. It is this: Education will not have permanent solutions to its problems, we will have no "breakthroughs," no enduring discoveries that will work forever. We are "stuck" with temporary resolutions rather than with permanent solutions. What works here may not work there. What works now may not work then. We are not trying to invent radar or measure the rate of free fall in a vacuum. Our tasks are impacted by context, riddled with unpredictable contingencies, responsive to local conditions, and shaped by those we teach and not only by those who teach. Those who want something easier to do for a career should go into medicine.

But it is the very complexity and uncertainty of education that gives it its exciting presence. Clinical skills and artistry will always be required to do something really well and the field of education in the variety of its manifestations—teaching, curriculum development, educational leadership, assessment practice—will always provide a place for artistry. Considered pragmatically, there will always be work to do!

The concept of artistry has not received a great deal of attention in education's scholarly literature. We have been more enamored with developing a science of practice than an art of practice—until quite recently. Yet, even now there is an ambivalence in the quest for an art of practice. It is science that reveals dependable regularities, it is science that discovers causes and effects, it is science that provides precision, it is science that produces trustworthy generalizations, it is science that offers cogent explanations that satisfy our curiosity and assuage our rationality. What can the arts do for us?

It has become increasingly clear, even by those most ardent about the uses of scientific knowledge in education that the contingencies of local circumstance cannot be addressed adequately by the general claims that any of the social sciences provide for scientific conclusions are not only partial—each social science addresses less than what needs attention in making wise and prudent decisions—they cannot take into account the unique particulars with which the practitioner must deal. As Joseph Schwab colorfully once put it, science tells us about the Gurnseyness of Gurnsey cows, not about Old Betsy. Teachers deal with Old Betsy. In dealing with Old Betsy teachers must rely on sensibility, imagination, prudence, and technique, as well as whatever theoretical considerations suit the situation. Theory without artistry is feckless, and artistry without theory is uninformed. We need both. The educational scholar's task is to see the educational world through the lenses of both the arts and the sciences. As Ernst Cassirer once mentioned, that's the only way we secure binocular vision and through it, depth of field.

If the emphasis in my writing has focused on the *what* that the arts have to contribute to education it is because the sciences have been almost exclusively in the limelight; they needed no help from me. I am trying to correct an imbalance. It is also because—if truth be told—the arts have been a central part of my life. I work best when I play to my strengths. But I do not want to be read as a one-eyed theoretician; as Cassirer said, we need binocular vision to have depth of field. I hope my work has contributed to the sharpness of at least one of the lenses.

COGNITION AND REPRESENTATION

Education can be regarded as a process concerned with expanding and deepening the kinds of meaning people can have in their lives. The construction of meaning depends upon the individual's ability to experience and interpret the significance of the environment, including the ways in which others in the culture have constructed and represented meaning. Forms of representation—visual, auditory, kinesthetic, linguistic, mathematical—are ways in which members of a culture uniquely "encode" and "decode" meaning. The meanings that can be secured from music, for example, have no identical counterpart in any other form. Composers make sound meaningful by the way they organize it, artists by the way in which they compose visual images, writers and poets by the way in which they treat language, mathematicians in the forms they employ to describe quantitative relationships.

The ability to secure meaning from such forms is not innate; rather, it is developed and this development typically is affected by a school's curriculum.

In one sense, this ability to encode and decode meaning can be thought of as a form of literacy. (By literacy I do not simply mean skill in using language conventionally, but rather in expressing meaning through any medium.) Literacy, as I'm using the term here, does not refer to one type of meaning making, but many. And schools have as one of their important functions the development of multiple forms of literacy—that is, the development of the student's ability to secure meaning from the arts, the sciences, mathematics, and, indeed, from any of the social forms from which it can be construed.

The ability to "make sense" out of forms of representation is not merely a way of securing meaning—as important as that may be—it is also a way of developing cognitive skills. The forms of thinking that students are able to use are profoundly influenced by the kind of experience they are able to have. Thus the school's curriculum is important. Of course, no teacher or curriculum developer can ensure that one kind of experience will be had rather than another for any particular student; they can, however, control content and shape tasks in their classroom or school, organizing classroom conditions that influence the student's experience. These experiences, in turn, affect learning; they help shape the forms of intelligence that students have the opportunity to acquire. Thus, the student's cognitive development is affected by the forms of representation available to them.

To speak of cognition often conjures up a bloodless form of thinking that somehow is disconnected from matters of affect. Nothing could be further from the truth. All thinking, especially all productive thinking, is infused with feeling. Feeling permeates the forms of thinking we employ and provides us with the information we need to make judgments about the quality of our work. Mind is not separated from affect; affect is part and parcel of mind. Thus, for the refinement of cognitive skills to be fully developed, it must in some way be emotionalized. In Part 1, I address these matters by examining the connections between cognition and representation.

1

Rethinking Literacy

The term *literacy* conjures up an image of reading and writing. Its etymology relates to "tongue"; to be literate is to be able to do what the tongue makes possible: to speak, to inscribe language into text, and to decode text in order to secure the meanings embedded within it. To be literate in America is to be able to construe or express meaning in written language.

There is little doubt that many of the meanings we secure in our lives are derived from what we read, but there is even less doubt that meaning is not restricted to what we find in text and that text, in fact, constitutes a small portion of the stuff out of which meaning is made. The virtue of literacy is, of course, that it makes meaning possible. Neither reading nor writing would be of value if it did not serve as an instrumentality through which we create and share meaning. As processes, reading and writing are not employed *primarily* as sources of deep intrinsic satisfaction. While we may say we enjoy reading, what we mean is that we enjoy reading when the text is enjoyable to read. This means the way the text is formed, the content it possesses, and the images it helps us generate are the sources of our satisfaction. Reading dull material is not a satisfying experience. Thus, literacy serves an important cognitive function: constructing and sharing meaning.

Because meaning is the core of literacy, we can (and I believe we ought to) conceive of literacy in terms broader than is customary. Literacy can be conceived of as the ability to decode or encode meaning in any of the social forms through which meaning is conveyed (Eisner 1994). And just how is meaning conveyed? What forms are employed? What role can the school play in developing what might be regarded as multiple forms of literacy?

This article explores these questions in order to provide a broader, more generous conception of literacy and, through such a conception, to provide a foundation for creating more educationally equitable programs in our schools.

First, it should be noted that even when one's conception of literacy is restricted to language, the forms language takes are quite diverse. One form of language is propositional: it is designed to provide precise relationships between subject and predicate and to diminish ambiguity—to the extent possible—between the linguistic terms employed and their referents. The language of science is an exemplar of propositional language. Mathematics, a nonlinguistic language, is the most compelling example of a precise "propositional" form.

Although the language of science is at its best highly precise, it is not without its metaphors and images (see, for example, Nisbett 1976). But for the most refined use of metaphor, and for the exploitation of form in the service of meaning, we go not to science, but to the humanities, particularly literature. Here we have another form of language. Literary meaning is not simply a function of the truth of propositional claims or semantic precision, it is also a function of the way in which a writer crafts language. In literary forms, cadence and tempo matter. Voice counts. Tropes and allusions signify and suggest. Ambiguity may serve meaning, not detract from it. Being literate in literature means knowing how to construe meaning from the literary forms one reads. The skills required are not the same as those employed in reading the language of physics—or law for that matter. Most of us seek an attorney to read important contracts before we sign them. Even though we say we can read, we recognize that in some domains—contracts, for example—it is more accurate to say we cannot.

Poetry employs meaning systems that differ as much from literature as literature differs from science. Poetry may have no propositions whatsoever. Indeed, the primary meanings of poetry, like some of those in literature, are nondiscursive; that is, poetic meaning is obtained from the forms the language takes. These forms convey what, paradoxically, words cannot say. In the case of concrete poets, e. e. cummings, for example, the way words are arranged on a page—the visual composition of a poem—is a part of its meaning system. What we see increasingly are poets exploiting the capacities of space itself to serve poetic meaning. The genres are being blurred.

Poetry is a form refined from what might be called vernacular poetics. I speak here of the use of slang and the neologisms created by preschoolers. The term *yucky* conveys most aptly the sense of revulsion children express through its use; the sound of the word fits the experience children wish to convey. Similarly, slang is a linguistic invention that creates meanings that challenge and elude conventional discourse. In a sense, the invention of new slang words makes certain ideas, comments, observations, and feelings vivid. They *de*familiarize the objects or events they signify so that we can regard them in a fresh way; they diminish the stock response.

The acquisition of literacy in one form cannot be used to predict literacy in another. One might be able to "read" the meanings of slang, but not those of poetry. One might be able to experience the flight that literature makes possible and be stymied by poetry. One might find the language of biology lucid and experience literature as a morass of ambiguity that obscures rather than reveals. To talk about literacy as if it were a single skill applicable to all forms of text is to underestimate the special demands that different forms of language exact.

A useful set of distinctions between two major language forms has been offered by Jerome Bruner. He calls these *paradigmatic* and *narrative* (Bruner 1985). Figure 1–1 displays the distinctive features of each. The paradigmatic, most vividly exemplified in the language of science, places an emphasis on reference, that is, on the tightness of the connection between the symbol and its referent. Narrative, best exemplified in the arts and humanities, places its emphasis on sense; how a situation, person, or object "feels." The paradigmatic seeks precision through the singular, while the narrative emphasizes configuration. The paradigmatic tries to achieve what is definite and does this through denotation. It cherishes certainty, it emphasizes causality, and it defines meaning in terms of verification. Narrative, however, prizes the metaphorical, emphasizes connotation, exploits ambiguity to convey meanings that are suggested by it, and speaks of intention or purpose or agency rather than cause. What narrative provides is believability or "truth-likeness," rather than *truth* in a verified scientific sense. Unlike the paradigmatic, the narrative is context sensitive and applies, in Bruner's view, to local or particular situations, while works of science are considered context free and universal. Bruner indicates that in paradigmatic discourse, one attempts to mean what one says. In narrative discourse, one means more than one says; the text is open to interpretation.

The central point that Bruner makes is an epistemological one: different forms of language make different forms of knowing possible. What we can come to understand through literary forms cannot be revealed through the propositional discourse of science. Conversely, what science can help us understand cannot be disclosed through literary form. Each language form has its own epistemic function. (For an example of this argument, see Goodman 1976.)

Thus far, I have devoted my attention to the different meaning systems

Paradigmatic	Narrative
(Exemplified in Science)	(Exemplified in the Arts and Humanities)
Emphasis on:	**Emphasis on:**
Reference	Sense
The Singular	Configuration
Definite	Metaphorical
Denotation	Connotation
Certainty	Ambiguity
Cause	Intention
Verification	Believability
Context-Free	Context Sensitive
"Truth"	Truth-likeness

Figure 1–1. Forms of knowing

within language: scientific or paradigmatic and literary, poetic, and vernacular, or what Bruner calls narrative. Language, whether formed in poetry or science, is only one modality through which humans construe and convey meaning, as I indicated earlier. Literacy is broader than language because the meaning systems humans have invented to convey meaning are broader than language.

Just where are these other meaning systems to be found? Upon reflection it becomes clear that they are nearby: Meaning is conveyed in the visual forms we call art, architecture, film, and video. It emerges in the patterned sound we call music. It appears first in human experience in movement, then gesture, and then dance. It emerges in the ways in which social relationships are constructed through the rites and rituals that represent and express our highest aspirations and deepest fears. Becoming literate, in the broad sense, means learning how to access in a meaningful way the forms of life that these meaning systems make possible. What we ought to be developing in our schools is not simply a narrow array of literacy skills limited to a restrictive range of meaning systems, but a spectrum of literac*ies* that will enable students to participate in, enjoy, and find meaning in the major forms through which meaning has been constituted. We need a conception of multiple literacies to serve as a vision of what our schools should seek to achieve.

Why should such a vision guide educational policy and practice? What is it about such literacies that give them special value? To answer these questions we must turn to the biologically given features of the human organism; specifically, we must turn to the cognitive functions of our sensory system (Eisner 1982).

The newborn child entering the qualitative world we inhabit comes equipped to experience the world's qualities through all of his or her sensory modalities. Although there is some evidence that even the prenatal child responds to environmental stimuli such as sound, it is in the world that we share with the newborn that the child's sensory system develops most fully. For most developmental psychologists, the concept of development refers to a biological process that more or less unfolds according to a genetically planned program. Piaget, for example, trained initially as a biologist, thought of himself as a *genetic* epistemologist.[6] His core question was: How do children's conceptions of reality change over time? His aim was to describe the universal, structural regularities of cognitive development not specific to culture (Case in press). In a sense, his concerns with human development are like the concerns of ecologists or naturalists. Their main activity is descriptive, and out of description grows theory, the product of further reflection designed to account for what has been given an account. Educators, however, are not primarily concerned with development, although development is certainly an important educational consideration. Educators are concerned with facilitating learning and engendering intrinsically satisfying forms of experience and do so with respect to certain values. Education, fundamentally, is a normative enterprise. It is not concerned with the mere change, but with the enhancement of life.

The programs we provide in schools, what we include and what we exclude, what we emphasize and what we minimize, what we assign prime time and what we assign to the remainder, reflect the directions in which we believe children should grow. Educators help shape minds, and the curriculum we provide is one of the most important tools we use in this process. The curriculum is, in this view, a mind-altering device (Eisner 1985).

The biological features of the newborn provide resources in defining the direction development can take. Among the primary resources the child possesses is a sensory system that enables the child to experience the qualitative world he or she enters. I say *qualitative* world because the objects and processes which we eventually label are, at base, qualities. Sweetness is experienced by the child long before it is assigned a name. Sound is experienced before it is described as soft or loud. Touch is felt before it is characterized as a caress or a slap. The world of experience is a world rooted in qualities, and the ability to "read" these qualities is an ability that can be developed throughout life.

As children mature, their ability to read qualities grows. As they get older, their perceptions become increasingly differentiated and they see more and more of the qualities they attend to (Arnheim 1990). Along with this gradual development comes the acquisition of language. Children learn to label the qualities they explored so intensively earlier. The child who sucks, rattles, touches, tastes, and experiments with a toy or found object now assigns it to a nameable category. All too often when this occurs, exploration diminishes. Categorization replaces exploration. Recognition replaces perception (see Dewey 1934, Chapter 3).

It is interesting and significant that kindergarten teachers often encourage children to use their senses to explore materials and tasks. When the educational stakes are still modest, there is time and even merit for such activities, but once the child moves into the first grade, the grade in which the "real" business of schooling begins in earnest, teachers seem to have less time for such matters. Grade-earning and teacher-pleasing gradually become more important to children than securing the satisfactions a sensuous world makes possible.

There is no question that the acquisition of language has some important cognitive functions. Some ideas are neither thinkable nor knowable without language. At the same time, language, as a privileged form of representation, exacts a price (Rorty 1979). Language can homogenize; that is, it tends to treat things as members of a class—that is an oak tree, this is a cat, that is a house, . . . a cloud, . . . a dog. No doubt, classification is crucial. But oak trees are not all alike, nor are cats, dogs, houses, or clouds. To the extent that classification short-circuits the perceptual exploration of the individuality of objects and events, it undermines what can be known about them. In the ideal world we need to encourage and develop not only the ability to classify, but also the appetite to individuate (Arnheim 1990). Indeed, the child needs to learn—and he does learn—that his mother is not only his mother, but a woman. He also needs to learn that not every woman is his mother.

The particular aspects of the qualitative world about which we become aware depend on the degree to which our sensory system has developed an acuteness for the phenomena that populate some domain. One learns to make fine-grained discriminations about the conformation of English setters if one cares about English setters, has taken pains to attend to their conformation, has schemata with which to notice them, and is able to see. Collectively these skills enable us to experience what others are likely to miss. We gradually develop sophisticated levels of connoisseurship in those areas of life in which we have special interests. (For a full discussion of the concept of connoisseurship, see Eisner 1991.) This achievement is what provides consciousness with the content it needs to function. The sensibilities provide a fundamental means through which such consciousness is achieved. As Jacob Bronowsky used to say, "There is nothing in the head that was not first in the hand." Put another way, it is our sensory system that enables us to get in touch with the world. Each sensory modality enables us to experience the world in ways that are distinctive. What we come to know about autumn, for example, depends as much on our ability to experience the crispness of an October evening, the scent of burning leaves, and the warm tones of turning trees as it has to do with its location on the Gregorian calendar. What autumn means is intimately related to its qualities, and phenomenologically its qualities depend upon what we can experience. What we can experience depends upon an intact sensory system and how well we can use it. It is through experience that the content literacy makes possible is acquired.

In many ways it is odd that we often neglect this content when we talk about reading or writing. Words are so automatic a resource we forget that, aside from the forms they display, their meaning depends upon referents. We tend to take the map to the territory. It is wiser to regard language as cues to referents that are nonlinguistic. Indeed, imagination is central in the process, for we cannot know through language what we cannot imagine. The image—visual, tactile, auditory—plays a crucial role in the construction of meaning through text. Those who cannot imagine cannot read (Broudy 1987).

But literacy, as I have indicated earlier, is not limited to text. It relates to the ability to construe meaning in any of the forms used in the culture to create and convey meaning. What cannot be conveyed or constructed in words is often possible in visual images or in music. Becoming literate in the broad sense means learning how to read these images. The reason the ability to read these images is so important has to do with three critically significant educational aims. The first is the aim of increasing the variety and depth of meaning people can secure in their lives. The second pertains to the development of cognitive potential and the third to the provision of educational equity in our schools.

Aristotle wrote long ago, "All men by nature desire knowledge" (McKeon 1941). Knowing, at base, is a personal form of human experience. This experience is guided, evoked, stimulated, and cued by both nature and culture. Nature provides resources in terms of the world as it naturally occurs, and culture provides those forms created by human beings that serve as amplifiers for our cognition. The natural world that we encounter is experienced through our own developed sensibilities, and these, in turn, are assisted by the tools that culture has made available. For example, we learn to think about human development more acutely by understanding psychological theories and other ideas about the course of its growth. We learn to see the patterns of light and shadow on a city street by seeing photographs and paintings of such qualities made by artists. We come to understand the depths of tragedy by reading novels and seeing plays. We come to comprehend the organization of families and schools through the tools that sociological and organizational theory make possible. Each cultural device functions as an amplifier for capturing and examining some aspects of the world we inhabit. In fact, Nelson Goodman (1978) has argued that there are as many worlds as there are ways to describe them. If education as a process is aimed at expanding and deepening the kinds of meanings that people can have in their lives, and if literacy is conceptualized as a process concerned with the construction and communication of meaning, then school programs must attempt to provide time for the development of multiple forms of literacy. Not to do so is to create an epistemological parochialism that limits what people can experience and, therefore, what they can come to know.

Literacy is far more than being able to read or to write. Such conceptions are educationally anemic and shortchange children in the long run. The development of human sensibility and the provision of programs that address the several ways in which experience has been represented—propositional, literary, poetic, visual, auditory, choreographic—ought to be fundamental educational aims. Regrettably, many of these representational forms are made marginal in our programs.[1] We simply do not see far enough.

The second aim, the development of cognitive potential, is predicated on the belief that human cognitive abilities are not simply given and fixed at birth; they are achieved. What people are able to do in the course of their lives, in large measure, is a function of the opportunities they have to learn. The school curriculum is the major vehicle through which we define those opportunities. When we include forms of representation such as art, music, dance, poetry, and literature in our programs, we not only develop forms of literacy, we also develop particular cognitive potentialities. What one does not or is not permitted to use, one loses. Mind is a form of cultural achievement, and the school programs we develop and implement help define the kinds of minds that children will be given an opportunity to own. The curriculum also represents symbolically the cognitive virtues that we value. Thus, the realization of cognitive potential depends upon the opportunities that children have to use their minds in the variety of ways minds can be used. Access to a wide variety of forms of representation not only makes the development of multiple forms of literacy possible, it cultivates the forms of skilled thinking in which children can be engaged.

The distilled forms of thinking that I refer to are developed most especially through the process of representation. Each array of qualities— visual, auditory, gestural, as well as linguistic and numerical—requires different forms of attention and imposes demands peculiar to its "nature." Musical cognition requires the individual to think about, experiment with, and control patterned sound. The ability to write poetically requires skill in the creation of allusion and an ear for the melody of language. Visual art makes demands upon the student's ability to perceive emerging opportunities on the canvas, paper, or clay and to control material well enough to mediate the possibilities he or she conceives.

It is noteworthy that the syntactical structures of poetry, music, and visual art are open-ended and depend upon the creation of figurative relations. There are no specific rules to follow and no algorithms to employ to determine when a solution is correct. Indeed, the notion of correctness itself is inappropriate in such matters. "Rightness of fit," as Nelson Goodman (1978, 109–40) calls it, is much more apt. What students must do is to think in a form that allows them to judge rightness of fit. This process requires attention to patterns or configurations, it focuses on wholes rather than on discrete elements, and it obeys no conventional set of rules. Tasks such as these are extremely demanding. Indeed, one of the most difficult tasks a student confronts is answering the question, When am I finished? The development of literacy in those forms we call the arts makes an important contribution to the development of such cognitive skills.

But these contributions do not exhaust the matter. The very act of representation is a transformation of an internal state into the public world. In a sense, representation involves externalizing the internal, making public what is private. The virtue of this process is that it stabilizes what is evanescent. Nothing is so slippery as a thought; here one moment, gone the next. Through inscription, image construction, recorded movement, and sound, a permanence is conferred upon an idea that makes another intellectual virtue possible.

The virtue I speak of is secured through the editing process. Once an idea is fixed in the public medium, it becomes possible not only to stabilize thought, but to increase its precision. Editing is concerned with the refinement of one's thinking and representation makes refinement possible. Another cognitive function of representation is that once ideas are made public, they can be shared with others. We often take such matters for granted, but we should not. There is an enormous mystery in the transformation of our internal life into its public equivalents and in our ability to share with others the meanings we have constructed.

The overlap, of course, between public interpretation of our ideas and our own is never perfect, yet communication—literally, the holding of something in common—is made possible through this process. Finally, representation as a process is not simply an activity that provides a channel for ideas to pass from the head, through the hand, into the material, it also provides an arena for the discovery, or, better yet, the occasion for the creation of ideas one did not have at the outset: The act of representation is also an act of invention. Representation is not a monologue; it is a dialogue between the individual actor and the material acted upon. These four processes—stabilization, editing, sharing, and the discovery of new ideas—make extremely important contributions to the development of our cognitive capabilities.

Third, although I have argued that mind is largely made, I do not assume that children come into the world with blank slates in their cortexes, awaiting the impression of the cultural environment. Children differ genetically with respect to their intellectual proclivities (Gardner 1983). And because they do, the differences among them need to be taken into account in educational policy and practice. Each child in our schools should be given an opportunity to find a place in our educational sun. This means designing educational programs that enable children to play to their strengths, to pursue and exploit those meaning systems for which they have special aptitudes or interests. Educational equity is provided to the young not simply by giving them access to our schools, but by providing programs that enable them to become what they have the potential to be once they pass through the schoolhouse door. Indeed, I would argue that the genuinely good school increases individual differences, it does not diminish them.[2] A genuine educational process cultivates productive idiosyncrasy, it does not homogenize children into standardized forms. Neither the cookie cutter nor the assembly line is an apt model for education. The studio is a much more congenial image. Teachers define opportunities and stimulate direction. They lead children and, at times, take their lead from them. Providing opportunities within school for children to pursue what they have a feel for—to follow their bliss, as Joseph Campbell used to say—is not an inappropriate policy for guiding educational practice.

There are two other points that need to be made. First, attention to the distinctive functions of various forms of representation has been provided by a number of important philosophers. Ernst Cassirer (1961), Susanne Langer (1942), and, more recently, Nelson Goodman (1978) have addressed the epistemic functions of symbol systems. Educators, in contrast, and especially educational psychologists, have paid comparatively little attention to such matters. Most studies of cognition focus on word and number as if these forms exhausted the means through which thinking and representation occur. In other words, the argument I have developed here is rooted in a body of scholarship that is not new.

Second, although I have emphasized the need for a broader, more generous conception of literacy, the argument I have developed is, in my view, wider than the argument advanced by E. D. Hirsch (1987) in his book *Cultural Literacy.* I am not primarily concerned with making sure that students possess a large pool of cultural icons, as important as this might be. I am concerned with developing the intellectual skills necessary to know how to read a wide variety of forms through which meaning is conveyed. This aspiration is both more ambitious and less prescriptive than the acquisition of the content of a cultural dictionary (Hirsch 1988). It is concerned with the development of skills that can be employed whenever poems, paintings, products of science, history, and other such materials are publicly available. In other words, my concerns are aimed at developing a versatility in language systems, not simply acquiring a codified canon of content.

It should be said that Hirsch's aims are not limited to such a canon, but since he underplays the skills of inquiry I believe are important, our views on this matter take different turns and have a different cast.

Throughout this article, I have tried to argue a case for a broader, more catholic conception of literacy than the one that prevails both in our professional literature and in our schools. There is no reason whatsoever why literacy should be restricted to the decoding of written text. Humans are makers of meaning, and the forms that culture contains have been invented to convey meanings that could not be conveyed in any other way. If we are concerned with cultivating in the young a broad capacity to construct meaning, we must provide in our schools the opportunities they need in order to learn how to do so. This, in turn, will require a fundamental reconceptualization of how we think about our educational priorities and how we conceptualize human cognition. Humans think not only in language, but also in visual images, in gestural ones, and in patterned sound. The surest way to create semiliterate graduates from American secondary schools is to insure that many of the most important forms through which meaning is represented will be enigmas to our students, codes they cannot crack.

I know that the agenda I am suggesting is formidable. It is much easier to write about such aspirations than to realize them. It is simpler to formulate educational policy than to alter educational practice. Yet, who among us wishes to devote his or her adult life to practices that inadvertently limit rather than expand human potential? Who among us prefers succeeding at the educationally mediocre to failing—if we must—at the genuinely important? The development of multiple forms of literacy is one goal worth our efforts. The first step on the road toward that goal is more certain with clarity of vision. This article is intended to describe the contours of that vision.

Notes

1. Unfortunately, many universities do not consider students' grades in the fine arts when they calculate grade point averages for purposes of making admissions decisions. This practice not only assigns a second-class status to the arts, but conveys to students, teachers, and parents that course work in these areas can be regarded as educational liabilities.

2. For a lovely argument concerning the importance of cultivating individual differences, see Herbert Read, *Education Through Art* (London: Pantheon, 1944). Read argues that there are two principles that can guide education: one is to help children become what they are, the other is to help them become what they are not. The latter is pursued by fascist societies that try to mold children into an image defined by the state. The former is pursued in democratic cultures in which individuality is prized and fostered.

2

The Celebration of Thinking

Celebration has a spirit that is rare in discussions of American schooling. Celebration connotes joy, ceremony, something special in experience. Celebrations are events we look forward to, occasions we prize. The celebration of thinking suggests honoring and joy in a process we all consider central to education. Yet, there are schools without celebration. Those of us who work in education today are admonished to get serious, to tighten up, to excise the so-called soft side of school programs. This can be done by specifying a common curriculum or prescribing the steps that teachers should take to teach students. Both Alan Bloom in *The Closing of the American Mind* and E. D. Hirsch in *Cultural Literacy: What Every American Needs to Know* come close to such solutions, the former in the name of intellect, the latter in the name of culture.

Specifying a common curriculum neglects student idiosyncrasies and aptitude differences by assuming that in curricular matters one size fits all. The specification of teaching method appeals to our sense of technic, a technology of practice that is deduced from research that aims to assure, if not guarantee results.[1] The most common pedagogical procedure for such a technology is the breaking up of content into small units, prescribing a uniform sequence among those units, and using an objective, multiple-choice test to measure learning. Both approaches to school improvement, if they celebrate anything, celebrate standardized content, standardized method, standardized objectives measured by standardized tests.

The idea that education is best served by standardizing method, content, goals, and evaluation procedures leads to another consequence. It tends to convert education into a race. Those who achieve goals most quickly win.

This attitude is expressed in the proliferation of preschools, the academic formalization of kindergarten, the creation of better baby institutes, and the all too common syndrome of the hurried child (Elkind 1981). At more advanced levels, this attitude is represented in the growth of Stanley Kaplan schools and the specialized high school courses on the SATs. Yet, speed in accomplishing tasks is not particularly compatible with the concept of celebration. Events that we celebrate are events we like to prolong. Efficiency and speed in completing a task are characteristic of tasks that are distasteful. We look to clean our kitchen or the toilet bowl efficiently, but who likes to eat a great meal efficiently? What we enjoy, we wish to savor.

My argument here is not to prolong teaching and learning for its own sake, but rather to recognize that speed is no necessary virtue. Getting through the curriculum in the shortest possible time is a virtue when the program is noxious. Thinking should be prized not only because it leads to attractive destinations, but because the journey itself is satisfying.[2]

Language and Knowledge

It is the nature of thinking and the forms through which it occurs that I wish to focus on in this article. In American schools, as in European schools, thinking is often conceptualized as both an abstract and linguistic process. Thinking, like knowledge itself, is argued by some to depend on language. To have true knowledge, one must be able to make a claim about the world that can be verified. The truth or falsity of a belief can be determined only if the belief can be stated in words, not just any words, but propositions. Without propositions there is no claim. Without a claim there is no test; without a test there is no verification. Without verification there is no knowledge (Phillips 1983). The argument goes further. To state propositions one must be able to think in a propositional form. Indeed, some claim it is language itself that makes thinking possible (Schaff 1973).

For schools, such a view has meant that language has been assigned a place of privilege in our educational priorities, in our time allocations, and in our concept of intelligence itself. I need not remind you that the best predictor of IQ is the vocabulary subtest on the IQ test. The SATs have two sections, verbal and mathematical. So do the GREs. Human intellectual ability, the ability to think, is made almost isomorphic with the ability to use language or number.

My aim here is to challenge that view. I wish to portray a concept of mind, of thinking, of intelligence that is not restricted to language. Any limited view of intellect will penalize students whose aptitudes reside outside its boundaries. If schools aim at cultivating intellect, those whose aptitudes lie in forms of thinking that are excluded from the accepted concept of intellect will also be excluded from a place in our educational sun. So will students whose aptitudes are in the use of language; for language itself, I will argue, depends on forms of thinking and intelligence that relate to the qualitative aspects of our experience.

A Biological Basis for Thinking and Learning

Humans do not enter the world with minds, but with brains. The task of education, acculturation, and socialization is to convert brains into minds. Brains are born, and minds are made; and one of the privileges of the teaching profession is to have an important part to play in the shaping of minds.

The major means through which this feat is accomplished is through the curriculum and the quality of the process through which it is mediated, teaching. Together they define the quality of what students learn in school, at least its formal or explicit part. The curriculum, in this sense, can be thought of as a mind-altering device, a way of changing minds; and teachers are those who help define the direction of the change and mediate and monitor its processes.

Our definition of school curricula reflects views of mind that we believe are important. Our culture regards language skills as important and defines intelligence as the ability to handle abstract, language-based tasks. However, I will argue here that the senses are part of thinking and intelligence and, hence, another basis for deciding about the content and goals of our school programs.

Traditionally we have separated mind from body. The separation is Platonic. For Plato, mind was lofty and body was base (*Republic,* Book Seven [Plato 1941]). Working with one's head was different and more noble than working with one's hands. Today, we have manual trade schools for those who are good with their hands, but really bright students take physics. The separation, this unfortunate dichotomy, is philosophically naive, psychologically ill-conceived, and educationally mischievous. There is no competent work of the hand that does not depend on the competent use of mind. The mind and senses are one, not two.

Our world is first a qualitative world. We are able to experience color, texture, smell, and sounds—qualities that permeate our world. Becoming conscious of that world or some aspect of it depends on a *skilled* and intact sensory system. We often do not think of the senses as being skilled; they just are there. However, the qualities of the world are not simply given to human experience, they must be won. Experience is not simply an act or event, it is an achievement. We learn to see and hear. We learn to read the subtle qualitative cues that constitute the environment. We learn to distinguish and differentiate between kittens, squirrels, and puppies. Eventually, if we care enough, we are able to see qualities in Irish setters, golf clubs, fine wines, antique cabinets, Japanese pots, and the complex nuances of American football that others miss. If we care enough and work hard enough we *achieve* experiences. We become connoisseurs of some aspect of the world.

Making such distinctions, noticing, becoming perceptive, depends on sensory differentiation. Our first avenue to consciousness, the refinement of sensibilities, ought to be a prime aim of education. It is through cultivated and refined sensibility that patterns in nature and culture are distinguished. From these patterns, works of science and art are built. The centrality of this process of mind was articulated more than forty years ago by one of America's greatest aestheticians, Susanne Langer. Writing in *Philosophy in a New Key,* she said:

> The nervous system is the organ of the mind; its center is the brain, its extremities the sense-organs; and any characteristic function it may possess must govern the work of all its parts. In other words, the activity of our senses is "mental" not only when it reaches the brain, but in its very inception, whenever the alien world outside impinges on the furthest and smallest receptor. All sensitivity bears the stamp of mentality. "Seeing," for instance, is not a passive process, by which meaningless impressions are stored up for the use of an organizing mind, which construes forms out of these amorphous data to suit its own purposes. "Seeing" is itself a process of formulation; our understanding of the visible world begins in the eye. (1942, 84)

Alas, the lesson Susanne Langer was trying to teach, not only in this paragraph, but in her remarkable book, never took hold in American educational theory or in American public schools. It has only been in recent years that psychologists such as Howard Gardner (1983) have re-emphasized the multiple nature of human intelligence.

Remembering and Imagining

The development of the sensibilities not only provides us with access to the qualities of the world, it is through the content of such experience that we are able to perform two very important cognitive operations—remembering and imagining. The sensibilities, a part of our *minding*, provides recall with its content. What we have not experienced, we cannot remember. Therefore, the ability to remember is significantly influenced by the qualities of the world we are able to experience in the first place. The differentiation of the sensibilities is key to providing the mind with content.

The ability to remember is a critical aspect of our cognitive capabilities, but to remember without the ability to imagine would leave us with a static culture. The engine of social and cultural progress is our ability to conceive of things that never were, but which might become. The central term in the word *imagination* is *image.* To imagine is to create new images that function in the creation of a new science, a new symphony, and in the design of a new bridge. It is a process critical to the creation of poetry and for innovation in our practical lives. But imagination, like recall, works with qualities we have experienced. What was not first in the hand, cannot be later in the head. Try to imagine something you have never experienced. You will find that while you are able to imagine new forms of animals, automobiles, devices for seating, and the like, the components of these entities are made up of qualities you once encountered. Our imaginative life is built from experience. That imagination is essential to human progress is evident in comparing human architectural achievements with the architecture of bees.

Some people claim that bees are the most inventive and skilled architects. Out of soft material they create a structure that is not only strong but elegant. Huge honeycombs built with mathematical precision, and capable of holding weight many times their own, constitute a remarkable architectural achievement. Such structures pale what humans have been able to create, particularly considering the material with which bees work.

This argument is attractive, but I think it is inaccurate. Bees are not architects. They do build magnificent honeycombs, but they have been building the same honeycombs year, after year, after year. Bees build what they build because they must. They have no options. They are genetically programmed to do the same thing, over and over again. They have no imagination that enables them to do other than what they have done from the beginning. Architecture without choice, without imagination, is a contradiction in terms. When bees create a cathedral, a skyscraper, a curtain-walled building, when they are able to produce pyramids, the Golden Gate Bridge, or even a simple bungalow—even one for bees—I would be willing to call them architects.

The power to imagine is central to our culture's development. It not only provides for cultural development, it provides for our own development; because, through culture, our own development occurs. Like an upward spiral, we receive from the culture in which we live and give back to it more than we receive so that others born later can have what we did not. There is no such culture among animals. All of them, generation after generation, start from the same place as their predecessors and go no farther than they. The tricks you teach old Rex, he cannot teach to his puppies.

One would think, given the importance of imagination, that it would be regarded as one of the basics of education. As you know, it is not on anyone's list of basics, at least not in any national report on the state of our schools that I have read. We are far more concerned with the correct replication of what already exists than with cultivating the powers of innovation or the celebration of thinking. Perhaps a little parity among these educational goals would be appropriate.

Everything that I have said thus far about the sensibilities and about recall and imagination pertains to events that occur inside our heads. Recall and imagination are qualities of human experience that are internal and private. I can enjoy my own fantasies and you can enjoy yours, but you cannot access mine, nor me yours. If things were left that way, culture would be static. Even worse, it would eventually cease to exist because culture depends on communication, and communication requires a shift through which what is private is made public.

Using Forms of Representation

The process of making the private public is a process that we take too much for granted. It is an extraordinary achievement, one that is still evolving. It requires more than language as a means of giving thoughts, feelings, and imaginings a public face. It requires what I have called "forms of representation" (Eisner 1982). Becoming acculturated means acquiring the multiple forms of literacy that enable one to encode or decode the public vehicles through which meaning is represented or recovered. One major virtue of any particular form is its capacity to convey or express unique meanings.

Forms of representation are visual, auditory, tactile, gustatory, and even olfactory. They manifest themselves in pictures, speech, the movements of dance and gesture, in word and in number. Each social device carries meanings that represent qualities we have experienced directly or through recall or imagination. Hence, experience that is visual may be uniquely represented by forms of representation that exploit the visual—a picture is better than a paragraph when we want to know what someone looks like. If we want to know about a sequence of events over time, a story is usually better than a picture. If we want to convey the vital and dynamic experience of our emotional life, dance and music are probably better than a string of numbers. Our curricula could be designed to help children acquire these multiple forms of literacy. Inability to think in any particular form means that one is unable to access the meanings that are projected in that form.

The use of any form of representation has at least four important educational functions.

First, it is important to recognize that there is nothing so slippery as a thought. The great articles and books I have written—on my way to work or just before rising in the morning—come and go with a flick of an eyelid. The process of externalization is a process of stabilization. Working with a form of representation provides the opportunity to stabilize what is ephemeral and fleeting. It gives students an opportunity to *hold onto* their thinking. This "holding onto" provides a second important benefit. Thoughts in one's head are difficult to edit, but thoughts on paper, or portrayed on canvas, or in notation, or on a recorded tape can be edited. Editing allows one to refine one's thinking, to make it clearer, more powerful, and, not least, to appreciate the happy results of creativity. It allows one to confer a personal signature to a public product.

The editing process, whether in writing, painting, or making music, is not emphasized in our schools. Students write, not to communicate what they care about, but to answer questions posed by the teacher who already has the answers (Applebee 1981). Their responses tend to be brief. No premium is placed on clarity and elegance, but rather on being right. The stabilization of thinking in a form of representation makes the editing process possible. We need to make it probable in our classrooms.

The third function of using a form of representation to externalize the internal is that it makes communication possible. For our thoughts to be known, they must be made public. Imagine how impoverished our musical life would be if Mozart, at age thirteen, had decided not to notate his magnificent music, or if Cezanne had only enjoyed the views of Mount St. Victoire rather than painting them, or if Isaac Newton had decided not to tell. The history of art and western science would have been ineluctably altered. It is its public status that makes our thinking socially valuable.

The fourth function of using a form of representation is that it provides opportunities for discovery. Earlier, I discussed representation as if it were a process that proceeded from the head through the hand and out onto the paper. In fact, the creation of anything is more like a dialogue than a monologue. The act of making something is not only an occasion for expressing or representing what you already know, imagine, or feel, it is also a means through which the forms of things unknown can be uncovered. The creative act is an act of exploration and discovery.

All of this means that thinking should be celebrated by giving students opportunities to try to represent what they think they know. And because what they know cannot always be projected through the logical use of language, they should have a variety of options available and the skills with which to use them.

Forms of Representation Have a Syntax

All forms of representation have a syntactical structure. The term *syntax* comes from the Latin, syntaxis, which means to arrange. For example, forms of representation used in painting or drawing require the student to arrange the qualities within the work so that they cohere. The same is true of musical composition or choreography. The syntactical structure of these forms are structure-seeking or figural.[3] What the individual seeks is a coherent, satisfying form. Other forms of representation such as the use of word and number must also be arranged. However, mathematics and much of language, particularly in the early grades, is more rule abiding than structure-seeking. That is, there are strict conventions that must be met. To use the English language correctly, one must put letters in the proper order. To calculate correctly, one must perform operations according to rule. Such conventions allow us to communicate with precision.

The problem in our schools is that activities whose syntactical structure is rule-abiding dominate the curriculum to the virtual exclusion of figural or structure-seeking activities. As we all know, students never learn one thing at a time. While they are learning to write and to compute, they are also learning to be good rule followers. They are also learning that for most tasks, and especially the most important ones, the correct answer is known. The teacher knows it or it can be found in the back of the book.

We should be concerned about curricula that place a heavy emphasis on limited forms of learning and thinking. When limited forms of learning dominate curricula, they also cultivate a disposition. Following rules and applying algorithms do not match the kinds of problems with which most people must deal in life outside of school (Eisner 1986). Life's problems almost always have more than one solution, and they typically require judgment and trade-off.

Ironically, the arts, an area of thinking that has the most to offer, is the most neglected in our schools. The arts are models of work that do emphasize the creation of coherent structure, that do encourage multiple solutions to problems, that do prize innovation, that do rely on the use of judgment, and that depend on the use of sensibility. In short, the arts are a most important means of celebrating thinking.

I am painfully aware that the current educational climate for the ideas that I have expressed are not as hospitable as they might be. As I indicated earlier, we do not typically pay much attention to celebrating thinking, or curiosity, or imagination, or creativity in our schools. In addition, we have a strong tendency to want to monitor the quality of schooling by implementing a common program and applying common standards to determine who wins. The results, like the results at the Belmont race track and the Kentucky Derby, are published in the newspapers. Yet, I see no virtue in supporting what is educationally questionable; and, in any case, Pi Lambda Theta is concerned not simply with sustaining the status quo, but with educational leadership. And even if the educational aims and concepts of thinking I have described here cannot be completely achieved, movement in their direction would be salutary. Let me indicate a few things that might be done to make such moves.

Developing Multiple Forms of Literacy in Our Schools

First, consider the matter of content and the ways in which students display what they have learned. Let's say that the content that we care about is helping students understand the life and times of the slaves just prior to and during the Civil War. This material is common fare for fifth graders in many elementary schools in our country. What students learn about slavery will be shaped by the forms of representation that we choose to use. If the students read an artistically crafted historical text, they will not only be given access to the facts, but the language itself will enable them to learn something about how the slaves felt and what those who kept slaves felt about their own lives. Through narrative and prose that exploits the capacity of language to generate images and to foster feeling, an affective picture of the period can be rendered and secured. Of course, to secure this picture, students must know how to read. They must know how to read not only clipped, factual accounts, but literary accounts. They must be sensitive to the melody, cadence, and metaphor of language if the text contains them.

But even when students possess such high levels of reading comprehension, literary text cannot tell it all. The music of the period, the hymns, the chants, the rhythms of Africa, can also help students gain access to the period. And so can Matthew Brady's photos and Lincoln's Emancipation Proclamation and Gettysburg Address. So too can the mythology of the slaves and their homespun stories. Further, it would be useful for students to create their own plays about the period and to act them out. It might be useful for them to perform the dances and to eat what the slaves of the period ate.

What I am getting at is a model of curriculum that exploits the various forms of representation and that utilizes all of the senses to help students learn what a period of history feels like. Reality, whatever it is, is made up of qualities—sights, smells, images, tales, and moods. Firsthand experience is simply a way of getting in touch with reality. In our schools we often rely on conceptually dense and emotionally eviscerated abstractions to represent what in actuality is a rich source of experience. To compound things further, we require students to tell us what they have learned by trying to fit it into one of four alternatives to a multiple-choice question. Harriet Beecher Stowe told us how she felt about the period in *Uncle Tom's Cabin;* D. W. Griffith told a very different story in *A Birth of a Nation.* There is no reason to restrict communication to a single form, except to facilitate comparability among students. Here a standardized form of assessment is an asset. Multiple-choice tests put everyone on the same scale. But is this what we are really after? Is our most precious technical achievement or educational aim being able to determine where our students are in relation to others? I think not. Such practices foster a racetrack concept of schooling.

The use of multiple forms of representation in the construction of curriculum is not limited to social studies; good math teachers use them in the teaching of math. Graphics, charts, histograms, and number diagrams are ways of helping students access mathematical ideas through forms that many find easier to grasp. The fact that charts, diagrams, schemata, and spreadsheets are very useful ways to display information has been quickly understood by IBM, Apple, and Toshiba. They waste no time pointing out to prospective customers how much more readable and saleable their products will be if they use graphics. In this respect, they are far ahead of us.

English, music, and the visual arts are also enhanced by curricula that portray the content of these fields in different forms of representation. Scientific concepts and generalizations—DNA, for example, or Newton's Third Law—are more likely to be meaningful if they are represented in several, rather than in one form. What language can carry is not all that we can know. Ultimately, what we know is rooted in qualities encountered or images recalled and imagined.

Schools with Celebration

The celebration of thinking should be returned to our classrooms. It should be given a seat of honor in its own right, for its own rewards. The forms in which thinking occur should not be subjected to the status differences and inequities of our society. Is a first-rate piece of science really better or more important than a first-rate symphony? Is knowledge of geometry more important than understanding and appreciating poetry? I am not urging a displacement of science for art, or math for poetry. I am not arguing for the creation of a new privileged class, but rather for a decent conception of what our students are entitled to. Without opportunities to acquire multiple forms of literacy, children will be handicapped in their ability to participate in the legacies of their culture. Our children deserve more than that. I hope the membership of this important organization will celebrate thinking in its many forms and help build school programs that do justice to the richness and the scope of our children's minds.

Notes

1. Technological approaches to teaching and school improvement are represented by much of the research on effective teaching and on effective schools. In both cases factors are identified that purportedly constitute effectiveness in these areas, and teachers and policy-makers are encouraged to replicate those factors in their own teaching. The operating assumption is that the factors that make for educational effectiveness are common across situations, replicable, and relatively context independent. In addition, little or no attention is paid to matters of interaction or curvilinearity.

2. Unless students receive satisfaction from their work, the likelihood of pursuing such work outside of the classroom is low. The only robust outcomes of schooling are those internalized by students and pursued because of the satisfaction they provide.

3. The distinction between structure-seeking and rule-abiding is found in Gabrielle Lusser Rico, *Writing the Natural Way* (Los Angeles: J. P. Tarcher, Inc., 1983).

3

Aesthetic Modes of Knowing

So gorgeous was the spectacle on the May morning of 1910 when nine kings rode in the funeral of Edward VII of England that the crowd, waiting in hushed and blackclad awe, could not keep back gasps of admiration. In scarlet and blue and green and purple, three by three the sovereigns rode through the palace gates, with plumed helmets, gold braid, crimson sashes, jeweled orders flashing in the sun. After them came five heirs apparent, forty more imperial or royal highnesses, seven queens—four dowager and three regnant— and a scattering of special ambassadors from uncrowned countries. Together they represented seventy nations in the greatest assemblage of royalty and rank ever gathered in one place and, of its kind, the last. The muffled tongue of Big Ben tolled nine by the clock as the cortege left the palace, but on history's clock it was sunset, and the sun of the old world was setting in a dying blaze of splendor never to be seen again.

—BARBARA TUCHMAN, *THE GUNS OF AUGUST*

An examination of the relationship between the form and content of the opening paragraph in Barbara Tuchman's *Guns of August* will help us understand what the phrase "aesthetic modes of knowing" alludes to. Before examining this relationship I wish to mention now a theme that I will return to later. The phrase, "aesthetic modes of knowing," presents something of

I wish to acknowledge with gratitude the very useful critique of this chapter by my student, Lynda Stone.

32

a contradiction in our culture. We do not typically associate the aesthetic with knowing. The arts, with which the aesthetic is most closely associated, is a matter of the heart. Science is thought to provide the most direct route to knowledge. Hence, "aesthetic modes of knowing" is a phrase that contradicts the conception of knowledge that is most widely accepted. I hope to show in this chapter that the widely accepted view is too narrow and that the roads to knowing are many. Let us return to Tuchman.

"So gorgeous was the spectacle on the May morning of 1910 when nine kings rode in the funeral of Edward VII of England that the crowd, waiting in hushed and black-clad awe, could not keep back gasps of admiration." What does Tuchman do in this, the opening line of her book? In the initial phrase, "So gorgeous was the spectacle on the May morning," Tuchman creates a rhythm, which is then punctuated by a staccato-like "when nine kings rode in the funeral of Edward VII." She then follows with contrasts between "gasps" and the soft sound of "hush." And then again, with the phrase "in scarlet *and* blue *and* green *and* purple, three by three the sovereigns rode through the palace gates," Tuchman creates a syncopation that recapitulates the sound of hoofs pounding the pavement as the horses pass by. Again, "with plumed helmets, gold braid, crimson sashes, jeweled orders flashing in the sun"—another series of short bursts filled with images as well as sound. And later in the paragraph, the "muffled tongue of Big Ben tolled nine by the clock." Here, the paired contradictions of "hushed gasps" and "muffled tongue" appeal to our sense of metaphor. And for a finale Tuchman writes, "but on history's clock it was sunset, and the sun of the Old World was setting in a dying blaze of splendor never to be seen again." Like the coda of a classical symphony, Tuchman brings the paragraph to a slow declining close.

What occurs in the paragraph occurs throughout the book, and what occurs throughout the book is what makes literature literary. It is in the use of form, especially in the cadence and tempo of language, that patterns are established among the "parts" of the sentence and between the sentence and the paragraph that create their counterpart in the reader's experience. "After them came five heirs apparent, forty more imperial or royal highnesses, seven queens—four dowager and three regnant—and a scattering of special ambassadors from uncrowned countries." Like a partridge in a pear tree, the cadence of the sentence captivates and carries the reader off on a ride.

What also occurs in the paragraph is the generation in the reader's mind's eye of an array of visual images. The writing is vivid and it is vivid because it is designed to elicit images of scarlet and blue and purple and of the plumed helmets and the gold braid. The writing evokes the scene Tuchman wishes the reader to see. We are able to participate vicariously in events that occurred when we were not yet born.

Consider again her use of language: "the muffled tongue of Big Ben" and "black-clad awe." The language is shaped to help us see and feel the day and hence to know it as participants. Its form and content transport us to another time, another place. The literary in literature resides in the aesthetic capacities of language to influence our experience.

The reader should not assume that the aesthetic treatment of form for purposes of vicarious participation in events not directly available is limited to literature. Poetry, dance, the visual arts, and drama all employ form for such purposes. The drama within drama is created through the tensions that writers, actors, stage designers, lighting experts, and directors produce. What happens on the stage is the result of a collective effort. What occurs in literary works and in the visual arts is usually the product of individuals. Whether collective or individual, the common function of the aesthetic is to modulate form so that it can, in turn, modulate our experience. The moving patterns of sound created by composers, in turn, create their counterparts in the competent listener. The physically static forms produced by visual artists create in the competent viewer a quality of life analogous to those in the forms beheld. In sum, the form of the work informs us. Our internal life is shaped by the forms we are able to experience.

The phrase "we are able to experience" is a critical one. If the forms that constitute the arts or the sciences spoke for themselves we would need no programs in the schools to help students to learn how "to read" them. What we are able to see or hear is a product of our cultivated abilities. The rewards and insights provided by aesthetically shaped forms are available only to those who can perceive them. Not only is competence a necessary condition for experiencing the form in works we have access to, but the particular quality of life generated by the forms encountered will, to some degree, differ from individual to individual. All experience is the product of both the features of the world and the biography of the individual. Our experience is influenced by our past as it interacts with our present.[1] Thus, not only must a certain kind of competence be acquired in order to perceive the qualities of form in the objects available to us, but the nature of our experience with these forms is influenced not only by the form itself but by our past.

I have thus far directed my remarks to the aesthetic functions of form as a source of experience and understanding in the fine arts and in literature. But I do not wish to suggest that the aesthetic is restricted to the fine arts and literature. All scientific inquiry culminates in the creation of form:

taxonomies, theories, frameworks, conceptual systems. The scientist, like the artist, must transform the content of his or her imagination into some public, stable form, something that can be shared with others. The shape of this form—its coherence—is a critical feature concerning its acceptability. The adequacy of theory is not simply determined by experimental results. Experimental results can often be explained by competing theories. The attractiveness of a theory is a central factor in our judgment of it.

Viewed this way, both artist and scientist create forms through which the world is viewed. Both artist and scientist make qualitative judgments about the fit, the coherence, the economy, "the rightness" of the forms they create. Readers of these forms make similar judgments. It was his recognition of the universal character of formmaking in every sphere of human life that prompted Sir Herbert Read to say that the aim of education was the creation of artists. What he meant was that all students should be enabled to produce good forms. He writes:

> Having established the relevance of aesthetics to the processes of perception and imagination, I shall then pass on to the less disputed ground of expression. Education is the fostering of growth, but apart from physical maturation, growth is only made apparent in expression—audible or visible signs and symbols. Education may therefore be defined as the cultivation of modes of expression—it is teaching children and adults how to make sounds, images, movements, tools and utensils. A man who can make such things well is a well educated man. If he can make good sounds, he is a good speaker, a good musician, a good poet; if he can make good images, he is a good painter or sculptor; if good movements, a good dancer or laborer; if good tools or utensils, a good craftsman. All faculties, of thought, logic, memory, sensibility and intellect, are involved in such processes, and no aspect of education is excluded in such processes. And they are all processes which involve art, for art is nothing but the good making of sounds, images, etc. The aim of education is therefore the creation of artists—of people efficient in the various modes of expression. (1944, 10)

There is another sense in which form and the aesthetic experience it engenders can be considered. I have used the term *form* thus far to refer to the products made by both artists and scientists. Both, I have argued, create forms, and these forms have aesthetic features that appeal. But the term *form* can be conceived of not only as a noun, but as a verb. Following Read, we form groups, we form sentences, we form structures. Form, in this sense, refers to something we do. Indeed, in Norway visual arts education is called *Forming*. To form is to engage in an activity occurring over time, guided by attention to changing qualities whose end is to produce a structure, either temporal or spatial, that gives rise to feeling. To be able to produce such forms the qualities that constitute them must be appraised by their contribution to the life of feeling. The maker, in this case, must know what he has before him in order to make decisions that will yield the hoped for results. A satisfying end is achieved only if appropriate choices are made in process. To make such choices one must be aware of the qualities of form as well as the content as one proceeds. One must know the qualities of life that the qualitative components engender and know they will function within the whole when it is completed.

In this view the aesthetic is both a subject matter and a criterion for appraising the processes used to create works of science as well as art. The aesthetic is not simply the possession of completed works. The sense of rightness or fit that a scientist or artist experiences in the course of his or her work is crucial to the quality of the final work. But not only does the aesthetic function in this way. The ability to experience the aesthetic features of the process has been regarded as a prime motive for work. Alfred North Whitehead once commented, "Most people believe that scientists inquire in order to know. Just the opposite is the case. Scientists know in order to inquire." Scientists, Whitehead believed, are drawn to their work not by epistemological motives but by aesthetic ones. The joy of inquiry is the driving motive for their work. Scientists, like artists, formulate new and puzzling questions in order to enjoy the experience of creating answers to them.

The distinctions I have made concerning form and the aesthetic as a mode of knowing can be summed up thus far as follows. First, all things made, whether in art, science, or in practical life, possess form. When well made these forms have aesthetic properties. These aesthetic properties have the capacity to generate particular qualities of life in the competent percipient. In literature and in many of the arts such forms are used to reveal or represent aspects of the world that cannot be experienced directly. Second, form is not only an attribute or condition of things made; it is a process through which things are made. Knowing how forms will function within the finished final product is a necessary condition for creating products that themselves possess aesthetic qualities. Such knowing requires an active and intelligent maker. Third, the deeper motives for productive activity in both the arts and the sciences often emanate from the quality of life the process of creation makes possible. These satisfactions are related to the kinds of stimulation secured in the play process and from the aesthetic satisfactions derived from judgments made about emerging forms.

My comments thus far have been intended to free the aesthetic from the province of the arts alone and to recognize its presence in all human formative activity. All subjects have aesthetically significant features, from the process of making to the form the product finally takes. I have also argued that what we find satisfying in both art and science is a function of the coherence the things we make possess. The creation of coherence is a central aim in both art and science. The aesthetic as a mode of knowing therefore can be regarded in two senses. First, it is through aesthetic experience that we can participate vicariously in situations beyond our practical possibilities. The aesthetic in knowing, in this sense, performs a referential function; it points to some aspect of the world and helps us experience it.

Second, knowledge *of,* rather than knowledge *through,* the aesthetic is knowledge of the aesthetic qualities of form per se. We become increasingly able to know those qualities we call aesthetic by our developed ability to experience the subtleties of form. We come to know aspects of music and literature and science by being increasingly able to experience their nuances. The music of Mendelssohn and the paintings of Pollack contain certain unique features; they possess an "aesthetic." To know these features is to know aspects of the world. To achieve such knowledge the percipient must be aesthetically literate. He or she must be able to read their subtle and often complex aesthetic features. Knowledge within the aesthetic mode is therefore knowledge of two kinds. First, it is knowledge of the world toward which the aesthetic qualities of form point: we understand the emotional meaning of jealousy through the form that Shakespeare conferred upon *Othello.* Second, it is knowledge of the aesthetic in its own right, for no other purpose than to have or undergo experience. Such motives are often the driving force in the creation of both science and art.

One might well ask why the aesthetic should play such an important role in the arts and sciences. What is it that confers such a significant function upon what is often regarded as an ornamental and unnecessary aspect of life? One reason is related to our biological nature. I speak here of the deep-seated need for stimulation. Humans have a low toleration for homeostasis. We seek to use our capacities, to activate our sensory systems, to vary our experience. When our life is without stimulation, as it is in sensory deprivation experiments, we hallucinate. When we are sated with one type of experience, we seek other kinds. Rather than being a stimulus-reducing organism, the human is stimulus-seeking. The aesthetic is one important source of stimulation. Secured within the process of coping with the problematic, its satisfactions arise as the problematic is explored and eventually resolved. The making of a form from the simplest sandcastle to the most advanced architectural achievement is a process in which aesthetic satisfactions are pervasive. Our need for variety and for stimulation is met, in part, through the aesthetics of human action.

The aesthetic is not only motivated by our need for stimulation; it is also motivated by our own need to give order to our world. To form is to confer order. To confer aesthetic order upon our world is to make that world hang together, to fit, to feel right, to put things in balance, to create harmony. Such harmonies are sought in all aspects of life. In science it is extraordinarily vivid: theory is the result of our desire to create a world we can understand. The scientist conceptualizes a theoretical structure, defines its parts, and arranges them in a configuration that appeals to our sensibilities so that the theoretical form helps us make sense of our world.

The need for coherence in things made is not, of course, limited to science or art; it manifests itself in all walks of life from the setting of a table to our social interactions (Dewey 1934, Chapter 1). The exquisite creation of either is a very high aesthetic achievement.

The aesthetic, then, is motivated by our need to lead a stimulating life. Related to the need to explore and play, the aesthetic is part and parcel of what these processes are intended to yield, not only practical outcomes related to premeditated goals, but the delights of exploration. The aesthetic is also inherent in our need to make sense of experience. This sense-making is located in the choices we make in our effort to create order. Both scientists and artists, to take paradigm cases, are makers of order—the former through the relationships created within theoretical material and the other through the ordering of the qualitative. Our sense of rightness, like our sense of justice, is rooted in that ineffable experience to which the word "aesthetic" is assigned.

I said at the outset that I would return later to a theme I introduced at that time. That theme was the contradiction in our culture between the terms aesthetic and knowing. The polarities we encounter between these terms hark back to Plato's conception of the hierarchies of knowledge. Plato believed that episteme—true and certain knowledge—could not be secured if one depended upon the information the senses provided (1941). The reasons, he thought, were clear enough. Sensory information is dependent upon the stuff of which our universe is made, namely, material things. Since material things are in a state of constant decay, any knowledge derived from them must, of necessity, be short-term at best and misleading at worst. Second, sensory information is not trustworthy. To illustrate how the senses mislead consider how a perfectly straight rod placed in a glass of water appears to be bent. Knowledge derived from what the senses provide, as such a case reveals, is misleading. The rod is straight, not bent, even though it *appears* bent. To secure knowledge that is dependable, Plato believed, one must move away from the empirical world that our senses come to know and move into the world of abstraction. The most secure and dependable form of knowledge is achieved not through empirical investigation or sensory information, but through the exercise of our rationality. Through our rational powers we can conceive of a perfect circle even though we will never see one in the world in which we live. Dependable knowledge is more likely as we move from the concrete to the abstract. The more we advance toward the abstract the more we achieve episteme.

Plato's views have had a profound effect not only upon our conception of knowledge, but upon our conception of intelligence. To be intelligent means in our culture—especially the culture of schooling—to be able to manipulate abstract ideas. One of the most vivid examples of this is to be found in the status of mathematics as a school subject. Mathematical ability is commonly regarded as a prime manifestation of intelligence. Ability in mathematics is considered prima facie evidence of one's suitability for the rigors of university work. Mathematics, the queen of the sciences, is the apotheosis of human intelligence.

Subjects that depend upon empirical information such as the natural and social sciences are a step lower in the intellectual hierarchy. Again, the reason is clear. Truth in mathematics does not require empirical evidence but rather rational comprehension. Claims to truth in the sciences look toward a decaying empirical world for evidence of validity.

When it comes to the arts and to things made, the level of intelligence employed is even lower in rank. And should emotion or feeling enter the picture, the likelihood of achieving dependable knowledge is smaller still. For Plato the life of feeling was, like the passions, an impediment to knowledge (*Republic,* Book Six [1941]). What one wanted was pure mind, unencumbered by emotion or by the misleading qualities of the empirical world.

This view of knowledge and intelligence did not terminate with Plato's passing. Our current view of knowledge is based largely upon it. Consider, for example, the distinction we often make between intelligence and talent: talent is displayed primarily in things related to the body, the arts, and sports, for example. Intelligence is used to describe those who are good at abstraction. The highly intelligent enroll in college preparatory courses—the more abstract the better. Those who are talented are good at making and doing things. We are less apt to view these doings and makings as examples of intelligence at work.[2] Consider further the typical distinctions between the cognitive, the affective, and the psychomotor. We create tidy psychological domains, keep our categories clean, and assign the aesthetic to affect: its presence in human experience, we tacitly hold, is not a function of thinking.

Consider still further what our tests assess in the way of achievement.

The Scholastic Aptitude Test, for example, focuses upon two areas of human performance, verbal and mathematical. Both of these areas are regarded as abstract rather than concrete in character. We assess a student's aptitude for the heady work of college by defining aptitude in terms of verbal and mathematical skills. To be sure, verbal and mathematical skills are relevant for college; my point is not that they are irrelevant. It is that these abilities are considered the primary surrogates of human intelligence and symbolize an entire constellation of assumptions about the mind, knowledge, and human ability. These assumptions are so pervasive in western culture and so dominant in our own professional culture that few of us have the psychological distance to regard them for what they are, human constructions, something made and, therefore, something that could be otherwise.

Given these assumptions, the aesthetic becomes a casualty in American education. It is embedded in a historical context that has underestimated the role it plays in man's effort to know. The aesthetic aspects of human experience are considered luxuries. And luxuries, as we all know, can be rather easily foregone in hard times.

The aesthetic is also diminished by our belief that we *search for* knowledge. Knowledge is considered by most in our culture as something that one discovers, not something that one makes.[3] Knowledge is out there waiting to be found, and the most useful tool for finding it is science. If there were greater appreciation for the extent to which knowledge is constructed—something made—there might be a greater likelihood that its aesthetic dimensions would be appreciated. To make knowledge is to cast the scientist in the role of an artist or a craftsperson, someone who shapes materials and ideas. The making of something is a techne, and for good techne one must be artistically engaged, and if artistically engaged, then aesthetic considerations and criteria must operate to some extent.

What does the argument I have provided imply for education? One implication pertains to the way in which we think about what we teach. The curriculum of the school performs a variety of important functions. One such function is to convey to students what we regard as important for them to learn. These values are expressed in what we choose to assess in school, in the amount of time we devote to various subjects, and in the location of the time that is assigned to what we teach. Our educational priorities are not expressed by our testimonials or our publicly prepared curriculum syllabi, but in our actions. By our works we are known.

If we believe that the aesthetic values of a subject are important for students to appreciate and experience, then we must, it seems to me, try to figure out how these values can be purposely introduced to them. We often recognize, in our conversations at least, that mathematics has an aesthetic dimension. What does this mean for designing curriculum and teaching? Are students aware of the aesthetic aspects of mathematics, and if not, what can we do about it?

Mathematics is, in some ways, far removed from what we usually regard as a subject having aesthetic dimensions, but clearly literature is not. Yet, how do we help students experience the aesthetic aspects of language? What kind of work would they be asked to do if we gave the aesthetic aspects of writing and reading a significant priority in the teaching of English? What kind of sensibilities would we cultivate—indeed must we cultivate—if writing and reading are to be more than simple encoding and decoding? One cannot write well if one has a tin ear. It is necessary to hear the melodies of language (as Barbara Tuchman obviously does) in order to use language in graceful and informative ways. While few students will become as skilled as Tuchman, all students can learn how to attend to the cadences of language. How do we help them do this?

Do students recognize the aesthetic features of inquiry in science and in the social studies, or do they separate the aesthetic from what they study in general and assign it to the realm of the arts alone? What would we need to teach in each of the fields students study to help them understand the role that the aesthetic plays in a particular field? How might we design tasks within a field of study so that inquiry in that field provided aesthetic satisfaction? Such questions point in a direction quite opposite to the direction in which curricula and teaching have been moving over the past ten years. Pedagogical practices in American schools have become increasingly fragmented. Because of pressures upon teachers to become "accountable," there has been a widespread tendency to break curricula into small units of instruction.[4] The result of this fragmentation is to make it increasingly difficult for students to see how each piece is a part of a larger whole. When the content taught for each small fragment is tested, the test is a signal to the student that he or she can forget what has been "learned" after the test has been taken. By using such teaching and testing procedures it is believed the teacher will secure an objective record of what a student knows and the student will have unambiguous feedback of how well he or she is doing. The educational liability of such teaching and learning procedures is that they emphasize short-term memory; it is difficult to remember small bits and pieces of information when there is no larger conception or armature upon which they can be placed. Indeed, this orientation to teaching and testing is formidable; it may make it difficult for students to achieve meaningful learning.

Another factor that undermines the aesthetic is that the rewards that are emphasized in class are rewards emanating from test performance. What far too many teachers and students care about almost solely is how well they do on tests.[5] Again, the focus is on the short-term and the instrumental. Yet the enduring outcomes of education are to be found in consummatory satisfactions—the joy of the ride, not simply arriving at the destination. If the major satisfactions in schools are high test scores, the value of what is learned tends to decline precipitously after the tests are taken. The only confident way to have a bull market in schooling is to turn students on to the satisfactions of inquiry in the fields into which they are initiated.

There is another implication of signal importance that pertains to the formation of curriculum and teaching in our schools. The implication I described earlier regarding the place of the aesthetic in the school curriculum is related to what we convey to students about what we value for them. The absence of a subject or its de facto neglect in the curriculum teaches students implicitly that we do not value that subject.

There is, finally, one more implication regarding the absence of a subject. This implication has to do with the fact that the curriculum is a mind-altering device. When we define the content and tasks that constitute the curriculum, we also define the kind of mental skills we choose to cultivate. The absence of attention to the aesthetic in the school curriculum is an absence of opportunities to cultivate the sensibilities. It is an absence of the refinement of our consciousness, for it is through our sensibilities that our consciousness is secured. If our educational program put a premium on the aesthetic as well as on the instrumental features of what is taught, students would have an opportunity to develop mental skills that for most students now lie fallow. Attention to the aesthetic aspects of the subjects taught would remind students that the ideas within subject areas, disciplines, and fields of study are human constructions, shaped by craft, employing technique, and mediated through some material. Works of science are, in this sense, also works of art.

Such an orientation to knowledge would reduce the tendency for students to regard the textbook as sacred and knowledge as fixed—not a bad outcome for a nation that prides itself on being a democracy. The more students conceive of their roles as scholars and critics, as makers and appraisers of things made, the less tendency they will have to regard the world as beyond their power to alter.

But for me the most important contributions of the aesthetic to education pertain to what I have called its referential and its consummatory functions. The referential function is performed as students acquire the ability to read the forms that aesthetic qualities convey: we can learn from aesthetically rendered lives what words, paradoxically, can never say. As Langer puts it:

The arts, like language, abstract from experience certain aspects for our contemplation. But such abstractions are not concepts that have names. Discursive speech can fix definable concepts better and more exactly. Artistic expression abstracts aspects of the life of feeling which have no names, which have to be presented to sense and intuition rather than to a word-bound, note-taking consciousness. (1957, 94–5)

The consummatory function of the aesthetic provides delight in the inquiry itself. The durable outcomes of schooling are not to be found in short-term, instrumental tasks. Such outcomes must penetrate more deeply. When school programs neglect attention to the aesthetics of shaping form, they neglect the very satisfactions that reside at the core of education. If students are not moved by what they study, why would they want to pursue such studies on their own? But one has a hard time keeping them away from things that do provide them with deep satisfaction. Can we aspire for less in education?

The aesthetic in education has two major contributions to make, neither of which is yet a purposeful part of our educational agenda. First, it tells us about the world in ways specific to its nature. Second, it provides the experiential rewards of taking the journey itself. These potential contributions must surely be important to those who wish, as we do, to improve the quality of schooling for the young.

Notes

1. The concept that most succinctly captures this notion is John Dewey's term "interaction." See his *Experience and Education* (New York: Macmillan, 1938).

2. It is telling, I believe, that the best overall prediction of intelligence test scores is the vocabulary section of group intelligence tests. The ability to know and use words is, in our culture, a mark of intelligence. This view is now being challenged by several psychologists. See, for example, Howard Gardner, *Frames of Mind* (New York: Basic Books, 1983).

3. Even some constructionist views of knowledge employ terms, in the books in which they appear, suggesting that knowledge is discovered. See, for example, Barney G. Glaser and Anselm Strauss, *The Discovery of Grounded Theory* (Chicago: Aldine Publishing Co., 1967) and Karl Popper, *The Logic of Scientific Discovery* (New York: Harper and Row, 1968).

4. Recent studies of classroom practices in secondary schools have revealed this tendency. See John I. Goodlad, *A Place Called School* (New York: McGraw-Hill, 1984).

5. Current studies of secondary schools undertaken at Stanford University suggest this quite clearly.

4

Cognition and Representation
A Way to Pursue the American Dream?

In some ways it's an old idea. I'm talking about the idea that the forms we use to represent what we think—literal language, visual images, number, poetry—impact how we think and what we can think about. If different forms of representation performed identical cognitive functions there would be no need to dance, compute, or draw. Why would we want to write poetry, history, literature, and factual accounts of what we have experienced? Yet this apparently obvious idea has not been a prominent consideration in setting curricular agendas in America's schools or shaping educational policy. This article is intended to illustrate the ways in which *forms of representation,* or what are sometimes called symbol systems, function in our mental life and to explore their contributions to the development of mind.

Among the various aims we consider important in education, two are especially so. We would like our children to be well informed, that is, to understand ideas that are important, useful, beautiful, and powerful. And we also want them to have the appetite and ability to think analytically and critically, to be able to speculate and imagine, to see connections among ideas, and to be able to use what they know to enhance their own lives and the desire to contribute to the culture. Neither of these two goals are likely to be achieved if schools are inattentive to the variety of ways humans have represented what they have thought, felt, and imagined nor will these goals be achieved if we fail to appreciate culture's role in making these processes of representation possible. After all, human products owe their existence not only to the achievements of individual minds, but to the forms of representation available in the culture, forms that enable us to make our ideas and feelings public. Put another way, we can't have a musical idea without

44

thinking and representing what we have thought musically. We can't have a mathematical idea without mathematics and neither is possible without a form of representation that affords our ideas the possibility of life. It is the school as a representative of culture that provides access to those forms. It is the school that fosters their skillful use among the young.

Minds, then, in a curious but profound way are made. Their shape and capacities are influenced by what the young are given an opportunity to learn. The curriculum is, given this conception of the genesis of mind, a mind-altering device. Decisions policy makers and educators make about what children will be given access to help shape the kind of minds they will come to own. The character of their minds, in turn, will help shape the culture in which both they and we live.

Brains, in contrast to minds, are biological—brains are given by nature; minds are cultural, they are the result of experience and the kind of experience the child secures in school is significantly influenced by the decisions we make about what to teach. As I indicated, as important a consideration as this might be, reflection upon the role that forms of representation play in the creation of mind has been all but neglected in framing curricular policy. We need to remedy that.

Ours is a school system that gives pride of place to the skillful use of language and number; the venerable three Rs. No one can cogently argue that the three Rs are unimportant. Clearly, competency in their use is of primary importance. But even high levels of skill in their use is not enough to develop the variety of mental capacities children possess. The three Rs tap too little of what the mind can do. Where do we learn what the mind can do? We learn about its potentialities not only from psychologists who study the mind, but by looking at the culture—all cultures—because culture displays the forms humans have used to give expression to what they have imagined, understood, and felt. Each product humans create symptomizes the forms of thinking that lead to its realization, each one of them provides testimony of what humans can achieve, each one represents a silent but eloquent statement concerning the scope and possibilities of the human mind, and each one comes into being through the use of one or more forms of representation.

If culture is, as I have suggested, the most telling repository of human capacity, I suggest that we inspect the culture to discover what might be called cognitive artifacts—the products of thought—that we use these products of thought to understand what we can of the forms of thinking that led to each, and that we try in the process to grasp the kind of meaning that each provides. I am saying that it is the sciences and the arts, the architecture, the music, the mathematics, the poetry, and the literature found in culture that give us the clearest sense of what humans are capable of thinking about, the heights their thinking can reach, and which, in turn, tell us about the kinds of meaning humans are capable of creating. Understanding these achievements can, and in my view ought to, provide a basis for making decisions about what we teach.

Let's now turn to some of the core ideas you will find elaborated in the papers to follow.

First, the form of representation we use to represent what we think influences both the processes of thinking and its products.

Imagine a white horse. Imagine a white horse standing in the corner of a green field who slowly begins to move. As the horse moves it gradually turns from white to a brilliant blue. Imagine as it begins to move from walk to trot, from trot to gallop, large gold wings emerging from its back. Now imagine those wings moving as the blue horse rises slowly into the sky above, getting smaller and smaller and slowly disappearing into a large soft white cloud.

Now imagine writing a poem that conveys to a reader your experience with that image, or a painting that depicts it, or a literal description that describes it, or a set of numbers that represents it—a set of numbers? A problem emerges. Poetry, yes; painting, yes; a literal description, yes. But numbers, in this case, numbers won't do.

This scenario is not an argument against the representational capacities of numbers, it is an effort to demonstrate graphically that you can't represent everything with any thing. What you choose to use to think with effects what you can think about. Furthermore the ability to represent experience within the limits and possibilities of a form of representation requires that you think *within* the material with which you work. When such thinking is effective you convert that material into a medium, something that mediates. Mediates what? Mediates your thinking. The choice of a form of representation and the selection of the material to be used imposes both constraints and affordances. When the material is employed skillfully meanings are made that become candidates for interpretation by the "reader."

Reading a form that carries meaning is by no means limited to those who are spectators, reading the form is required of the maker, the individual who attempts to use a form of representation to say something. The maker must be able to read the work as it unfolds and through such a reading be able to make adjustments. It is in this monitoring and editing process that attention to nuance becomes especially important and through such attention, when the necessary skills are available, the process is modified to yield a product worth making. In short, the processes of thinking are engaged in the process of making and the process of making requires the ability to see what is going on in order to make it better. When we modify what we have made as result of such inspection we call it editing. The editing process is employed in all forms of representation.

What is particularly important in this process is that the "standards" the maker uses to make judgments about his or her work are often personal or idiosyncratic, that is, the standards for the work, although influenced by the culture, are often sufficiently open—especially in the arts—to allow the maker to depend upon an internal locus of evaluation. Thus, thinking is promoted by the character of the task.

Second, different forms of representation develop different cognitive skills.

Think about what is required to write a poem or to paint a watercolor or to choreograph a dance. What must someone be able to do? What must a child learn to think about in order to become proficient? First of all an idea must be framed that at the very least functions as a launching pad for one's work. Second, the idea itself must be transformed within the parameters of the medium, that is, the child must be in a position to conceive of the idea in terms that the medium permits. Think again about the horse. To render the experience in dance, what we might call choreographic thinking is required. To render it in paint another form of thinking is involved. Dance requires movement, painting the illusion of movement. While both require attention to composition, the terms or conditions of composing in each form are quite different. The choreographer composes through movement framed by a proscenium arch, the artist composes on canvas, a static surface intended to receive a physically static image. The ability to cope successfully with the demands of the former provides no assurance that one will be successful with the demands of the latter. Each form of representation, although both visual, is mediated through its own materials and each material imposes its own demands. And because the demands of different forms of representation differ, different cognitive skills are developed to cope with them.

Let me offer a specific example of one of those demands in order to better appreciate the forms of cognition it engenders. I turn to watercolor painting.

Watercolor painting is an unforgiving process. By this I mean that watercolor requires a directness and confidence in execution that helps one avoid costly mistakes. Unlike working in oil paint where changes can be made by over-painting a section of a canvas, over-painting in watercolor is not a happy solution for correcting unhappy decisions; colors muddy and spontaneity is lost. Thus the person using watercolors must work directly and often quickly and this means becoming sensitive to a wide array of qualities including the weight of the tip of the brush for its weight when charged with color tells one about the amount of paint it holds and this is important to know because the amount of paint on the brush's tip will effect the kind of image that will flow from it. But that is not all. The kind of image that flows from the brush is also influenced by the wetness of the paper that receives it. The artist or student has to take that interaction effect into account as well.

In these assessments of the conditions of one's work there is no rule to follow and no metric with which to measure weight or to determine wetness. The artist knows through sight and through feel. A unified body and mind must be fully engaged with the material at hand to have a basis for making such judgments.

I have described only a minuscule part of the process of watercolor painting; I have not mentioned any of the formal or expressive considerations that are at the heart of making an art form. These considerations present particularly complex cognitive demands. To regard what is euphemistically called "art work" as "non-cognitive" is to reveal a massive misunderstanding of what such work requires. The task of the teacher is to create the conditions through which the student's thinking about these matters can become more complex, more subtle, more effective. In a word, more intelligent.

Third, the selection of a form of representation influences not only what you are able to represent, it influences what you are able to see.

E. H. Gombrich, the noted art historian was said to have said, "Artists don't paint what they can see, they see what they can paint." Gombrich's point, of course, is that people look for what they know how to find and what they know how to find is often related to what they know how to do. When what one knows is how to measure, one looks for what one can measure. If the only tool you have is a hammer, you treat almost everything as if it were a nail. Tools are not neutral. Forms of representation are tools. They are not neutral. If one sees a city in terms of the poetry one wants to write about it, one seeks in one's travels through the city what has poetic potential. If one searches the city for images to record on black and white film, one seeks images in light and dark. Put color film in the camera and another set of criteria emerge with which to search the city's landscape. When we emphasize the use of particular forms of representation we influence what counts as relevant.

Fourth, forms of representation can be combined to enrich the array of resources students can respond to.

I alluded earlier to the fact that our schools are deeply immersed in teaching language and number. Focusing on each separately as is often done in school has the benefit of providing for focused attention to a specific task. There is virtue in such a focus when trying to learn something complex. At the same time displays that make available to students ideas couched in visual, verbal, numerical, and auditory forms increase the resources available to the student for making meaning; When resources are rich, the number and avenues for learning expand.

The kind of resource-rich environment I am talking about is much closer to the conditions of life outside of schools than inside of them. We live our daily lives in a redundant and replete multimedia environment in which opportunities for iterative forms of learning are common. This means that if we have difficulty learning something one way, there are often other routes that can be taken. Observing preschoolers explore the worlds they inhabit through all of their sensory modalities is evidence enough of the variety of ways through which they come to understand the world. Preschool teachers and kindergarten teachers know this and the environments they create for their students reflect their understanding of the multiple ways through which children learn. These environments also reflect their belief in the importance of providing a wide variety of forms through which their students might represent what they wish to "say."

It is unfortunate that the resource-rich environments that characterize good preschools and kindergartens are typically neutralized as young children move up into the grades. We would do better, I believe, to push the best features of kindergarten upward into the grades than to push the grades into the kindergarten. In many ways the good kindergarten displays features that could serve as a model for the rest of schooling. Kindergarten teachers can create such environments because normally—at least in the past—kindergarten is not regarded as "serious" education. As a result kindergarten teachers are able to utilize the central role sensory experience plays in learning, and are free to afford their students many opportunities to find and use forms of representation that stimulate, practice, and develop different cognitive skills.

For older children imagine programs in science, history, and the arts coming together to provide students with a replete picture of scientific, historical, and artistic content; the relationships between discoveries in physics around the turn of the century, the innovations in visual art and music—Picasso's cubism and Stravinsky's "Firebird" for example—with Einstein's work on his special theory of relativity, and all of this occurring during a period in which Freud's exploration of the unconscious was taking place. What would it mean to students to be given the opportunity to experience these connections *through* the representational forms in which they were realized; listening to Stravinsky, seeing Picasso's cubism, reading Einstein's comments on his own thought processes? A curriculum unit designed to introduce students to such material, designed to ground such material in time and in representational form, would multiply the number and types of "cognitive hooks" or forms of scaffolding that students could use to advance their own learning. The enrichment of the environment by the provision of a variety of forms of representation would also increase the array of cognitive abilities that students could develop. The curriculum would become not only a mind-altering device, it would become a mind-expanding one as well.

There is another issue that also needs to be recognized. This one pertains to matters of educational equity. The selection of the forms of representation that an institution emphasizes to determine who succeeds and who does not is related to the fit between the aptitudes of the students and the affordances of the forms they are to use. When the primary game in town is the denotative use of language and the calculation of number, those whose aptitudes or whose out of school experience utilize such skills are likely to be successful; there is a congruence between what they bring to the school and what the school requires of them. But when the school's curricular agenda is diverse, diverse aptitudes and experience can come into play. Educational equity is provided not merely by opening the doors of the school to the child, but by providing opportunities to the child to succeed once he or she arrives. The provision of the resource rich environment I have described is an extremely important way in which genuine educational equity can be achieved.

This way of thinking about the relationship between the development of cognition and the forms of representation through which it is realized has implications for how we conceive of a successful school. In the conception implicit in what I have said the mission of the school is decidedly not to bring everyone to the same place but, rather, to increase the variance in performance among students while escalating the mean for all. The reason I believe this is an important aim for schools in a democracy is that the cultivation of cognitive diversity is a way of creating a population better able to contribute uniquely to the common weal. Look at it this way. If by some magic everyone was transformed into a brilliant violinist, the convocation of all the brilliance among all the violinists on the planet would not make possible the kind of music that equal competencies would achieve if they were distributed among all the instruments; sometimes you need woodwinds, or percussion, or brass. Schools that cultivate the differences among us while escalating the mean for performance in each of the forms of representation provides for the richness of the full orchestra. We do better as a culture when we are not all violinists—even brilliant ones.

Fifth, each form of representation can be used in different ways and each way calls upon the use of different skills and forms of thinking.

We tend to talk about forms of representation as if each of them called upon a single set of specific cognitive skills. At a general level they do. Dance, in contrast to computation or the writing of poetry, makes use of the body in motion; thinking must be realized within the capacities of a moving body. But such parameters are general parameters and within movement itself there are a wide array of options; *how* one chooses to dance, *what* one wishes to express, the *genre* within which one works also imposes requirements that are specific to the particular task to be performed. In the field of painting the pathos expressed in the drawings of Käthe Kollwitz required her to make use of a marriage between mind, emotion, and body that made the power of her images possible; in a sense, her aesthetic center is located in her guts. Her work is not what one might call cerebral, though surely there are ideas in it. Other artists, for example, the abstractionist Josef Albers was concerned with color relationships. His paintings deal with what might be called visual vibration. Their source is located in a different part of the body compared to Kollwitz. And when we look at the work of Salvador Dali, other sources become dominant, these in the meanderings of the unconscious. My point here is that as Snow (1997) has pointed out, many forms of thinking are at play in any single form of representation, even though one may dominate.

What does the foregoing mean for American education? Do the ideas we have examined have any implications for what we do in schools or for the policies we create to guide them? Do they have relevance for how we think about the meaning of education? I think they do and I believe their implications pertain to matters of *process, content, equity,* and *culture.* I address each briefly here.

By process I refer back to where we began, namely with the idea that mind is a cultural achievement, that the form it takes is influenced in significant degree by the kind of experience an individual is afforded in the course of a lifetime. In school, a major locus of experience for children and adolescents is the curriculum. It performs a major function in shaping those experiences. Decisions regarding which forms of representation will be emphasized, which will be marginalized, and which will be absent constitute decisions about the kinds of processes that will be stimulated, developed, and refined. In short, in schools we influence the forms of cognitive competency that students will develop by providing opportunities for development to occur. In education we are in the construction business.

Process is one side of the coin, content is the other. Competency in the use of a form of representation provides access to particular forms' experience and therefore to ways of understanding. The ability to read a poem, an equation, a painting, a dance, a novel, a contract constitutes distinctive forms of literacy where literacy means, as I intend it to mean, a way of representing and recovering meaning in the form of representation in which it appears. Given this conception of literacy, a conception far broader than its commonly held root "logos," referring to the word, we ought to be interested in developing multiple forms of literacy. Why? Because each form of literacy has the capacity to provide unique forms of meaning and it is in the pursuit of meaning that much of the good life is lived. Schools serve children best when their programs do not narrow the kind of meanings they know how to pursue and capture.

Equity is a third notion that can summarize the contributions that attention to multiple forms of representation can help achieve. The equity question is related to aptitude differences among students and to the opportunities they will find in schools that make it possible for them to play to their strengths. Equity of opportunity does not reside as some people seem to believe in a common program for all. It resides in school programs that make it possible for students to follow their bliss, to pursue their interests, to realize and develop what they are good at. Of course there will need to be parameters set with respect to what is possible—a school cannot do everything—nevertheless, I am talking about ambitions, desiderata, principles. We ought to try to grasp what may be beyond our reach—or what's a heaven for?

Finally, we come to culture. What kind of society do we want? What kind of life do we want to be able to lead? What kind of place will America become? The quality of life that America as a culture will make possible will not only be a function of diversity of traditions and values, it will be a function of the quality of the contributions rooted in the differences among us. In totalitarian societies, Herbert Read (1944) reminds us, children are to be shaped by schools to fit an image defined by the state. In democratic societies and in those societies seeking to create a democratic way of life, children are helped to realize their distinctive talents and through such realization to be in a position to contribute to the culture as a whole. The presence of multiple forms of representation in the school is a way to try to achieve that democratic ambition.

Ultimately I believe we need to build a culture reflecting the two senses in which the term "culture" can be used. One sense is biological, the other is anthropological. In the biological sense a culture is a medium for growing things. In the anthropological sense a culture is a shared way of life. Our schools should be cultures in both senses. They should be media for growing things and what they should grow are minds. They should try to achieve that noble ambition through the shared way of life they make possible, a way of life that recognizes both the differences and the commonalities among us. Understanding the relationship between cognition and representation and its relevance for policy and practice in our schools is one place to begin. It is also one way to pursue the American dream.

THE ARTS AND THEIR ROLE
IN EDUCATION

How should we think about the role of the arts in our schools? For centuries the arts have been regarded as marginal to the central mission of schooling, which has been considered the development of intellect. As the story goes, the arts are thought to be matters of play rather than work, matters of body rather than mind; they are thought to traffic in emotion rather than in the cool rationality that is supposed to characterize mature, rational beings. It's not that the arts are not nice to have when you can, they simply are not necessary for the conduct of education and therefore an add-on that often is thought of as "co-curricular" or, even worse, "extra-curricular."

In some ways it is strange that the arts should be marginalized in our schools when their position in our culture is so important. We build palaces called concert halls and museums to house them and travel halfway around the world to experience their delights. Yet when it comes to our schools, other subjects take priority.

Making the case for the arts may very well be not only a matter of rectifying misconceptions, but of altering constraints that affect school programs. For example, our achievement testing practices typically focus on forms of performance that are distant from those the arts employ. And since the reputation of schools, teachers, and administrators often hinges upon their students' performance on such tests, our most precious resource, time, is assigned to the subjects we test.

But testing practices are not the only dominant influence affecting the arts in our schools. Consider university admission requirements. Here too priorities reside elsewhere. Selective institutions of higher education often disregard performance in the arts in secondary school transcripts when calculating the student's grade point average. Counselors, teachers, and students and parents themselves understand where the rewards will be secured and define their educational priorities not so much in terms of the subjects they would like to pursue, but those they feel they must pursue. Thus, it is not unusual for students to be pressured into enrolling in courses that have little to do with their deepest interests in order to satisfy the requirements of college admissions committees.

The need to develop a conception of both the arts and education that addresses the intimate relationship between them and the need to alter, politically if necessary, the constraints upon school programs imposed from above by testing programs and admission practices are tasks that have yet to be completed.

Part 2 addresses the contributions the arts make—when well taught— to the educational development of the young. These essays attempt to correct misconceptions and to locate the arts within the central mission of education. The arts inform as well as stimulate, they challenge as well as satisfy. Their location is not limited to galleries, concert halls, and theatres. Their home can be found whenever humans choose to have attentive and vital intercourse with life itself. This is, perhaps, the largest lesson that the arts in education can teach, the lesson that life itself can be led as a work of art. In so doing, the maker himself or herself is remade. This remaking, this re-creation is at the heart of the process of education.

5

What the Arts Taught Me About Education

What follows is a personal, autobiographical statement. To write about how the arts have influenced my thinking about education demands, at least for me, an examination of the role they have played in my life. I can see no other way to do it.

I must confess that I have thought about this matter many times, but it was not until I was invited to *write* this chapter that I confronted the task of thinking systematically about it. As almost all academics know, writing forces you to reflect in an organized and focused way on what it is you want to say. Words written confront you and give you the opportunity to think again. Thinking on its own, without the commitment that writing exacts, makes tolerable—even pleasurable—the flashing thought, the elusive image. When one writes, the public character of the form demands organization, and when autobiographical, the problems of appearing egoistic or saying too much or seeming self-promoting are constant threats.

I share these concerns with you because I want you to know that for me this is not the usual academic paper; the topic of the paper is me.

Let me begin with a confession that art—the visual arts—was a source of salvation for me in the two elementary schools I attended between five and thirteen years of age. I did not do well in elementary school: arithmetic was problematic and frustrating, my handwriting was and is at present not particularly good, spelling was a relentless bore, and English grammar—the diagramming of sentences whose features remain before me as vividly now as they were then—was largely meaningless, even when I was able to correctly indicate the difference between a direct and an indirect object. But art—ah, that was another story. I was good at art; indeed, I was the "class artist," and appreciation for this achievement motivated my third-grade teacher, Mrs. Eva Smith (at that time a nearly ancient fifty-year-old), to suggest to my mother that I should be enrolled in art classes at the School of the Chicago Art Institute.

My mother was both an intellectual woman and someone who prized the arts, particularly music. She wasted no time enrolling me in Saturday morning art classes which I continued to attend throughout elementary school and into the beginning of high school. Art was then, as it is today, a deep source of pleasure.

High school was even more frustrating for me than elementary school. Aside from art, sports, and girls, my high school classes were dull at best. I did not do well. Out of a class of about 430 graduates, I managed to graduate in the 32nd percentile of my class. The prospects for my future would be lackluster if I graduated today in the same position as I did then.

After graduating from high school, I enrolled in the School of the Art Institute of Chicago to study painting, and then attended Roosevelt College in Chicago to complete a B.A. in art and in education. It was during those four years—between seventeen and twenty-one—that the marriage of art and education occurred. Let me tell you how.

I grew up in a Jewish community on Chicago's West Side. Although there was an exodus of Jews in the 1950s from this part of Chicago to the northern suburbs, our family was among the last to leave. The neighborhood that was once populated with delicatessens and synagogues—virtually one on every corner—became a haven for African American not only from Chicago, but from other parts of the country. "My" neighborhood had as one of its community resources a boys club, the American Boys Common-wealth, where as a child I spent countless happy hours working with clay, plaster, and paint, and learning to weave and draw. I returned to the ABC during my college years to teach arts and crafts to the children and adolescents who had moved into the neighborhood. In fact, I taught my arts and craft classes in the very same art room in which I had spent such happy days during my own childhood.

The children I encountered, and particularly the adolescents with whom I worked, were poor, and, as they were described at that time, were either "pre-delinquents" or "juvenile delinquents"—not all, to be sure, but enough of them to help me understand what those terms meant. Establishing rapport was tough but achievable, and such victories were very satisfying. My work with these children and adolescents, motivated initially by a desire to learn more about art by examining its sources, soon was converted into an interest in how art could be used to help children grow. My master's thesis at the Illinois Institute of Technology was titled "The

Therapeutic Contributions of Art in Group Work Settings." I became as much interested in the children with whom I worked as in their art; no, even more so.

The opportunities to work with "children at risk," as we say today, and to teach art in the Chicago Public Schools after finishing a master's degree in art education provided a part of the foundation for my commitment both to art and to education. The other part of that foundation was built from the kind of social conscience that growing up in the home of a socialist father and an artistically interested and intellectual mother generated. Discussions about "society," "the working man," and "equality," as well as the importance of education, were almost daily fare.

As important as these two particular sources were, they do not tell the whole story. For example, while at Roosevelt College I had the good fortune of having some superb neoprogressive professors of education who were interested in "deep" learning and who cared about children. What they were concerned about I had become interested in years earlier, and so the congruence between their ideas and my interests were very close. My work as a student in the School of the Art Institute of Chicago taught me invaluable lessons about the importance of both intellectual and emotional commitment to one's own work. Painting was difficult, complex, challenging, and demanded time and the ability, even if one was only nineteen, to commit oneself to its seriousness. In its own special way the School of the Art Institute of Chicago was a deeply intellectual place, as I think the really well-run high school auto mechanics program can be for today's adolescent. I learned at the Art Institute of Chicago to take work seriously. The fact that some of my fellow students were a decade older than I, veterans of the Second World War going to school on the G.I. Bill, helped in this regard.

Also contributing to my views about education was my experience as a neophyte art teacher working on the fourth floor (where few administrators ventured) in Chicago's Carl Schurz High School. A school for thirty-six hundred students and middle class throughout, this setting gave me the opportunity to discover the deep satisfactions I could receive not only from seeing or making paintings and sculpture, but from helping fourteen- and fifteen-year-olds immerse themselves in the process of creating their own art. I discovered at a level different from what I learned in the American Boys Commonwealth that initiating the young into the pleasures of art and the visual world was for me a very important source of satisfaction. These satisfactions and interests continued and provided a major theme during my doctoral studies in the Department of Education at the University of Chicago. No one on the faculty had a specialized or even a special interest in art education, but my professors provided the space and the support that made it possible for me to continue my interests in this field. I was very lucky.

Chicago also provided the theoretical tools and the intellectual climate that I needed; much of it was like my life as a child at home; ideas were prized almost for their own sake. Analysis, debate, and speculation were common. Much of my experience there was familiar and comfortable. More moments than one has a right to expect were like peak experiences. At Chicago, art and intellect had a happy marriage.

So much for foundations. What difference have these experiences made in the way in which I think about education?

Perhaps the most important contribution that my immersion in the visual arts has made to my views of education is the realization that neither cognition nor epistemology can be adequately conceptualized if the contributions of the arts to these domains are neglected. Those of us professionally socialized in education, not to say the culture at large, have lived in a sea of assumptions about mind and knowledge that have marginalized the arts by putting them on the back burners of mind and understanding. To engage in cognitive activities, we have been told, is to mediate thought linguistically, to use logic in order to monitor thinking, and to escape the limiting concreteness of the particular in order to experience the loftiness of the general. Plato's conception of knowledge as thought liberated from the senses and Piaget's ideal of formal operations as the apotheosis of cognition represent for most in education what it means to engage the mind (Gardner 1989).

As for knowledge, the legacies of Compte and positivism in its various forms put the arts beyond the margins of knowledge (Ayer n.d.). To know, the positivists tell us, is to make meaningful assertions—that is, to state propositions or make claims about the empirical world whose truth (or falsity, at least) can be tested. What one cannot say one cannot know. Given this view, how can a nonpropositional form—and these forms include not only the visual arts, music, and dance, but also literature and poetry—be regarded as having any epistemic functions at all (Phillips 1987)? The answer is clear: they cannot.

The result of such beliefs—often unexamined, at that—is to promote a hierarchy of knowledge that enthrones scientific knowledge and expels the arts from cognition entirely. The arts, as everyone knows (given these beliefs), are affective, not cognitive, and in our educational institutions we are hell-bent on cognition. Given the prevailing view, the arts are nice, but not really necessary (Broudy 1979).

My own experience in the arts as a painter contradicted these narrow views of what the thinking mind did or how it was we come to know. It was clear to me, as a doctoral student at the University of Chicago, that the creation of a successful painting or an expressive sculpture could in no way be dismissed as a consequence of emotion finding its release in a material. The job of making a painting, or even its competent perception, requires the exercise of mind: the eye is a part of the mind and the process of perceiving the subtleties of a work of art is as much of an inquiry as the design of an experiment in chemistry. As a painter I grappled with the problem of trying to make a picture "work"—often unsuccessfully. Painting was no easy task. Matters of visualization, technique, composition, sensibility, and inventiveness were required. And all of these skills and abilities were employed on a dynamic configuration; things were always changing, and the most subtle alteration of a passage in one section of an image required attention to a variety of others as well. To conceive of the arts as the discharge of affect was to miss the point of what they were about and, more important, to neglect a resource that could have a major contribution to make to the developing mind. Such ill-conceived notions, I thought, must surely be apparent. Yet all around, the arts were a nonissue. Even the educational scholars I respected the most paid little attention to their potential role in our schools.[1]

My work in the arts as a painter made it perfectly clear that cognition, by which I mean thinking and knowing, is not limited to linguistically mediated thought, that the business of making a picture "that works" is an awesome cognitive challenge, and that those who limit knowing to science are naive about the arts and, in the long run, injurious to the children whose educational programs were shaped by their ideals.

I must confess that the foregoing beliefs were, early in my academic career, convictions that were derived intuitively from my experiences as a painter. It was not until I read the work of Rudolf Arnheim (1990), Susanne Langer (1942), and John Dewey (1934) that I encountered respected scholars whose work supported my intuitions. And when I read Michael Polanyi's *Personal Knowledge* (1958)—a book I encountered years after it was first published—my sense of being vindicated grew.

My appreciation for the kinds of thinking that qualitative mediation and qualitative problem solving elicited led quite quickly to the view that if education was to do more than develop a small part of human cognition, it had to give the young opportunities to work in the arts. The arts were mind-altering devices and the curriculum the major means through which such alteration could be fostered. To underestimate their importance in the array of cultural resources that the school could make available was to do a significant disservice to the young. Making a place for the arts in our schools became for me a kind of cause, a cause in the name of a balanced and equitable education.

It is both interesting and gratifying to find that both developmental and differential psychologists have discovered the arts. Gardner (1983), for example, argues the case for a multiple theory of intelligence and makes place for the arts within the seven modes of intelligence he describes. Snow (1986), likewise, recognizes aptitude differences in learning and the importance of formulating curricula that allow children to play to their strengths. The newfound cognitive pluralism and the greater willingness of psychologists to recognize "practical knowledge"[2] harkens back to an Aristotelian distinction between the ways in which knowledge is secured and displayed. The upshot of these interests is the liberalization of views about the nature of intellect and the provision of a wider and more generous conception of what it means to be smart. I confess that I sometimes feel like someone standing on the sandy beach of a fog-swept sea watching a rowboat filled with cognitive psychologists searching for the shore. I sometimes see myself waving to those aboard and shouting to them, "Over here! Come over here! What's taken you so long?"

I know that such personal revelations make me appear smug; I do not intend for that impression to be conveyed, but those of us who have devoted so much of our professional lives to trying to make a place for the arts in education have been waiting for a very long time. To be perfectly candid, although the rowboat is closer now to the shore than it once was, it has not yet docked.

You will recall that I said that cognition referred not only to skills, but also to knowledge. The creation of a picture, or a poem, or a musical composition requires, at minimum, knowledge of the unfolding qualities with which one works. These cognitively mediated qualities must be seen, modulated, transformed, and organized in the course of one's work. It is clear to anyone who has struggled with the task of doing so that there are no linguistic equivalents to the qualities experienced in this process. To reduce knowledge to warranted assertions, true propositions, or falsifiable claims that have withstood falsification is to be oblivious to the fact that, insofar as such claims refer to empirical qualities, they are never their equivalent. The map is not the territory. In order to draw the map, the territory first has to be known in other ways.

I was not willing to reduce knowledge to the kinds of truth tests that positivists or neopositivist philosophers required. Furthermore, knowledge of the qualities of works of art is not limited to the qualities found in works of art alone. It was clear that the qualitative subtleties of the world outside of art—the comportment of people, the look of a city street, the tone of voice as it speaks, and an infinite array of others—were objects of knowledge by a seeing eye and a hearing ear. Language is, in a way, our heroic effort to transform what we have come to know directly into that public surrogate we call *text*. When text is itself artistically rendered, we can begin to approximate the virgin experience it is intended to convey.[3]

Appreciation of qualitative sources of knowledge led me to reject conventional wisdom: why restrict knowledge to what verificationists *or* falliblists demand? To do so would be like limiting the content and aims of education to what psychometricians are able to measure. It made no sense to me to try to consign knowledge to a piece of paper the size of a bubblegum wrapper, all in the service of verification. Thus, it becomes increasingly important to me not only to broaden our view of what it means to think, but also to enlarge our view of what it means to know. In this effort cognitive pluralists such as Nelson Goodman (1978) became important allies.

To illustrate the ways in which the arts enlarge our knowledge of the world, consider two complementary processes that they engender: individuation and generalization (Arnheim 1990). The refinement of the perception of idiosyncratic features of objects or events is one of the two major lessons that learning to draw, sculpt, compose, or write artistically focused language develops. To draw a tree or the particular comportment of a seated figure, the artist must not only notice that the object to be drawn is a tree or a figure, but a *particular* tree or figure. To do this, the artist must avoid the premature classification that is typically fostered by schooling and instead remain open to the particular features and overall conformations of individual forms. No tree, no oak tree, no young oak tree is the same as any other young oak tree. The task the artist faces is to experience individual features of *this* tree, of *this* person, and to create a form that succeeds in revealing the essential and unique features of the object seen. In the process of revealing what is individual, the work also—ironically—becomes what Arnheim (1990) calls a canonical image through which the features portrayed through the visual rendering of a distilled particular can be used as a generalizable image to locate similar features found elsewhere. In this process the image becomes a concrete universal, a means through which perception is sensitized so that it can locate like qualities. Such functions are performed through literature, poetry, dance, as well as the visual arts. *Othello* is about more than Othello.

It is ironic, to say the least, that schools should pay so much attention to the process that Dewey (1934) called *recognition*, and so little attention to the processes of perception. All so-called abstract knowledge depends upon the ability to relate language to images: infinity, kindness, masculinity, envy are imagistic in character; the sources of these images are in the extrapolation of qualities seen: infinity—time and space; kindness—subtle degrees of care experienced; masculinity—the features we learn in our culture to stand for maleness; envy—the way in which individuals respond to each other. In fact, we have no words that can adequately reveal the meanings to which these terms refer. To the extent to which our imagination is impoverished, the meanings of these terms also will be. Imagination is fed by perception and perception by sensibility and sensibility by artistic cultivation. With refined sensibility, the scope of perception is enlarged. With enlarged perception, the resources that feed our imaginative life are increased. Thus, one of the lessons I have learned from art that has influenced my views of education is that it is through the refinement of sensibility that language secures its semantic character; another is that the eye is a part of the mind; a third, that not all that we can know, we can say. Polanyi (1967) was right: we know more than we can tell.

The practical and normative implications for curriculum of these ideas I believe to be more than substantial. Like the arts, the school curriculum is a mind-altering device; it is a vehicle that is designed to change the ways in which the young think. If the arts develop particular mental skills—the ability to experience qualitative nuance, for example—and if they inform about the world in ways unique to their form, then their presence in our programs for the young are likely to foster such outcomes; their absence, the opposite. Thus, when we think about the arts not simply as objects that afford pleasure, but as forms that develop thinking skills and enlarge understanding, their significance as a part of our educational programs become clear. Curricula in which the arts are absent or inadequately taught rob children of what they might otherwise become.

Thus far I have spoken of the contributions of the arts within the curriculum in fairly general terms. While it is true that all art forms share some common features, there are significant differences as well. The cadences of poetic language are not those of symphonic form; the rhythms of visual form are different from those found in literature or dance. At the most obvious level, differences among the arts are (usually) differences in the sensory modalities appealed to. They are images experienced through the funded perception of the form or genre in which any particular work participates. What this means is that the development of sensibility and judgment profits—indeed, often requires—a memory of forms related to the one being encountered (Eisner 1991). The curricular implications of this observation are that the educational benefits of the arts are secured not simply by their short-term presence, but by sustained experience with like forms. It takes time, effort, and experience to learn how to read a complex and subtle array of qualities. Each of the different art forms participates in a different history, has its own features, and utilizes different sensory modalities. By learning to create or perceive such forms, the arts contribute to the achievement of mind.

The differences among the various arts are not only differences that count in calculating their educational value. There are important differences *within* a specific art form. Different forms of visual art, for example, may be said to appeal to different parts of our body. Surrealist art, in both its perception and creation, calls upon the individual to take leave of reality and to enter into a *sur-real* world. Fantasy, dreams, reverie are the stuff that the surreal depends upon. Children introduced to such work or to activities that invite them to create it experience a different kind of "ride" than those working with the French impressionists. My point here is that styles of art—cubism, de Stijl, constructivism, minimalism, realism, pop and op art, expressionism—call upon different aspects of ourselves. Which art forms are selected and what tasks are set in the curriculum have consequences for that aspect of our being to which the form speaks. The same case can be made for music, dance, and literature.

Thus, another of the lessons I've learned from the arts is that while they share commonalities, different forms of art put me in the world in different ways. They speak to different aspects of my nature and help me discover the variety of experiences I am capable of having. I believe that such lessons have implications for educational policy and for deciding about what knowledge is of most worth.

As fundamental as curriculum is, no curriculum teaches itself. The curriculum is always mediated. It is in the description and improvement of teaching that the arts have a special contribution to make.

It has been relatively recent that it has become legitimate to think about teaching as an art form. The dominant image and ideal has been, and in most quarters still is, a technical one. The general model is for educational researchers to do the basic social science, to pass on to teacher trainers what they have discovered, who in turn inform would-be and practicing teachers of "what works." This model has increasingly been regarded as oversimplified and, by some, downright wrong (Broudy 1976). New and, I believe, more adequate views talk about the epistemology of practice (Atkin 1989) and about the differences between theoretical knowledge and practical deliberation (Schwab 1969). The importance of the context is recognized even by cognitive scientists when they talk about "situated knowledge" (Greeno 1989). Yet, for all of these developments, it is telling to note that the *Handbook of Research and Teaching* (Wittrock 1986), a tome weighing over four and a half pounds and containing over eight hundred entries in its index, has no listing under the heading "Art" with respect to teaching. To be sure, there is a heading referring to art, but it is to the teaching of art, not to the art of teaching.

My work in the arts has influenced my view that teaching is an artistically pervaded activity—at least at its best. Teaching is artistic in character in many of the ways in which all art is artistic: it provides a deep sense of aesthetic experience to both perceiver and actor when it is well done (Eisner 1982). It requires the teacher to pay attention to qualitative nuance—tone of voice, the comportment of students, the pervasive quality of the teaching episode. It requires the teacher to attend to matters of composition in order to give the day or lesson coherence. It often requires flexibility in aims and the ability to exploit unforeseen opportunities in order to achieve aims that could not have been conceptualized beforehand. Teaching is a constructive activity whose efforts result in forms that can provide what the fine arts are intended to provide: a heightened consciousness and aesthetic experience.

Because theoretical models are idealized structures, and research results, abstractions referring to absent populations, no teacher can rely upon them exclusively for dealing with particular students in particular classrooms in particular schools. Like all artistic activities, the features of the specific material or situation must be addressed without relying upon algorithms for decision making.

These features of teaching seem perfectly plain to me. They are less clear to many others, although, as I have indicated, the field of education is moving toward a more artistically conscious view of the nature of teaching than it has in the past (Kagan 1985). When there is a willingness to recognize the artistic nature of excellent teaching and to acknowledge the inherent limitations of the social sciences in guiding teachers, possibilities emerge for treating the improvement of teaching in ways that are not unlike those used to improve individual performance in any art (Atkin 1989). When such ways are examined, attention to nuance in performance becomes crucial, and the use of a language through which it can be revealed, essential. These processes are examples of connoisseurship and criticism (Eisner 1985).

What the arts have taught me is that nuance counts in teaching no less than in painting. It has taught me that not everything can be reduced to quantity and that the attempt to do so creates a destructive form of reductionism and a misleading sense of precision. I have learned from the arts that poetic language is often needed to *render* a performance vivid, and that suggestion and innuendo are often more telling than stark statement of fact.

The logical categories and operational definitions that appear so attractive in the social sciences are, in my view, often misplaced in so fragile and delicate an enterprise as teaching. Although the traditional ambition of nailing down the facts and measuring the outcomes have long been sources of cognitive security for some, they are beginning to give way to a more elastic but relevant form of disclosure. That is one of the reasons why ethnography is now seen as a useful way to understand classrooms and schools. When Clifford Geertz (1988) says that anthropological authority often emanates from the ways in which some anthropologists write, he recognizes the artistic contributions to anthropological scholarship. Geertz is by no means alone. The previously sacrosanct methods and criteria for social science inquiry, methods that once aspired to those of physics, are being reconceptualized and widened in the process. The direction is toward the arts.

The conceptualization of teaching as an artistic activity and the acceptance of epistemological pluralism have opened the door to a form of evaluation that is rooted in the arts and humanities. Educational connoisseurship and educational criticism (Eisner 1985) are efforts to use and extend aims and methods employed to heighten awareness of works of art to educational practice. Connoisseurship is the art of appreciation; criticism, the art of disclosure. They are means with which to see and to articulate the qualities and values of particular works of art by using a language that helps others see those works more completely. The genre of educational criticism is literary. While an educational critic might use some of the techniques of the cultural anthropologist—interviewing students, for example—the aims of the critic's work are not anthropological, but educational. It is intended to heighten awareness of the classroom or of teaching or of the materials students and teacher use. It is critical, interpretive, and often poetic in flavor. From the arts I have learned that such efforts can amplify perception and expand consciousness of what otherwise might go unseen. Much of my own work over the last two decades has been aimed at elucidating that model and fostering its legitimation in the field of education. I believe much progress has been made.

Another lesson I learned from the arts deals with how we think about the outcomes of educational practice. In the standard model of rational educational planning, the task confronting the planner is, first, to be clear about his or her objectives, to specify them in detail and, if possible, to define them in measurable terms.[4] By using this model, curriculum development is believed to be made easier because clarity of aims is thought to facilitate the invention of means for their achievement. In addition, aims, by and large, are to be common among students of the same age levels, as are the tests they are to take to demonstrate competency. The education summit talk of September 1989 about national goals for America's schools, defined in measurable terms, is nothing less than the rationale I have described directing educational policy at the highest levels of our government. Clarity of expectation subjected to a common form of examination using standardized criteria meet the accepted canons of rationality and objectivity.

My experience in the arts has taught me a different lesson. From the arts I have learned that not only cannot all outcomes be measured, they frequently cannot be predicted. When humans work on tasks, they almost always learn more *and* less than what was intended. Furthermore, teaching that is not hog-tied to rigid specifications often moves in directions and explores ideas that neither the students nor the teacher could envision at the outset. In addition, virtue in education is much more than achieving uniformity in outcomes among students. Such an aim might be defensible in a training program, but when one values individual vision and personal creativity, the specter of all fourth graders marching at the same pace to the same drummer toward the same destination is a vision that better fits the current People's Republic of China than a nation aspiring to become a genuine democracy. In short, educational practice does not display its highest virtues in uniformity, but in nurturing productive diversity. The evocation of such diversity is what all genuine art activities have in common. Even art forms as apparently restrictive as the music of the baroque or the brush painting of the Meiji Period in Japan made it possible for artists to improvise in order to reveal their own personalities in their work. Educational programs, I learned from the arts, should not be modeled after the standardized procedures of the factory; the studio is a better image.

When one seeks not uniformity of outcome, but productive diversity, the need to create forms of evaluation that can handle uniqueness of outcome becomes increasingly apparent: the multiple-choice test will no longer do. Any approach that prizes such outcomes foregoes commensurability, a source of deep security for many. When we cease putting all children on the same statistically derived distribution, we have to think and judge, we have to interpret what it is that they have done. We move more and more toward connoisseurship. And when we talk to others about what we have learned, we move more and more toward criticism, that age-old process of interpretation and appraisal. An artistic perspective, once taken, colors the way we see all facets of the educational enterprise; it is not restricted to a bit here and a piece there.

What, then, have I learned from the arts that has influenced the way I think about education? I have learned that knowledge cannot be reduced to what can be said. I have learned that the process of working on a problem yields its own intrinsically valuable rewards and that these rewards are as important as the outcomes. I have learned that goals are not stable targets at which you aim, but directions toward which you travel. I have learned that no part of a composition, whether in a painting or in a school, is independent of the whole in which it participates. I have learned that scientific modes of knowledge are not the only ones that inform and develop human cognition. I have learned that, as constructive activity, science as well as the fine arts are artistically created structures. I have learned these lessons and more. Not a bad intellectual legacy, I think. And not a bad foundation on which to build better schools for both children and teachers.

Notes

1. Two exceptions were Jacob Getzels, whose background in literature permeated his observations about education, and John Goodlad, who intuitively knew that the arts were an important aspect of programs for children and adolescents. Both Getzels and Goodlad supported my interest in the arts, although neither taught courses in the arts in education.

2. The concept "practical knowledge" reverberates in current discussions of "situated knowledge," a phrase being used increasingly among cognitive psychologists to underscore the differences between learning within an academic setting and the kind of knowledge that students can act upon in situations outside of the classroom. The family resemblance, it seems to me, between Aristotle's distinction between practical and theoretical knowledge is quite apparent, even when psychologists do not harken back to its roots.

3. Susanne Langer's point that both literature and poetry are nondiscursive is directly related to her argument that the artistic formation of language presents a form of feeling that can be known only through the way in which a form—language—has been shaped. Artistic form, for Langer, has an important epistemic function.

4. The salience of hyperrationalized views of educational planning as represented in the work of Robert Mager and James Popham has diminished in recent years. However, it is well to recall how oversimplified conceptions of "intelligent" professional planning undermined genuine professionalism among teachers by its failure to appreciate the need for what Dewey referred to as "flexible purposing." As teachers have a larger say in schools, the acknowledgment of artistry and the need for flexibility is likely to increase.

6

The Education of Vision

Since the seventeenth century, that is since René Descartes separated mind from body, educators in the western world have regarded the senses as *cognitio inferior*—minor resources in the human's quest to understand. Understanding at its best requires the pure, clean light of reason and reason among all of the human faculties belongs to the mind, not the body.

This view of the locus of reason and the function of mind marginalized the senses as instruments in reason's pursuit. That marginalization has, in turn, become a basic feature in American educational policy. Fields dealing with sensory material—the arts especially—are given only a brief, passing nod in the creation of educational priorities. For example, it was only after the intense lobbying of arts educators that those individuals who formulated the educational policies embedded in *America 2000* (United States Department of Education 1991) acknowledged the arts as one of the fields that students ought to address. The horse, however, had long since left the barn and although this acknowledgment reached the ears of arts educators—who were intently listening—I doubt that it reached the ears of those who were not.

Visual learning is a concept broader in character than learning in the visual arts. Nevertheless, there are many features of visual learning that also appear in learning in the visual arts and I will in this essay be shuttling back and forth between these two areas.

The thesis I advance attempts to reintegrate mind and body. Indeed, I hope for an integration so pervasive and secure that distinctions between the two become impossible to draw. I argue here as I have elsewhere (Eisner 1994) that the human organism in common with most living organisms possesses a sensorium that is responsive to the qualitative environment it inhabits and that it is this responsiveness—our capacity to see, to hear, to touch, to smell, and to taste—that makes consciousness possible. Indeed, I believe the information that these capacities provide makes possible the images and icons that we too often glibly refer to as concepts. Concepts, a term that is often used in both educational and psychological literature, is just as often un- or under-analyzed as a human resource for thinking. Concepts are often thought to be the terms we use to refer to a set of common qualities rather than the qualities to which the terms refer. It is our capacity to experience sweetness, to hear loudness, to imagine infinity, that makes the terms we use to refer to these forms of consciousness meaningful: Images precede language. Our conceptual life is filled with what Arnheim (1990) has called canonical images: sensory distillations of the sensory experience we secure from a qualitatively rich and always changing environment.

Visual learning represents a particular form of human achievement, one that includes our ability to notice what is visually subtle and to use it in ways that are personally or socially meaningful. Consider a simple example. Our ability to discern the visual qualities of a piece of fruit makes it possible to use those qualities as signifiers of its degree of ripeness. In this example and a host of others, visual qualities become meaningful, in part, because we regard them as indicative of other states of affairs. But this is not the only way in which visual qualities become meaningful. They also become meaningful in and of themselves; they yield meanings that are immediately enjoyable. Thus, an abstract painting or a gnarled old branch can be a source of meaningful experience as we notice and respond to the particular visual qualities that it possesses: its color, form, and composition, for example. Whether the painting or the branch signify a state of affairs beyond themselves is less important than what they yield as sources of consummatory experience. Visual learning makes such forms of experience possible. In so doing, it becomes a means through which we make sense of the world we inhabit and learn to experience and enjoy visual forms for their own sake.

In speaking about visual learning in these ways, I have addressed the receptive, or appreciative, side of the equation. Visual learning pertains not only to our growing capacity to construe meaning from the visual forms around us. It also pertains to our capacity to *create* visual forms that will carry the meanings we intend forward. At a simple level, we all recall from Ross Perot's campaign for the presidency his use of pie charts and diagrams that made plain the economic state of America. He was shrewdly able to display a set of complex relationships in a visual form that enabled millions of people to grasp what he believed to be the condition of our economy.

Pie charts, histograms, scattergrams, trend lines, spread sheets, maps, and models all perform similar functions. They all represent. The ability to create these forms and to interpret those available are important communication skills. In fact, it is so important that computer companies have not missed the opportunity to market their wares more effectively by calling to the customer's attention their computer's versatility in providing spreadsheets and other visual means through which the customer can recover and represent information more easily.

One of the reasons why such forms work is that they simplify. They simplify by distilling complex information into spatial analogues that display the structural features of the phenomena people wish to understand. They function as synchronic media. Language, unlike visual images, is a diachronic medium; language is a medium that carries a message over time. Images are presented at once. To understand language, one needs to "hang on" to accrued meanings so that the meanings to be encountered can be related to the network of meaningful utterances that preceded them. When matters become complicated, language often becomes a complicated means for holding or conveying the information one wishes to possess or share.

Reflect for a moment on the task of describing to someone who has never done so how to tie a bow with shoelaces. Can you imagine the linguistic somersaults you would need to perform in order to provide an accurate rendering of that performance? Parents know intuitively, as do teachers, that the best way to help a child learn how to tie a bow is to show the child how it is done. In the showing, a complex task is divided into parts and a kind of scaffolding provided so that the parent's performance can be successfully imitated. Here is an example of visual learning in action. A set of relationships is displayed visually rather than described linguistically. Through display, the task is more easily grasped and the child's performance more likely to be successful.

Teachers have long known that when verbal explanations do not suffice, examples need to be given. In fact, observing teachers at work makes it plain that example after example is sometimes needed to help a particular child grasp the meaning of a set of ideas. What the example does is to make vivid the referent that less descriptive language failed to provide. Examples have been used forever to help people grasp meaning. Do examples carried by language foster visual learning? I would argue that they do. I believe they do because examples illustrate. They illustrate not by providing visual images directly but by inviting the child to use his or her imagination to create them in order to "see" what previously was not understood.

It is revealing that in the English language we use metaphors that disclose the power of visualization as a source of human understanding.

Someone who doesn't understand something is in the dark. Someone who does has just seen the light. Someone who grasps meaning is bright. Someone who doesn't is dull. Someone who understands, "sees" what you mean. Our intuitively generated vernacular discourse reveals our tacit recognition that the capacity to see, in this case through our imaginative life, is a fundamental resource for understanding aspects of the world in which we live. In fact, that highly valued human capacity called intuition is derived from the Latin and means "to look upon." See what I mean?

Visual learning has other features besides those I have already identified. Recall that synchronic forms display patterns and relationships simultaneously and that diachronic forms display relationships over time. The display of a set of relationships that can be examined simultaneously often facilitates their comprehension and manipulation. Thus, model-making in science and the use of holography are potent resources for invention. In mathematical forms of invention, visualization is essential.

Still another feature of visual form is that it presents information directly. Visual form, *when artistically encountered,* is not mediated through language. Susanne Langer (1976) made a distinction years ago between *discursive* and *nondiscursive* knowledge. For Langer, knowledge carried by propositions is discursive in character; science represents a paradigm for discursive knowledge. We use propositional language in order to learn *about* the facts of the world; in a sense, propositional language functions as a pointer or instrument that directs our attention to qualities other than itself. We read a set of scientific generalizations or grasp the meaning of a scientific theory and test their utility by what the generalization or theory enables us to anticipate or to control. In science the subject matter of those anticipations are qualities.

Nondiscursive forms of knowledge are those forms that present meaning directly. For Langer, the arts are the paradigm case for this form of knowing. Forms that present their meanings directly are linguistically unmediated. Writing on this topic, Dewey (1934) indicated in *Art as Experience* that, while science states meanings, art expresses them. What Dewey meant is that the meanings of art are found directly within the medium itself while scientific meanings are found in the relationship between propositions and the referents to which scientific statements refer. Some kinds of meaning, both Langer and Dewey believed, could not be represented through discursive form. Each form, discursive and nondiscursive, possesses its own cognitive utilities. While both scientists and artists share the task of creating meaning, the means through which they do so and the kinds of meanings they are able to create are not the same. If they were, one of them would be redundant.

One other point regarding visual learning and that point deals with matters of abstraction. Normally, abstraction is associated with the use of language and number at their most obtuse. Abstract thinkers are supposed to be those who rise above the empirical world in order to grasp realities that transcend that world. Plato's philosopher king was a paradigm case of someone who, according to Plato, had the "genetic" capacity to grasp meanings the senses could never have access to. Those meanings were located in the forms *(eidos)* that Plato believed to be eternal and nonmaterial.

Yet restricting abstraction to what language makes possible is too limited. Abstraction is inherent in the act of perception itself and always present in any act of symbolic representation. One of the primary features of perception is that it is selective. Individuals who are incompetent in a domain are often profoundly confused about what to look for. As individuals become more sophisticated, their capacity increases to focus and select, to abstract from a complex array of competing qualities those that are useful for the achievement of some function or the accomplishment of some goal. This process is an abstracting process. Out of a world of relatively infinite possibilities, only certain ones are abstracted. Without the ability to abstract, focus is lost.

Similarly, in the process of representation, say in creating a drawing or a painting, the child must decide which aspects of the world are relevant. Further, the child must invent a symbol that distills what the child considers relevant so that it displays the features he or she wishes to convey (Arnheim 1957). The inventive symbolic representation of the visual qualities of the world requires a high level of skill in abstraction. It also requires a high level of skill in relating an abstracted image to the space on which one works as well as to the other elements within that space. Put simply, both the selection and creation of images *require* the use of abstraction. The extent to which one is intelligently engaged in that abstracting process is displayed in the character of the work that is created. Put another way, human intelligence is displayed in the quality of what we are able to make or do (Dewey 1934).

There is another important cognitive function of abstraction, one I alluded to earlier. I want to underline its function once again. The function I refer to is one of distillation. When the qualities of the world are abstracted and transformed into a symbolic representation there is often an intensification of "normal" experience. This is most clearly seen in art. Artists not only reduce aspects of the world through a process of abstraction, they create a presence through abstraction that is more intense, more vivid, more "real" than the features of the day-to-day world we all inhabit. Thus, Monet's paintings of water lilies intensify the color that we would see if we visited

Giverny. Similarly, John Steinbeck gives us in *Grapes of Wrath* an intensified experience of the travails of those eking out their living from the land during the Great Depression. The artist's ability to distill and display experience enables us to see what we have learned to ignore: It enables us to elude the customary quality of our own perception and the proclivity to provide stock responses to those perceptions.

Given the cognitive functions I've described, what can we say about the place of visual learning in our educational system and what can we do to foster its development? It is to these issues that I now turn.

The argument that I have developed thus far emphasizes a number of important aspects of visual learning. First, it emphasizes the point that visual learning requires an individual to abstract from the world at large those visual qualities that are relevant to some purpose. Creating a painting or a drawing, generating a map or a diagram all require abstraction. In the perception of visual form there is also a process of abstraction employed. It consists of seeing relationships among qualities themselves. Learning how to see these relationships means learning how to select and focus. When those relationships are subtle, this can be a complex and difficult task.

A second aspect of visual learning is that visual form is used in at least two major ways. First, visual forms are used to signify. Red, yellow, and green on a stop light signify certain meanings concerning our behavior when crossing a street. In this sense, we use visual form in a way that is similar to the way we use words. Some visual forms, like words, are arbitrarily defined and culturally coded. Through visual learning we come to understand what those codes mean. A second way we use visual form is to perceive or create images whose expressive properties afford us a certain quality of life as we perceive them. The visual arts represent the quintessential realization of this use of visual form.

Another aspect of visual learning I wish to recount is the important role that it plays in helping us secure meanings that are not translatable into other terms. The kinds of understanding we are able to secure depend upon the forms of representation we are able to decode. Becoming visually literate is a way of comprehending what visual forms say and how they work. The ability to, for example, intelligently and reflectively decode the commercial ads we see on television requires an understanding of how they are composed and the functions that their properties perform in our experience. It is not for nothing that warm and fuzzy images of camaraderie are often used to sell beer.

For American education, serious attention to the cultivation of visual literacy would represent a fundamental expansion of our educational agenda. We simply have not taken this aim seriously. The arts, as I indicated at the outset, are marginalized in education. They are marginalized because we have historically associated the arts and visual phenomena in general with matters of the body while we have assigned to schools responsibility for the development of mind. Unless we can reintegrate these two domains by recognizing their inherent unity, it will be difficult to create a secure place for the arts and other forms of visual learning in our schools.

If we were to utilize visual forms to foster learning in our schools, we would need to pay attention not only to the arts as such, but to the *pedagogical* presence of visual forms (and I would include other sensory forms) in the materials and tasks that were provided in our curriculum. This would require attention to curriculum development. It would require us to think about the ways in which the child's sensory system could be engaged to facilitate the learning of any subject—history, physics, mathematics, the social studies. In other words, we would need to think about the teaching and learning of these subjects not only through text, but through resources upon which students can place their hands and eyes.

To be more than mere novelty, the creation of such materials would need to rest upon a fuller conception of mind than is now prevalent. We would develop and use these resources because of our understanding that human intellectual capacity is extraordinarily diverse, that the varieties of meaning are many, and that the comprehension of a subject profits from more than one perspective and form of representation (Eisner 1982). Such a reorientation to mind and meaning would lead to a significant enrichment of the tools we use to teach. It would redefine the resources we employ in our curricula in all areas. Finally, the use of such resources in our classrooms would contribute to greater educational equity for our students. The single-minded narrowness inherent in the dominance of text in teaching impedes the life chances of students whose aptitudes are more attuned to nontext forms. Diversifying the resources we use to teach would give more of our students a chance to succeed.

The agenda before us is as broad as it is challenging, as promising as it is complex. There is much to be done. The practical task is to get on with it. To be successful will require the engagement of teachers and others who understand what is needed and why. It will require us to learn how to create the necessary curricular resources and pedagogical practices. It will also require the willingness of school boards and state departments of education to provide the time and the financial resources for teachers and others to do such work. Perhaps a first step is to initiate a dialogue with those who make and implement educational policy and through that dialogue to frame a new agenda for our schools, one that does justice to the capacities of our students' minds. This new agenda, most certainly, will include the education of vision.

7

The Misunderstood Role of the
Arts in Human Development

In America 2000 the American people are presented with a reform agenda for their schools in which the arts are absent. Should they be? To provide an intelligent answer, one needs a concept of the arts and a view of the functions of education. What conception of the arts do people who shape education policy have? What image do they have of the aims of education? What kind of culture do they prize? What do they feel contributes to a life worth living? I believe that prevailing conceptions of the arts are based on a massive misunderstanding of the role of the arts in human development and education. This misunderstanding is rooted in ancient conceptions of mind, knowledge, and intelligence. Collectively, these conceptions impoverish the programs of schools and the education of the young.

Make no mistake, the curriculum we prescribe for schools and the time we allocate to subjects show children what adults believe is important for them to learn. There is no more telling indicator of the importance of the subjects students study than the amount of time allocated to them (Bernstein 1971). In American schools, the arts receive about two hours of instructional time per week at the elementary level and are generally not a required subject of study at the secondary level. The allocation of time to what we teach has other consequences as well. The amount of time allocated to a field of study influences the kinds of mental skills children have the opportunity to acquire.

Thus time represents both value and opportunity: value, because it indicates what is considered significant; opportunity, because the school can be thought of as a culture of opportunity. A culture in the biological sense is a place for growing things. Schools, too, are cultures. They are cultures for growing minds, and the direction this growth takes is influenced by the opportunities the school provides. These opportunities are defined by the school's program—its curriculum—and by the artistry with which teachers mediate that program. A school in which the arts are absent or poorly taught is unlikely to provide the genuine opportunities children need to use the arts in the service of their own development.

To speak of mind as developed or, even more pointedly, as grown may seem strange. Yet, in a basic sense, mind is a form of cultural achievement. We are born with brains, but our minds are made, and the shape they take is influenced by the culture in which that development occurs. For children, the school constitutes a primary culture for the development of mind. Therefore, decisions that are made about the school's priorities are also fundamental decisions about the kinds of minds children will have the opportunity to develop. Since our educational priorities are significantly influenced by our conceptions of mind, knowledge, and intelligence and since I believe that prevailing conceptions of the arts misconceive their primary features, I will briefly identify five widely held but fundamentally flawed beliefs about mind, knowledge, and intelligence that give direction to our schools. I will then describe what the arts can contribute to the educational development of the young.

1. Human conceptual thinking requires the use of language. Perhaps no belief shapes our understanding of cognition more than the conviction that language plays a necessary role in its operation. Indeed, thinking itself has sometimes been thought of as a kind of subvocalizing, a physical process that accompanies the chain of language activity that best represents the higher mental processes. Language and thought are inseparable.

There are many reasons why this belief will not stand scrutiny. First, to argue that language is a necessary condition for cognition is to conclude that children cannot think until they are able to speak. Yet anyone who has lived with a child knows firsthand how inquisitive a child can be before speech has developed and how intelligent such a child can be in solving problems: a child who cannot think cannot survive.

Second, language as we normally use it is a symbolic device, and symbolic devices that do not have referents do not symbolize. To symbolize, a symbol must be connected to a referent—that is, to an array of qualities one can experience, or that one has experienced, or that one has imagined. To speak meaningfully of baroque music—or of an oak tree or of a jet airplane—requires a conception of these objects and events, and these objects and events exist as qualities in our experience prior to the labels we assign to them. Contrary to popular opinion, in the beginning there was the image. It is the image that gives meaning to the label. The information of the image is a cognitive event.

2. Sensory experience is low on the hierarchy of intellectual functioning. The genesis of this belief can be found in Plato's ideas about the nature of human understanding. You will recall that in the sixth book of *The Republic,* Socrates asks Glaucon to imagine a single vertical line divided unequally into an upper and a lower segment. The longer upper half of the line represents the intelligible world; the bottom portion, the visible world. The intelligible world is grasped through rational procedures; the visible world, through perception. Rationality is high; perception is low. Plato's hierarchy was not diluted by the expansion of the Roman Empire. It is alive and well in the schools and universities of modern America.

But is it true that the perception of qualities is a low-level cognitive activity? When those qualities are complex and subtle, as they are in the arts, the perception of their relationships and nuances can be daunting. To put this matter in context, listen to Rudolf Arnheim:

> By "cognitive" I mean all mental operations involved in the receiving, storing, and processing of information: sensory perception, memory, thinking, learning. This use of the term conflicts with one to which many psychologists are accustomed and which excludes the activity of the senses from cognition. It reflects the distinction I am trying to eliminate; therefore I must extend the meaning of the terms "cognitive" and "cognition" to include perception. Similarly, I see no way of withholding the name of "thinking" from what goes on in perception. No thought processes seem to exist that cannot be found to operate, at least in principle, in perception. Visual perception is visual thinking. (1969, 13–14)

Ironically, indifference to the refinement of perception and inattention to the development of imagination have limited children's cognitive growth. Since no teacher has direct access to a child's mind, it is the child's ability to see the connections between the example the teacher uses, what the child already knows, and what the teacher hopes he or she will understand that makes the example instrumental to new meaning. In short, understanding depends on the child's ability to think by analogy and to grasp, often through metaphor, what needs to be understood. Poetry may indeed be closer to the most sophisticated forms of cognition than many people suspect.

3. Intelligence requires the use of logic. The importance of logic in the exercise of intelligence is clear *if* the form that is to be used to speak to the world is one in which the literal use of propositions is necessary. Mathematics and the sciences place a premium on a certain form of precision:

literal statement. Logical consistency in such forms of representation is a condition for meaning. But to regard logic as a necessary condition for the exercise of intelligence is to restrict intelligence to those forms of representation that require its use (Eisner 1994). The result of such a conception is to banish from the domain of intelligence those forms of representation whose meanings are not conveyed by and do not depend upon the use of logic. Poetry, for example, achieves meaning by employing language in ways that do not depend solely on logic; poetic meaning is often "extra-logical." The meanings conveyed by this extra-logical feature of poetry are what might better be thought of as the product of human rationality, and the same point pertains to the other arts.

Although rationality and logicality have been closely associated, rationality is a broader and more fundamental concept. Logic is one of the ways in which rationality is expressed, but it is not the only way. Individuals who manage human relationships well, those who draw or paint well, those who dance well, those who sing well—all do their thinking *within* the medium in which they work. Writing in 1934, John Dewey recognized that intelligence is usually regarded as the sole property of those whom we regard as intellectuals—especially, but not exclusively, in the academy. For those holding such a view, Dewey said:

> Any idea that ignores the necessary role of intelligence in the production of works of art is based upon identification of thinking with use of one special kind of material, verbal signs and words. To think effectively in terms of relations of qualities is as severe a demand upon thought as to think in terms of symbols, verbal and mathematical. Indeed, since words are easily manipulated in mechanical ways, the production of a work of genuine art probably demands more intelligence than does most of the so-called thinking that goes on among those who pride themselves on being "intellectuals." (46)

4. Detachment and distance are necessary for true understanding. Emotion has long been regarded as the enemy of reflective thought: the more we feel, the less we know. Now there certainly is a case to be made that such emotions as rage can radically influence one's perception and judgment. When running rampant, emotions can cloud vision, impair thought, and lead to trouble of all kinds.

But perception without feeling can do the same. Not to be able to feel, say, a human relationship is to miss what may very well be its most critical features. Not to be able to get a sense of history, not to be able to stand with Columbus on the deck of the *Santa Maria* and experience the pounding of the vessel by the relentless sea and the excitement of the first sighting of land is to miss—and perhaps even misunderstand—that aspect of history. And in failing to experience the emotion of such moments, we miss out on an aspect of life that has the potential to inform. Detachment and distance have their virtues, but they are limited resources for understanding, and any conception that assigns them dominion in cognition misconceives the ways in which understanding is fostered.

5. Scientific method is the only legitimate way to generalize about the world. The traditional, flawed conception of the arts claims that, when they are about anything, the arts are only about particulars: they yield no generalizations. Their virtues reside in delight rather than insight. They provide nothing that can reasonably be regarded as knowledge or understanding. Since the instrumental value of the products of science is considered greater than the delight derived from the arts (which in any case is usually thought to be merely a matter of personal taste), the value of the arts in comparison to the sciences is set low.

This conception of generalization defines much too narrowly the sources through which generalizations are actually made. The need to generalize is fundamental. Human beings generalized long before either science or statistics were invented. Generalizations are not only scientific and naturalistic; they also emerge from those intense forms of experience that we call the arts: concrete universals they are sometimes called.

Consider the paintings of Francis Bacon, Velásquez, or Picasso, or consider the novels of John Steinbeck or Cervantes. Even fiction—perhaps especially fiction—can help us grasp the meaning not only of Don Quixote, the particular man, but of what we all share with him as we tilt at our own windmills, struggling to overcome seemingly insurmountable obstacles (Goodman 1978). Cervantes helps us understand such travails, and, because he succeeds so well, we come away from his work with a new view, a view that enables us to recognize and reflect on one of the important features of our own lives. Through his work, we are also able to recognize these features elsewhere.

My argument thus far has focused on beliefs that have given direction to the educational enterprise. I have contended that the five beliefs I have described—that thought requires language, that sensory experience is a low-level function, that logic is necessary for intelligence, that detachment and distance foster understanding, and that science is the only legitimate way to generalize—create an intellectual climate that marginalizes the arts because what these beliefs celebrate seems to have little to do with what the arts provide. I will now focus on four contributions that I believe are central to all the arts. In doing so, I will not describe the specific contributions that each individual art makes to children of different ages. Instead, my aim is to identify the common, core contributions of the arts and their potential role in furthering the aims of education.

1. Not all problems have single, correct answers. One of the important lessons the arts teach is that solutions to problems can take many forms. This lesson from the arts would not be so important were it not for the fact that so much of what is taught in school teaches just the opposite lesson. Almost all of the basic skills taught in the primary grades teach children that there is only one correct answer to any question and only one correct solution to any problem. Spelling, arithmetic, writing, and even reading are pervaded by conventions and rules that, in effect, teach children to be good rule followers.

The arts teach a different lesson. They celebrate imagination, multiple perspectives, and the importance of personal interpretation. The last thing a modern teacher of the arts in America wants is a class full of standardized performances on a given task. The last thing an English teacher wants are idiosyncratic interpretations of how words are spelled. This is as it should be. Creativity in spelling is no virtue. But when the curriculum as a whole is so heavily saturated with tasks and expectations that demand fealty to rule, opportunities to think in unique ways are diminished. When carried to an extreme, the school's program becomes intellectually debilitating.

2. The form of a thing is part of its content. We have a tendency in our schools to separate form from content. Form is regarded as the shape something takes, and content is the meaning something conveys. In notational systems, we can live with such a dichotomy. In such systems, attention to form *as such* is largely irrelevant. For example, the number six can be symbolized in many ways, but its meaning is the same as long as one recognizes it as a six. The task is one of categorization. Early reading also emphasizes categorization. And when children learn to assign a form—say, a particular tree—to its category rather than to explore its distinctive features, perception is aborted. As Dewey pointed out, perception ceases when recognition begins. Assigning a label to an entity is an act of categorization, and when entities are assigned to categories, the exploration of their uniqueness stops.

The arts, however, teach the child that the grass is not simply green; it is lavender, grey, gold. And when it is green, its varieties are endless. Furthermore, in the arts and in much of life, the form something takes is very much a part of its content. In fact, what the content *is* often depends on the form it takes. The arts are prime examples of how this marriage of form and content is created and of the effect that it has on our experience.

I have made a special point here of emphasizing the function of the arts in human development. The arts are neglected resources and deserve attention in our schools. But I do not want to give the impression that at least some of the features that the arts possess are not also to be found in the sciences. The products of science have their own aesthetic features: the parsimony of theory, the beauty of conceptual models, the elegance of experiments, and the imagination and insight of interpretation. Indeed, the qualities for which a work of science is cherished are often related as much to its aesthetic appeal as to its explanatory power. A theory, after all, is a perspective about the way the world is. It is a way to secure a coherent view, and coherence is so important that we are often unwilling to give up the views we find attractive, despite contradictory evidence.

My point here is that, although my primary focus is on what may be called the fine arts, some of the features for which the arts are valued are also exhibited by the sciences. At the risk of oversimplifying the differences between the arts and the sciences, let me say that, in the context of creation, a work of science is a work of art.

3. **Having fixed objectives and pursuing clear-cut methods for achieving them are not always the most rational ways of dealing with the world.** There is a tendency in technologically oriented cultures to conceive of rationality as a method for tightly linking means and ends. To be rational, we tell children (and teachers), they must first formulate clear-cut objectives for their work, then use these objectives to define means for their achievement, and finally implement and evaluate the effectiveness and efficiency of the means for achieving the desired objectives.

Of course, there is a sense of sweet reason about such a procedure. Yet we often conceptualize and implement this process in mechanical ways: we give students goals for each lesson, we expect teachers to know exactly where they are headed, and we appraise classrooms and the quality of teaching on the basis of their achievement. We try to create a technology of management so that efficiency in learning and teaching is achieved and public accountability is provided. Our narrow conception of rationality is expressed in our incessant search for "what works"; it supports the belief that there is, in fact, a single best way, that the main task of researchers is to find it, and that the primary obligation of teachers is to use it. The entire effort to standardize educational outcomes is premised on a conviction that efficient and effective systems can be designed that will take luck out of the educational process.

These beliefs not only affect the conditions of teaching, they also create a climate that affects what and how students learn. Moreover, these views are antithetical to what the arts teach. The arts teach that goals need to be flexible and that surprise counts; that chance, as Aristotle wisely remarked, is something that art loves; that being open to the unanticipated opportunities that inevitably emerge in the context of action increases insight; and that purposeful flexibility rather than rigid adherence to prior plans is more likely to yield something of value. No painter, writer, composer, or choreographer can foresee all the twists and turns that his or her work will take. The *work* of art—by which I now mean the *act* of creation—does not follow an unalterable schedule but is a journey that unfolds. The relationship of the maker to the work is not that of lecturer to listener, but a conversation between the worker and the work.

In the context of much of today's schooling, the lessons taught by the arts are much closer to what successful and intelligent corporations do and to what cognitive psychologists are discovering constitute the most sophisticated forms of thinking (Resnick 1989; Greeno 1989). These recent psychological discoveries are lessons artists have long understood. What are these lessons? They are that solving complex problems requires attention to wholes, not simply to discrete parts; that most complex problems have no algorithmic solutions; that nuance counts; and that purposes and goals must remain flexible in order to exploit opportunities that one cannot foresee. These newly discovered cognitive virtues are taught in every genuine *work* of art. Yet, ironically, the arts are typically thought of as noncognitive.

What is even more ironic is that, while we say that the function of schooling is to prepare students for life, the problems of life tend not to have the fixed, single correct answers that characterize the problems students encounter in the academic areas of schooling. The problems of life are much more like the problems encountered in the arts. They are problems that seldom have a single correct solution; they are problems that are often subtle, occasionally ambiguous, and sometimes dilemma-like. One would think that schools that wanted to prepare students for life would employ tasks and problems similar to those found outside of schools. This is hardly the case. Life outside of school is seldom like school assignments—and hardly ever like a multiple-choice test.

4. In addition to their expressive function, the arts perform another function of critical importance. In all that I have said so far, I have emphasized the contributions that the arts make toward helping students recognize that problems are not restricted to those having single correct answers, that form and content interact, and that purposeful flexibility is a mark of fluid intelligence coping with the vicissitudes of the unpredictable. But I have neglected a contribution that is surely as important. That contribution hinges on a distinction between *expression* and *discovery*. In the arts, students learn that some kinds of meaning may require the expressive forms that the arts make possible. In this sense, the arts expressively represent; they provide the forms through which insight and feeling can emerge in the public world. Indeed, humans invented the arts to serve expressive functions. For most people who have thought about the arts, this particular function is the one most commonly recognized.

But the arts also make discovery possible. Discovery occurs as students learn through adventures in the arts something of the possibilities of human experience. The journeys they take through the patterned sound we call music, through the visual forms we call painting, and through the metaphorical discourse we call poetry and literature are means through which students can discover their potential to respond. In other words, the arts can help students find their individual capacity to feel and imagine.

While such journeys are experienced through the arts, they can also be secured through the ordinary aspects of daily life when it is approached aesthetically. The world outside of art can become something to explore and relish: through the arts students can learn how to discover not only the possibilities the world offers but also their own possibilities. Expression and discovery are two major contributions the arts make to human development.

Just how are such discoveries made? As children learn to manipulate, manage, and monitor the nuances of voice, movement, and visual form, they discover the effects that their own fine-tuning achieves. As form is modulated, so too is feeling. As imagination is given permission to rise, children have the opportunity to enter worlds not tied to the literal, to the concrete, to the practical. Discovery emerges in the appreciation of qualities examined and images pursued. The arts, more than most fields, put a premium on such activities, and those activities can help students discover the special qualities of experience we call aesthetic.

Let me close by returning briefly to my initial claim that prevailing conceptions of the arts are based on a massive misunderstanding of their role in human development. This misconception is reflected in the narrow educational priorities of America 2000. In turn, these priorities are rooted in beliefs that regard mind as fixed rather than developed, that conceive of knowledge as the exclusive property of science, and that consider intelligence as limited to forms of abstract thought dependent on the use of logic. These narrow and misguided conceptions are not ivory tower theories without practical consequences. They influence our educational priorities, shape what we teach, and affect our children's lives. They result in schools that have an antiseptic environment that seldom provides even a nod to our sensuous, poetic, or imaginative sides.

I hope readers realize that my argument here is an optimistic one. What is pessimistic is a fixed view of mind, a conception of knowledge limited to what literal language can convey, and a view of intelligence constrained by the rules of logic. Human intellectual capacity is far wider.

The realization of this capacity is surely more likely as we create a richer, more nurturant culture for our students. That culture, as I see it, ought to include significant opportunities for students to experience the arts and to learn to use them to create a life worth living. Indeed, providing a decent place for the arts in our schools may be one of the most important first steps we can take to bring about genuine school reform. Let's hope that, despite the priorities of America 2000, we have the courage and the wit to take it.

8

Does Experience in the Arts Boost Academic Achievement?

Those of us in arts education receive more often than we would like requests to justify our professional existence or the existence of the arts in our schools on the basis of their contributions to non-art outcomes. I cannot recall the number of times I have been asked about the contributions the arts make to increasing test scores in math, or in reading, or in any other academic subject that the inquirer believes to be more important than any of the arts—or all of them for that matter. What research, callers want to know, shows the relationship between experience in the arts and academic achievement? Does more exposure to the arts increase performance in academic subjects? Does more of the arts in school advance school reform?

All too often arts educators are all too ready to oblige. Those of us in arts education are apparently "faster than a speeding bullet, more powerful than a locomotive, able to leap tall buildings in a single bound . . ." I cannot help but wonder if we claim too much.

As someone who is the recipient of the requests I have described, I can say that I understand the drive of those who are desperately looking for ways to upgrade our educational system and to improve the performance of those within it. So many failed "solutions" have been tried: why not the arts? I sometimes ask myself if those who inquire ever considered reversing the question. Have they ever thought about asking how reading and math courses contribute to higher performance in the arts? I must confess I have never come right out and asked them—but I have come close.

That questions about the contributions of the arts to academic achieve-

I wish to thank Lissa Soep for first-rate assistance in preparing this paper. I also wish to thank Shiffra Schonemann for a very helpful critical reading.

ment are raised by those for whom the arts are personally marginal is understandable: When the arts are not a part of your own life it's hard to know what they can contribute to it. What *is* troublesome is the image of arts educators who know what the arts have to offer trying to give the customers what they want, whether or not there is evidence to support it. We too often promise more than we can deliver, a practice that by definition leads to disappointment.

What can we claim? What are the contributions that the arts can legitimately be expected to make to the education of the young? Just what does the research say about the relationship between experience in the arts and academic achievement? When pressures arise to justify the place of the arts in education, how shall we respond? These questions will occupy our attention.

Let's first start with what research has to say about the relationship between experience in the several arts and academic achievement. For our purposes here let's define experience in the arts as the number of courses taken in school—elementary or secondary—in any of the arts. Let's define the arts as courses in the visual arts, music, theater, and dance. I recognize that the definitions I have provided are to some degree arbitrary. Courses taken say nothing about the quality of experience secured or the kind of curriculum used. In addition, the quality of teaching matters and nothing that I have said pertains to the quality of teaching. I enter these caveats for two reasons; first, to indicate that I am aware of them and second, to adumbrate the complexities of the kind of research that is needed. The criteria I have just identified are general. Given these general criteria, what do we find?

Research on Experience and Academic Achievement

To review the research on the relationship between arts courses and academic achievement we turned to the literature published from 1986 to 1996. What we were looking for were studies describing the relationships between these two areas of human performance, experimental studies if possible, but correlational studies if necessary. What we did not include in our review were advocacy essays. Furthermore, we preferred publications that did not simply summarize the results of studies but presented the studies themselves so that the data and methods could be appraised. We also preferred studies published in refereed journals since we believe that refereed journals are more likely to provide the kind of methodological scrutiny that empirical studies deserve.

To create a pool of prospective publications we reviewed the contents for the past ten-year period of the following journals: *Art Education, American Educational Research Journal, Bulletin of the Council for Research in Music Education, Child Development, Journal of Aesthetic Education, Journal of Art and Design Education,* and a host of ad hoc publications that report research relevant to the topic.

Let's look at what studies in these journals and reports have to say.

First, we found that although there is much material published that *claims* the arts cause academic achievement scores to increase or that arts courses "strengthen" academic performance, it is often difficult to know the basis upon which the claims are made. One publication appears with histograms describing student performance and is accompanied by testimony from principals that arts courses "impact" test results on the Maryland Student Assessment Program in 1993–94, yet the material is impossible to evaluate. The conclusions are entirely unsupported by the research they are presumably based upon because the bases for the claims are not provided in the text nor is there a reference to a report one could consult. Nevertheless, the title of the document in which these claims appear is *The Arts and Children: A Success Story* (Maryland Alliance for Arts Education 1995). It is also of no small interest to note that what constitutes success is higher academic achievement scores as a result of enrolling in arts courses, not accomplishment in the arts.

Another publication claiming the arts increase academic performance is titled *Eloquent Evidence: Arts at the Core of Learning.* (Murfee 1995) Given the title one might expect to find eloquent evidence. The publication, which is a brochure, claims that "students of the arts continue to outperform their non-art peers on the Scholastic Assessment Test, according to the College Entrance Examination Board. In 1995, SAT scores for students who studied the arts more than four years were 59 points higher on the verbal and 44 points higher on the math portion than students with no course work or experience in the arts" (3). One cannot help but wonder if students who elect to study the arts for four or more years have the same academic background as those who never took an arts course. Clearly one factor that differentiates the two groups is that one group made such a choice. Is it the arts courses or other features related to academic performance that account for the differences in SAT scores? The information needed to know is not provided in the brochure. The reader is referred to the compendium in which a summary of the study is to appear. There is nothing in the compendium that refers to the study.

Another publication, *Building a Case for Art Education: An Annotated Bibliography of Major Research* (Kentucky Alliance for Arts Education 1990), lists twelve areas in which the arts are purported to make a contribution.

These areas include contributions to creative thinking, development of cognitive, affective, and psycho-motor skills; and learning styles, communication skills, literacy skills, cultural literacy, individual choice making, as well a group decision making, increase in self-esteem and so forth. One of the twelve areas is titled "The Arts Improve Student Performance in Other Subject Areas." What do we find?

We find that of the nineteen "studies" cited only two are published in journals. Of the two published in journals we find in a study (Forseth 1980) of the relationship between art activities and art attitudes and achievement in elementary mathematics, that although art activities seem to positively influence students' attitudes toward mathematics, they have little or no effect on their achievement.

In a study of the effects of two forms of reward on achievement in mathematics, Madsen (1981) found that rewarding students with books or with televised music lessons influenced their performance in mathematics. Each form of reward was effective. This study is essentially a study of the effects of reinforcement on learning in mathematics rather than a study of the contributions music makes to academic achievement.

Schools, Communities, and the Arts: A Research Compendium (Welch and Greene 1995), the compendium I mentioned earlier, was prepared on behalf of National Endowment for the Arts. This compendium is a selection of the best evidence collected from over 500 studies that were reviewed. It contains five sections the editors call Broad-based Studies, Targeted, Compilations, Attitudes and Public Opinion, and Status Studies. Of the studies summarized in the these two sections six studies are broad-based and seventeen are targeted. Of the six "broad-based" studies not one appears in a refereed journal. Of the seventeen studies that are "targeted," eight were published in refereed journals. Of the eight studies, five were relevant to the aims of this paper, only two of which we were able to obtain.

Analysis of these studies indicate in a study by Du Pont (1992) that the use of creative drama to enhance the reading scores of a population of remedial or low-ability fifth-grade readers enrolled in a compensatory program proved effective at the .05 level compared to the performance of two other groups of students using methods that did not include creative drama. It must be noted that the aim of the program was to increase reading performance, it was not to teach creative drama, and that the population was a special population of fifth graders in need of reading skills, not a population of average students. In short, given the aims of the study and the population studied, the results are limited to like populations.

In another study of narrative writing Moore and Caldwell (1993) found that experience in drama and writing increases the quality of writing of students in the primary grades. But again, the aim of the study was to try to improve writing. It was not to improve drama or drawing. Indeed, no assessment of growth in these ares was made. How shall we appraise an arts program whose effects are measured solely on non-arts tasks?

Perhaps the study that most closely addresses the topic is one carried out in 1992–93 by Richard Luftig (1993), titled *The Schooled Mind: Do the Arts Make a Difference?* The program tested is called Spectra. It was followed up with a second study in 1993–94 that purported to demonstrate that the arts influenced performance in a number of areas, including self-esteem, locus of control, creative thinking, appreciation of the arts, and academic achievement in the following: total reading score, reading vocabulary, reading comprehension, total math score, math application, and math comprehension. Results reported in this study which included experimental, placebo, and control groups showed no differences on any of the academic achievement measures, except in one school district where differences on total math scores were found by gender. Significant differences in favor of the experimental group were also found on creativity measures and on measures of art appreciation.

Despite these findings this study was offered up as providing evidence of the contribution the arts make to academic achievement. In fact *Eloquent Evidence* tells the reader that in this study "The most gains in total reading, reading vocabulary, and reading comprehension were made by elementary students in the 'Spectra' arts program in Ohio, compared to the control group" (4).

What *Eloquent Evidence* does not say is that the differences were statistically nonsignificant and, in my view, educationally trivial. Indeed the original report itself says, "For academic achievement in the A district there were no significant differences found in total reading, reading vocabulary, and reading comprehension" (25). For the B school district the experimental conditions needed to implement the experiment could not be employed, though as I said, differences were found in favor of performance in math by males. What is telling is that where differences were found, namely in creativity and in art appreciation, *Eloquent Evidence* does not say so. Are we to infer that achievement in these areas are of no account?

What about the follow-up study of Spectra?

What we find is that in school district A there were no statistically significant differences in reading scores on either the total test score or on the two subtests. Differences were found between experimental and control groups on math scores. In school district B differences were found in both math and reading scores. However, the design of the study was modified for school district B; it could be that a Hawthorne effect generated levels of motivation that account for the differences. Nevertheless, this is the only study in which the data are given to the reader and where a careful effort is made to describe the study's research methods. While its author is to be commended, the evidence, even when combined with other studies, provides a very slender reed on which to hang the claims that are made about the impact of the arts on academic achievement.

As for other research studies, Karen Hamblen (1993) published an article titled, "Theories and Research That Support Art Instruction for Instrumental Outcomes." In it she looked at both the research she could find and implementation practices of programs that were designed to have instrumental outcomes. She points out that the preponderance of evidence is anecdotal. She writes, "Teachers of art programs similar to those in Florida [where instrumental outcomes from art courses were sought] report increases in critical thinking skills, concept organizational skills, and applications of divergent thinking. However, specific assessments of academic achievement in these programs is weak or nonexistent" (195).

Where reports of the effects of arts education on academic achievement appear to be most notable are in programs that are specifically designed to help students with reading problems learn to read *through* the arts. As educationally virtuous as such effects might be, these programs are specifically designed to teach reading; the arts are resources to this end.

It must be granted that the achievement of transfer of learning is an ambitious and noble aim. It has been so since Thorndike (1914) did research to test his theory of identical elements around the turn of the century. Some contemporary social scientists such as Lave (1991) have little optimism that transfer can ever be very wide. Learning or cognition, they claim, is *situated* and its utility is limited, more or less, to contexts like the ones in which it is situated. Yet it seems obvious that some transfer must occur otherwise learning would be so situation specific that it would not occur elsewhere. After all, no two situations are ever identical; time changes among other things. However, when we talk about the effects of arts education on academic achievement in reading or in mathematics we are expecting transfer of wide scope. To expect that is to expect a great deal. At this moment I can find no good evidence that such transfer occurs if what we count as evidence is more than anecdotal reports that are often designed for purposes of advocacy.

What Would a Convincing Study Look Like?

If the studies that are now available are not as convincing as they might be, what would it take to make a study so? Let me describe the design features that such a study might have.

First, if someone claims that students who enroll in arts courses benefit academically from their experience in such courses one would need to compare the academic performance of students who have had arts courses in, say, secondary school with those who have not. We would expect that the more arts courses taken, the greater the effect on academic achievement. Thus the analyses would include performance on academic measures by the number of arts courses taken.

Since the academic accomplishments of the students in the two groups, experimental and control, need to be comparable at the outset of the experiment, the students will need either to be randomly selected and randomly assigned to experimental and control groups or matched on academic achievement on the relevant achievement variables. Where random selection and assignment are not feasible, gain scores—differences between pre-experiment and post-experiment scores—will be used to compare the performance of students in each group.

To know what might make a difference in the academic achievement scores between the two groups, the form and content of the experimental treatment, in this case the curriculum of the arts courses in which students in the experimental group were enrolled, would need to be monitored and described. In addition, the course aims and content of the students in academic classes would need to be monitored and described to insure that they were comparable, for if the experimental group's academic course's curriculum provided content that was more closely aligned with the achievement tests that were used to measure academic accomplishment than that used in the control group, differences in academic achievement scores could be due to a better fit between the academic content the experimental group was taught with what the test measured than because of the benefits of their arts courses.

Another feature of the design of such a study is the need to pay attention to the quality of teaching provided to students in each group. If, for example, the experimental and control group used the same curriculum but the experimental group had uniformly better teachers in their academic subjects, differences in academic performance could be due to differences in the quality of teaching the experimental group received.

Because the content and aims of the academic courses in which students enroll matter, it is necessary to use assessment procedures to assess achievement in content that matters educationally. It is not inconceivable that students could be assessed on tasks that have little academic or intellectual merit. Put another way, if the arts do contribute to academic achievement it only matters if they do so on academic accomplishments that have educational worth. Achieving higher scores on trivial outcomes is no victory.

Finally, appraising the educational effects of an experiment is not merely a matter of finding statistically significant differences between groups or correlations that are statistically significant. The differences, if differences are found, must also be educationally significant. Educationally significant differences may or may not be statistically significant. Statistical significance is an arbitrary level of a probable difference between two or more groups. The level required is specified by common agreement as the .05 or .01 level of probability that the difference between two or more groups is not a chance difference, but even when probabilities reach the required magnitude, a difference between two or more groups might be regarded as educationally significant at lower levels of probability. The main point here is that what matters educationally depends not upon statistics, but upon educational judgment. What is needed is an appraisal grounded in reasons that show the differences effected by the experimental conditions are educationally consequential.

These design conditions are at minimum necessary to produce a credible claim that arts courses influence in a positive way the academic performance of students.

What I have not mentioned is that in order to understand *why* arts courses have such effects, if in fact they do, requires a theory that relates the skills developed through the arts to the demands made upon students in academic classes. Perhaps it is not skills at all that arts courses develop, perhaps it's the promotion of certain attitudes, attitudes that promote risk taking and hard work. Perhaps the effects—if effects there are—of arts courses on academic achievement is due to the motivational effects of arts courses; perhaps students in arts courses enjoy school more and therefore attend more regularly. If higher motivation is the source of academic achievement it might be that other motivating experiences might have the same effects. What is needed is more than correlations or statistically significant differences between groups, what is needed is a theory that links experience in the arts with academic achievement. What we need is a theory that explains the connections between the cognitive skills work of all kinds in the arts develop and the function these skills perform in academic work of other kinds. To create these links the arts programs in which students are enrolled need to be carefully described, as do their academic programs.

Why Be Concerned About the Relationship of the Arts to Academic Achievement?

The title of the subhead above takes us back to first principles. Let it be said at the outset that when a body of work in a particular field of study makes significant and valuable contributions to a wide array of skills, dispositions, or understandings, the value of that field increases. We all like "toofers";

and if we can get them, so much the better. Thus, I have no objection whatsoever if experience in the arts makes contributions to achievement test scores in math, reading, or sentential calculus. Problems begin to emerge when the values for which the arts are prized in schools are located primarily in someone's version of the basics when those basics have little or nothing to do with the arts. The perils of such justifications, whether those justifications pertain to the so-called basics or to versions of arts education that regard its major function as fostering cross-cultural understanding, are profound. The core problem with such rationales for arts education is that they leave the arts vulnerable to any other field or educational practice that claims that it can achieve the same aims faster and better. If one wants to help students understand the life styles of other cultures it strikes me that anthropological studies would be a more direct route and even if we imagine for a moment that it wasn't, to use the arts *primarily* to teach what is not truly distinctive about the arts is to undermine, in the long run, the justifying conditions for the arts in our schools.

What instrumental justifications of the kind I have described also do is to legitimate the marginal position assigned to the arts by those looking for such justifications. When arts educators accede to their expectations it's a way of saying, "You're right, the arts are not really important in their own right, their importance is located in their contributions to more important subjects."

Let me turn now to a way of thinking about what the arts have to teach. What is it that the arts have to offer? What is their educational value?

Ways of Thinking About What the Arts Teach

Given the analysis I have provided so far it is possible to identify three levels or tiers to which arts education might be expected to make a contribution. I call the first tier *Arts Based Outcomes of Arts Education*. The second tier is called *Arts Related Outcomes of Arts Education*. The third tier is called *Ancillary Outcomes of Arts Education*. Tier 1 holds arts educators responsible for outcomes that are directly related to the subject matter that an arts education curriculum was designed to teach. For example, if an aim of the curriculum is to enable students to hear and be able to talk discerningly about the form and content of a piece of music, or a piece of architecture, or a cubist painting, or a play by Tennessee Williams, an Arts Based Assessment would disclose the extent to which those outcomes or outcomes like them were achieved. Such outcomes reside in perceptions and discourse unique to the arts. Outcomes like these, *including those outcomes pertaining to performance within the art form*, we shall call Arts Based Outcomes.

Outcomes that pertain to the perception and comprehension of aesthetic features in the general environment constitute Arts Related Outcomes. For example, arts courses that enable students to notice and respond to the aesthetic configurations of phenomena such as cloud formations, the dynamic flow of city streets, the cacophonies of a city during rush hour are examples of Arts Related Outcomes of Arts Education. The difference between responding to the qualitative and expressive features of the general environment and responding to works of art is significant. All objects and processes have formal features, including works of nature; the qualitative features of a tree or the pattern of shadows upon a wall can be perceived and described formally as completely and in as much detail as a sculpture by Louise Nevelson. A critical difference between the two is that Nevelson works within a tradition, Nevelson has intentions, Nevelson has something to say that she herself, working within her tradition, both constrains and makes possible. Trees, to consider a work of nature, have no intentions as far as I know, participate in no tradition save their own genetic necessities, and provide no symbolic meaning except those we assign. The difference between works of culture and works of nature are, as I said, critical. Arts Based Outcomes pertain to those outcomes that require an understanding of the culture and, indeed, the personal side of the artist's work. Formal analysis alone simply does not go far enough.

As you can see I am attempting to differentiate between the perception of forms as "mere" forms and forms that are members of a class we call art. This distinction does not mean that aesthetic experience cannot occur when interacting with cloud formations, it can. Art forms are those forms artists create that participate in a tradition that gives them a potential for meaning not found in works of nature or culture when those works are not created for artistic perception—*unless,* like Duchamp, they are construed that way by the percipient.

Thus far I have distinguished between Arts Based Outcomes and Arts Related Outcomes. The former pertains to outcomes specifically germane to works of art, the latter to outcomes germane to the aesthetic features of the general environment. But what about Ancillary Outcomes of Arts Education?

Ancillary Outcomes of Arts Education are those outcomes like the effects of arts education on student performance in reading, math, or other academic subjects. Ancillary outcomes of arts education pertain to outcomes that transfer skills employed in the perception, creation, and comprehension of the arts to non-arts tasks. For example, the kind of qualitative judgments required in the creation of any of the arts requires judgments made in the absence of formula or rule; one must judge, as Goodman (1978) calls it, "rightness of fit." What one typically seeks is coherence among relationships within a complex form. Does the ability to experience such relationships in any of the arts enable those to do so in other areas of life? Does such experience enable students to make better practical judgments where formulas do not work? If so, such outcomes can be counted among the ancillary outcomes of arts education.

The three tiers that I have described—Arts Based Outcomes, Arts Related Outcomes, and Ancillary Outcomes of Arts Education—allow us to sort out the kinds of justifications or rationales for arts education that are being advanced. Requests to demonstrate or justify arts education in our schools on the basis of advancing academic achievement in other subjects is a third tier ancillary rationale for arts education. In saying that such an aim for arts education is an ancillary rationale as contrasted with a primary or first tier rationale for arts education I am, of course, invoking a set of values, employing a conception, embracing a model of what matters in arts education. Others may hold other views. My claim, at base, is that arts education and the several art fields that constitute it ought to give pride of place to those unique contributions that only the arts make possible, that when justifications for arts education that are not distinctive become primary, the place of arts education in our schools and their potential contribution to the student's education is compromised. My argument is for arts educators to avoid becoming sidetracked onto paths that others can travel as well—and perhaps even better.

How does one justify arts education without using an ancillary rationale? One way to find out is to look to the arts themselves and to ask about the demands they make on those who would create, perceive, or understand them. It is to this agenda that we now turn. My attention to this agenda will address both first and second tier outcomes, that is, I am interested in both what students learn that pertains to the arts themselves and what they learn that pertains to the aesthetic aspects of the environment. In short, I am interested in the contributions arts education makes to both the arts and to life beyond them. There are four such outcomes I wish to identify.

1. Arts education should enable students to understand that there is a connection between the content and form that the arts take and the culture and time in which the work was created. This outcome is intended to situate the arts within culture and to advance students' understanding that the problems that artists tackle and how they do so are influenced by the setting in which they work, that art and artists participate in a tradition that both liberates and constrains, and that at times artists violate the expectations or norms of that tradition.

Why is such an outcome important? It's important because the quality of experience the arts make possible is enriched when the arts are experienced within a context of ideas relevant to them. Understanding the cultural context is among the most important ways in which such enrichment can be achieved. Such an outcome, I believe, is a reasonable expectation for students enrolled in arts programs.

To say that students should understand that the arts are culturally and historically situated is not to say that a student is expected to have an encyclopedic knowledge of the cultural context of every art form or individual work of art. It is to say that *the idea* of the relationship of culture and art at the level of principled generalization be understood and that at least one or more examples of that idea be a part of the student's intellectual repertoire. I believe this is a first tier outcome for which arts education should be responsible.

2. *Arts education should refine the student's awareness of the aesthetic qualities in art and life.* Here we have a first and second tier outcome at the very heart of arts education. If arts education is about anything it is about helping students become alive to the aesthetic qualities of art and life in the worlds in which they live. Put more directly, arts education should help students learn to use an aesthetic frame of reference to see and hear. What does this mean educationally? It means that students will know what they can listen for in music and what they can look for in the visual arts. It means also that when they are asked about the works or situations they encounter they will be able to say something about them with insight, sensitivity, and intelligence. It means that they will know not only what they like or respond to in a work—or a walk, for that matter—but why. This means that they will have reasons for their preferences, they will be able to bring to a work what they need to render the work intelligible.

As I suggested, the student's sensibilities should not be limited to what we call the fine arts. They should be applicable to the qualities of the general environment. Furthermore, at its best arts education should influence what psychologists call the connative aspects of cognition, that is, the *desire* to frame the world as an object of enjoyed perception. Both ability and desire are critical to the success of an arts education program.

3. Another first tier outcome of arts education is that *students should acquire a feel for what it means to transform their ideas, images, and feelings into an art form.* One could argue that at the core of arts education is the development of the students' ability to create art or, as some might say, art-like creations. Whether one calls students' work art or art-like, the point is that getting a feel for the process through which works of art come into being is fostered best by having experience trying to do so yourself, even if the most telling outcome of such experience is to recognize how much distance exists between our best efforts and the work of masters. But even

such a recognition is not an unimportant outcome of arts education. More important, to my mind, is the contribution experience in the studio provides for getting in touch with the arts. Having struggled to create compelling images, whether in sound or sight, becomes a part of the experiential continuum one brings to the work. Such experience can help the student recognize both the qualities of the work and the accomplishments of the artist.

You will have noticed that in writing about such outcomes I have resorted to metaphors such as "getting a feel" for the process and "getting in touch" with the arts. I do so because I have no literal words that will convey as well as these the meanings I intend. Both metaphors, getting in touch and getting a feel, relate to bodily processes. Both convey a sense of "getting into it." Both intimate a kind of carnal knowledge, of knowing in the biblical sense. Both convey a sense of knowing that is not reducible to words, certainly not the literal use of words, hence metaphor.

4. Finally. I wish to identify a particularly important set of outcomes for arts education. This one pertains to dispositions that are difficult to assess, let alone measure but they are dispositions that *appear* to be cultivated through programs that engage students in the process of artistic creation. I speak of dispositional outcomes such as the following: *a willingness to imagine possibilities that are not now, but which might become. A desire to explore ambiguity, to be willing to forestall premature closure in pursuing resolutions, and the ability to recognize and accept the multiple perspectives and resolutions that work in the arts celebrate.*

There is, of course, a question as to whether these dispositions are first, second, or third tier outcomes. After all, developing a willingness to cope with ambiguity, or to forestall premature closure, or to imagine a world that one might create are dispositions that could be applied to non-art domains. In this sense they could be considered third tier aims. Yet, if one regards such outcomes as essential to the process of artistic modes of thinking, something fundamental to the very act of making art, they could be seen not as second tier, but as first tier outcomes: Making art seems to require such dispositions. In that sense they are about the cognitive dispositions basic to the arts. Given this perspective they are first tier aims and outcomes.

What's the Point of It All?

What I have tried to do in this essay is to examine the research basis for claims about the effects of art experience on academic achievement. There is some, but it is very limited. The effects of the arts appear to be greatest when the arts are intentionally used to raise academic achievement in reading and writing. What I have also tried to do in this paper is to provide a fresh perspective, an analysis, an argument, and a set of distinctions I have called tiers that is intended to help sort out our reasons for being in arts education. I have tried to describe a way of recognizing the type of justification that is being advanced for the arts in education.

The four aims that I have described provide a broad educational agenda as demanding as it is important in arts education. It strikes me that we do the arts no service when we try to make their case by touting their contributions to other fields. When such contributions become priorities the arts become handmaidens to ends that are not distinctively artistic and in the process undermine the value of art's unique contributions to the education of the young.

Sometimes it is better not to give the customers what they want but, rather, to help them understand what they ought to want. Such a conception of our professional role is not paternalistic, I believe it is a part of our educational mission. We must interpret what arts education can contribute to the young. We need to help parents understand what the arts can mean as a part of their children's education, and we must cease trying to become whatever people want us to be. We would do well to go back to first principles. In the long run it's the only place where the arts can be made secure for the generation of students who populate our schools.

RETHINKING EDUCATIONAL RESEARCH

I believe the fourth quarter of the twentieth century will be seen as a watershed in the history of educational research. Since the turn of the century the dominant methodological orientation to educational research has been shaped by behavioristic and positivistic assumptions about the nature of knowledge. The laboratory with its tidy and controlled environment and measurement practices with their precise quantitative indices were seen as necessary accoutrements for meaningful research. The king of the hill was the "true experiment," a practice in which all variables that might confound or compromise the explanation of results were to be brought under tight experimental control. Educational research was regarded at its best as echoing physics.

Although the ideal of the experiment in the physical sciences is still embraced by some, it has been recognized increasingly that the very conditions that make experimental controls tight in the laboratory are the least likely to be replicated in the "messy" environment of the classroom and school. Researchers are seeking other approaches. In addition, our conception of what it means to know and to understand had also undergone modification. Once owned by scientific discourse, it is now recognized that the humanist and the artist can also enlarge human understanding and that the very phenomena that eludes literal meaning is often best revealed by poetic statement and by visual image. As a result, storytelling and narrative, for example, have emerged as potentially powerful means through which students and teachers can acquire knowledge. The critic of art, literature, and music has emerged as someone whose skills in adumbrating the subtleties of art forms might also be used to disclose the subtleties of teaching and learning. The construction of generalizations, once conceived of as the exclusive property of statistical analysis, is now conceived of in other forms as well. William Blake once commented that the universe resides in a grain of sand. Blake's point is that the particular embodies the universal, something that poets and playwrights have long known. Generalizations are not restricted to the products of randomly selected samples and experimental treatments, but can emerge in more aesthetically grounded practices; we have much to learn from stories, images, and poems.

The emergence of new paradigms for educational research has led to the development of research methods that were unavailable a quarter of a century ago. Qualitative methods, as they are called, are not restricted to matters of ethnography. Teachers, who are recognized as having an insider's understanding of schooling, now undertake action research. Arts based research has also attracted young researchers as a way to think about and do educational research. These new developments are welcomed as a corrective to previous research procedures that while useful for some purposes had been virtually useless for others. The emerging research paradigms are providing a rich array of methods for a more balanced understanding of what schools are and can be. Part 3 describes some of the major issues encountered in doing such research, it establishes links between new forms of assessment and changing views of what is important to assess, and it describes what artistically crafted research might help us understand about schools.

9

The Meaning of Alternative Paradigms for Practice

Although it's nice for academics to chew on epistemological questions and to debate normative and methodological issues, the aim of scholarship in education is not disinterested knowledge—even if there were such a creature—but the improvement of schooling. It is appropriate, therefore, to ask about the practical ramifications of the new models of mind, method, and knowledge we are so fond of discussing. I intend to do just that. I will address four areas in which the new paradigms can have significant implications: First, I want to discuss the conceptual implications of alternative paradigms; second, their implications for practice; third, their implications for policy; and, fourth, their normative implications.

I know, as you do, that no set of categories, dimensions, aspects, or features of a world as interactive as schooling can be neatly separated into the areas I have just enumerated. But you also know, as I do, that analysis requires separation, even if the parts are part fiction. Consider, therefore, the analysis that I am going to provide as analysis—a way of highlighting different aspects of a complex whole. I address each aspect separately because language itself is a diachronic, not a synchronic, medium. I bracket in order to illuminate and write in parts because I write rather than paint.

Conceptual Implications

Let's consider first the conceptual implications of alternative paradigms. By *alternative paradigms,* I refer to those ideational structures that portray humans as beings who generate different forms through which they hope to understand and represent the world they inhabit and who believe that

103

the different forms they use to understand and represent that world should be appraised by criteria appropriate to the form. Further, these paradigms hold that "truth" is ultimately a kind of mirage that in principle cannot be achieved because the worlds we know are those crafted by us and because we cannot uncouple mind and matter to know the world as it "really" is (Goodman 1978). By *alternative paradigms,* I refer to views of mind and knowledge that reject the idea that there is only one single epistemology and that there is an epistemological supreme court that can be appealed to to settle all issues concerning Truth.

One set of conceptual implications of alternative paradigms is a broader view of knowledge, a cultural view of mind (Cole 1985), a multiple view of intelligence (Gardner 1983), and a constructive view of cognition. Let's consider each in its turn.

By definition, the introduction of alternative paradigms for inquiry undermines the tacit but widely held belief that there is only one dependable way to know, something vaguely called "the scientific method." Acquiring a critical consciousness of method or knowledge is unlikely when a particular paradigm is so dominant that it has no competitors. What is pervasive often goes unexamined. When alternatives are suppressed or unavailable, we tend to accept what is accepted. When this occurs, we are in a poor position to know what we have. From this perspective, the emergence of alternative paradigms provides platforms from which to examine unexamined assumptions; in effect, their presence forces us to present our position, to defend it, and, therefore, to understand it better.

If this were the only contribution that alternative paradigms made to our conceptual life, it would be of profound importance. Professionally socialized doctoral students in schools of education are often unable to question the premises upon which accepted research methods rest. We usually do not encourage them to consider alternatives—or haven't until quite recently. The reasons for this neglect are many, but things are changing. The growing interest in alternative paradigms makes problematic the belief that one epistemology fits all or that nonscientific modes of inquiry are permissible only as reconnaissance efforts; if you "really" want to know, you need to conduct an experiment.[1] One conceptual consequence of alternative paradigms in education is their salutary effect on the research community. We are now less parochial than we once were.

The emergence of a broader and pluralistic view of knowledge can also contribute to a less dogmatic view in our schools of what it means "to know." Cognitive pluralism makes it more likely that students will understand that propositions, a necessary feature of scientific inquiry, are not by any means the only forms through which we come to understand the world.

Poetry and literature, for example, were invented to say what words can never say and, through what they say, we can come to understand what we cannot state. Science, Dewey (1934) reminds us, states meaning. Art expresses it. The meanings we are able to construct are influenced by the cultural tools we know how to use and the materials upon which we act. With the emergence of the new paradigms, "coming to know" in the school curriculum can take on a wider meaning. In the process, we are more likely to recognize the epistemic functions of fields we now dismiss as essentially "affective." [2]

Another conceptual consequence of alternative paradigms is a warming toward the idea that mind itself is a cultural achievement (Cole 1985; Eisner 1982). Everyone knows what a culture is—it is a place for growing things, and schools are places for growing minds (Cole 1985). The curricula we offer and the teaching methods we employ are means for creating minds. It is in this sense that the curriculum is a mind-altering device (Bernstein 1971) and the school a culture for growing minds. As this conception of mind takes root in our conceptual life, it creates an optimism for education for it emphasizes the possibilities of schooling, its capacity to make a difference in the kind of minds that students can come to own. The kind of culture we create in schools, the forms of thinking we cultivate, the forms of representation we make available (Eisner 1982), the recognition of the relationship between what we give students an opportunity to learn and the content of their experience is intimately related to a conception of inquiry that regards humans as creators of knowledge and makers of mind. Given this conception, we are more likely to cease seeking a fixed, measurable mental entity given at birth and seek instead to do what we can to grow minds as best we can.

Because alternative paradigms engender a pluralistic conception of knowledge, they share a family resemblance to what Gardner (1983) calls multiple intelligences. Intelligence is often conceptualized as something largely uninfluenced by culture, something biologically given. After all, what self-respecting psychometrician would choose to spend his or her time measuring what is fugitive or fleeting? The real task is to get at what is basic, what is enduring, what is fixed (Jensen 1969).

But when one entertains the notions of multiple ways of knowing and a cultural view of mind, it is not difficult to entertain the idea that intelligence itself is not one but many, that people cope with important problems in ways that depend on the kind of problem the problem is. Intelligence is, in this view, related to different kinds of action, which in turn is related to the kind of problem, task, or material one acts upon.

In addition to the implications that alternative paradigms have for our view of knowledge, mind, and intelligence, alternative paradigms also influence our conception of cognition. *Cognition,* a term that refers to the process through which the organism becomes aware (Statt 1981), has often been identified with linguistically mediated thought. To *cognize* is, for many, to think in language. Indeed, some writers believe no other form of conceptual thought is possible (Schaff 1973). Thinking and the use of language, for them, are synonymous. As our views of knowledge expand and our conceptions of the varieties of intelligence grow, it becomes increasingly difficult to restrict cognition to linguistically mediated thought. Thinking and knowing are mediated by any kind of experiential content the senses generate. Language, severed from semantics, is without meaning, and although images do not accompany every thought carried by language, our language refers to referents we are able to experience, recall, or imagine. Whether we are talking about unicorns, quarks, infinity, or apples, our cognitive life depends upon experience (Eisner 1988). Cognition is wider than words, and the forms through which our cognition is given public status are as diverse as the social forms of representation we use in culture to convey meaning. As Polanyi (1962) put it, "We know more than we can tell." Again, once we seek a pluralistic universe, we find differences we previously did not cognize; that is, we *re*-cognize the world and that world includes cognition itself.

Finally, with respect to the conceptual implications of alternative paradigms, I want to reiterate what I only touched upon earlier; the newfound appreciation of the epistemic functions of the subject matters of schooling. I refer here to our growing understanding that the forms of representation used in fields like art, poetry, literature, film, theater, and history, as well as those used in the natural and social sciences, were invented to convey meaning that would not take the impress of forms other than those employed: We are able to exemplify in art, for example, what words cannot articulate, and we are able to describe in words what we cannot exemplify (Goodman 1978). We are able to convey through analogy, prosody, innuendo, and metaphor what escapes the precision of literal language (Langer 1957). Forms of representation are functionally unique resources. The newfound appreciation of their contributions to cognition have potentially profound implications for curriculum, that mind-altering device I described earlier.

Implications for Practice

Given the conceptual shifts I have described, what might be their implications for the second of the four areas I wish to address, their implications for educational practice? One is that there is likely to be greater parity across the fields students study. By *parity,* I mean that literature, the visual arts, music, history, theater, and dance, as well as mathematics and science, would be recognized as cognitive in character, requiring intelligence and providing insight, understanding, and experience worth having. At present, this is clearly not the case, Some fields—the arts, for example—are marginalized in education. Some fields are regarded as "more cognitive" than others. Some fields are acknowledged by college admissions committees who count the grades secured by students in these areas when calculating GPA.[3] Other fields, such as the arts, regardless of the brilliance with which a student works in them, are simply discounted. As our epistemologies widen, the potential for rescuing curriculum from a hierarchy that reflects a more or less Platonic conception of knowledge and cognition increases. In short, the privileged place of a limited array of fields of study in our schools would give way to a more ecumenical and broadly arrayed set of curricular options.

Evidence of such a shift in curriculum would be displayed in that most telling indicator of our educational priorities—the way we allocate time to what we teach. Time allocation would reflect both a parity among fields and what Gardner (1983) calls individual proclivities. There would be less effort to put all children through the narrow eye of the same needle. Its details would also manifest themselves in our notion of what constitutes a core set of studies for all—what I refer to as a kind of *culturally referenced* curriculum balance and what individual students could elect without penalty, a kind of *personally referenced* curriculum balance. The general point here is that changes that take deep root in our conception of mind, knowledge, and intelligence can have very significant practical implications for what we teach.

What is taught is only one aspect of the practical consequences of new paradigms for education. How we organize what we teach is another.

School curricula, particularly at the middle and high school levels, are organized into what Basil Bernstein (1971) calls a "classification code." Subject fields have strongly bounded contours and are insular and essentially independent of each other. In addition, these subject fields are taught mainly through text and other propositional forms. As our understanding and appreciation for multiple ways of knowing grows, there is greater likelihood that a more synthetic, integrated curriculum will be developed. Within a curricular form that relates field to field, the use of multiple forms of representation is more likely. To illustrate the point, consider how a unit on slavery prior to the Civil War might be taught (Epstein 1989).

Students could, as they do now, rely mainly on textbooks to learn about the past. Yet, given the assumptions in the new paradigms, the textbook would be replaced or at least enhanced with films like *Roots,* with the music of the slaves, with the reading of their stories, their "folksay," with the food they ate; in short, students would encounter a wide range of curricular resources that serve epistemic ends to help them understand the life and times of the slaves prior to the Civil War. Hopefully, what becomes recognized in research circles will get reflected in curricular practice. The literal text is only one means through which the lives of others can be understood. Indeed, the novel may be a more powerful vehicle for transporting adolescents to Alabama, Mississippi, and Kentucky in the 1850s than a textbook rendition of the facts of the period.

Another implication of alternative paradigms for educational practice pertains to educational research and evaluation. We are already seeing in the field several vivid practical consequences of the appearance of the new kid on the block. We are debating issues and exploring methods that did not show a glimmer twenty years ago. The sacred cow has become a bit more profane. There is greater tolerance, even affection in some circles, for new ways to study educational practice and to assess its outcomes. We have new journals devoted to alternative paradigms,[4] more articles are appearing in learned journals that push deliberation a bit further, and conferences like the one on which this book is based and like the conference "Qualitative Inquiry in Education" that was held at Stanford in June 1988, are providing further legitimation. We have a qualitative special interest group in AERA that is not only alive and well but growing.[5]

But beyond these concrete practical manifestations of the new paradigms, we are inventing new ways to conduct research and creating new forms and methods with which to do educational evaluation. Whether it's Lincoln and Guba's (1985) naturalistic inquiry, Parlett and Hamilton's (1977) illuminative evaluation, Stake's (1975) responsive evaluation, or my own (Eisner 1985) educational connoisseurship and criticism, efforts are being made to weave a finer and wider net through which the processes and outcomes of educational practice can be understood and appraised. To be sure, we do not have the technical logic that has been developed for conventional approaches to research and evaluation. Furthermore, I do not believe we will ever create the kind of algorithms that are useful in treating quantitatively rendered data, but we have learned that there is more than one way to parse reality, and, with more refined approaches for describing, interpreting, and appraising the educational worlds we care about, greater confidence in methods that elude the security of rule will, I believe, develop. As the new paradigms really take hold, it will be increasingly recognized that Aristotle was correct when he said in his *Ethics:*

> Our discussion will be adequate if it has as much clearness as the subject-matter admits of, for precision is not to be sought for alike in all discus-

sions, any more than in all the products of the crafts . . . for it is the mark of an educated man to look for precision in each class of things just so far as the nature of the subject admits; it is evidently equally foolish to accept probable reasoning from a mathematician and to demand from a rhetorician scientific proofs. (McKeon 1941, 936)

Although we can argue with Aristotle about the meaning of precision—metaphor, for some things, may be more precise than measurement—the point of his statement is surely on the mark. Different forms require different expectations: Aristotle's biological interests served him well in matters epistemological.

It is difficult to imagine a more potent lever for changing the priorities of schools than the evaluative methods we employ. What we count counts. What we measure matters. What we test, we teach. After all, adaptation is a primary form of survival, and our appetite for assessment requires forms of adaptation in teaching that make survival possible. That is what it means to be accountable. Teachers and school administrators are expected to provide an account in forms that, for many, miss what they care about the most. The promise of new paradigms resides in their potential to provide methods and approaches that are both more equitable and closer to the values practitioners cherish.

In my experience, very few teachers value the tests they are required to administer to their students. They resent being held accountable through methods that they believe neglect what they feel is most important about their own teaching. With the new epistemology and new methods, we may be able to affect schools through assessment procedures that are more congruent with the educational values that I believe most teachers embrace. Should such consequences occur, it would be no small victory.

Thus far I have addressed two potential implications of the new paradigms for practice. One of these was their conceptual implications—the way they shift our way of thinking about knowledge, mind, intelligence, and cognition. The other was their implications for practice itself. Here I spoke of their consequences for curriculum content, for curricular form, and for the way in which we evaluate practice and we conduct research. Now I want to move up a notch and focus on the implications of the new paradigms for educational policy and then for our educational norms, that is, for what we hope to achieve in our schools.

Implications for Policy

Policy is a set of ideas reflecting certain values and beliefs that are created to guide decision making. The policies we form about education in general and about its components such as teaching and evaluation both constrain and stimulate practice. They constrain practice because policies legitimatize particular directions and values. They stimulate for the same reasons they constrain: Policies tell the educational world the direction decisions should take. For example, a school district policy that expects teachers to prepare a lesson plan each day so that the principal of a school can inspect it tells teachers something about how teaching is viewed and the importance of intentionality in their work. Policy that requires teachers to specify in behavioral terms the objectives toward which they aim articulates further what "the district" believes competent teachers do. Policy that requires that all teachers be evaluated once a year with an "objective" observation schedule by three appraisers independently observing a single 45-minute lesson conveys to those evaluated a tacit, if not explicit, epistemology and its application to the teaching process. Policy that publishes in local newspapers the achievement test scores of students on standardized tests on a school-by-grade basis reveals a set of values about what really counts in that school district and inevitably influences what teachers are likely to attend to in their classrooms.

The examples are endless and I do not want to perseverate. The point is that educational policy is shaped by beliefs about the kind of knowledge one can trust and the kinds of methods one can use to get such knowledge.

In contrast, consider the ways in which the new paradigms might influence how we think about policy pertaining to teaching. One potential consequence of the new paradigms is the way they encourage us to consider the sources of action. In conventional paradigms, action is idealized as a premeditated, goal-directed, cybernetically driven system. To act rationally, you have to have specific goals; the goals, in turn, determine the means you are to employ; the means you employ are then to be evaluated by their effects to determine the congruence between prespecified goals and the behavior of students. If the fit is not good enough, a new cycle is implemented.

What we have here is a recursive system, a means-ends model of rational behavior. Indeed, we have a very tidy world. As new paradigms have emerged in our educational discourse, our understanding of the sources of action in teaching has become less tidy and the role of intuition and qualitative thinking more salient. Body knowledge, as Johnson (1987) puts it, or reflectivity, as Schoen (1983) describes it, or craft, as Tom (1984) regards it, or artistry, as I think about it (Eisner 1983), have become a part of the way people think about teaching. The industrial model born of Taylorism (Callahan 1962) and implemented in a new garb in the 1970s and 1980s has become less attractive. There is a greater tendency these days to talk about reflective practitioners and clinical supervision (Sergiovanni 1983) and collaborative teaching. Although there is still plenty of appetite in the 108,000 American schools for formulaic approaches to the teaching act—the six steps to successful teaching—the picture today is more approximately complex than it was a few years ago.

The new paradigms have altered our conception of the sources of action, and we are recognizing that goals cannot always be specified; some are even difficult to articulate. We are recognizing that intuition is not some mystical process emanating from some Muse but the immediate grasp of field forces, of being able to read immediately the structure of the field in which one acts (Arnheim 1985), a feat wonderfully performed by a Larry Bird, or an Isaiah Thomas, and that the teacher's *sense* of what is needed, what is right here and now, are critical aspects of skilled teaching. In short, new paradigms that acknowledge the several ways in which humans think and know have loosened the corset that a narrow conception of human rationality imposes upon our conception of competent teaching.

The new paradigms make it more difficult to entertain the desiderata of teacher-proof curricula, or the use of a check-off observation schedule for evaluating teaching, or a Betty Crocker recipe for advancing teaching effectiveness. The new paradigms, I believe, contribute to more generous and more realistic educational policy affecting how teachers are to function. The longer-term consequences of such a policy are yet to come, but one place they might emerge is in the teacher's role in educational research.

The conventional role for research in education is built upon a paradigm that assigns to the specialist the job of studying teaching and learning in order to identify variables that have predictable effects on students. Once these variables are identified, the results of the research are published in journals and shared through inservice programs for teachers. The idea is that, once teachers learn about these studies, they will act upon their results in their own classrooms, that is, they will use what has been discovered by university researchers to do "what works" in their schools (U. S. Department of Education 1986).

This model is itself modeled after research in agriculture. The agronomist and the botanist do the basic research, the agricultural-extension agent carries the findings to the farmers, the farmers implement what the extension agent has provided, and, seven months later, a larger crop is harvested, all thanks to basic research. I know that this description is something of a caricature, but I also know that in its essentials it is the way we have proceeded. The *t* test, invented by William Gosset, was first used to determine the effect of fertilizer on the growth of corn.

What this paradigm has meant for research policy is a top-down orientation: Researchers create knowledge and pass it down to teachers. The knowledge that is transmitted is propositional and statistical in form. From such material the teacher—at least the really professional teacher—is to do things differently, and better.

The new paradigms advance another view. Although there is a place for conventional approaches, there is a difference between the kind of knowledge a teacher needs in a particular context and the abstracted generalizations found in learned journals or provided by inservice programs for teachers.[6] Teachers, some such as John Elliott (1986) in England and Mike Atkin (1989) in the United States argue, need themselves to conduct research. It's called action research. It's important that they do so, they argue, because the kind of knowledge secured by those on the inside, working in local contexts and needing to act upon what they know, differs in fundamental ways from the kind that will get an assent from three referees reviewing a manuscript submitted for publication to a learned journal. Research, given the new paradigms, is not likely to be the sole preserve of the university academic. At the very least, it will be a collaborative effort in which professors and teachers have parity.

Furthermore, what research yields is not to be regarded as dependable prescriptions for action but as analogues to increase the quality of teachers' deliberations. As Cronbach (1975) put it, it's to help practitioners use their heads. This is a significantly different view of the use of research. No longer are researchers in the business of sending to the social world information about cause-and-effect relations that ultimately direct action; instead, they provide ideas that can be creatively shaped by teachers in their own situations. This aspiration is at once more modest and more complex. It is more modest because it relieves researchers from the burden of finding the Holy Grail. It is more complex because it recognizes the need for creative rationality in teaching. It expands teaching rather than reducing it to rule. In the process, it confers professional status to the teacher. Behavioral prescriptions might work for bank tellers and airline attendants but they cannot work for teachers in schools concerned with education.

Alternative Paradigms and Educational Aims

I turn now to the fourth and final consideration on my agenda: the implications of the new paradigms for what we hope our schools will achieve. I suspect that the educational values implicit in the features of the new paradigms that I have described are not especially difficult to discern, but, to make them explicit, I address them here and now.

When one operates on the belief that there is one way to validate knowledge, it is not a long step to the belief that students should learn that knowledge. In other words, the primary mission of the school is to see to it that the transmission of knowledge occurs and that students get it right.

Knowledge transmission also means that knowledge not only can be discovered, it can be packaged and stored and transported and tested. In short, it has a life of its own. Furthermore, if there is a canonized body of knowledge, it seems reasonable that it be specified and transmitted to all students (except perhaps to those thought to be incapable of assimilating it; those unfortunates can always work with their hands). Because the same body of knowledge is to be transmitted to all, the same standards should be applied to all and the same criteria should be used to determine who graduates and who does not. The aim, whether intended or not, explicit or implicit, is to standardize curriculum and assessment and to diminish variability among students. Everyone is to have an equal (more or less) share in the same cultural legacy.

It takes no huge imagination to recognize that the recent efforts to specify the content of cultural literacy (Hirsch 1987), to develop a common curriculum, and to apply standardized "quality indicators" in schools participate mightily in the paradigm I have just described.

The new paradigms, yet again, provide more complex views of educational ends and make educational evaluation a much more daunting enterprise. You will recall that, when I was discussing the meaning of the new paradigms for practice, particularly for curriculum, I said that there were two kinds of curricular balance, a culturally referenced balance and an individually referenced balance. Culturally referenced balance encourages a common array of curriculum content for all students. I do believe that virtually all students ought to have *some* common program of education. An individually referenced balance fosters the development of those aptitudes, proclivities, and interests that individual students wish to pursue; in short, it fosters productive idiosyncracy. Given the new paradigms' acknowledgment of multiple intelligences and their recognition of parity across subject matters, it would be inconsistent to hold that all students should have nothing but a common educational diet and be assessed by the same set of standardized measures. The good school, given the values that permeate the new paradigms, would aim at increasing individual differences, not reducing them. The good school would seek to increase variance in performance, not to attenuate it.[7]

Such ambitions are, of course, at odds with prevailing lore about effective schools. Yet what the new paradigms imply for educational ends is productive diversity. They acknowledge and value different ways of learning and diverse forms of thinking. Once schools liberate themselves from the idea that the course to be run must be the same for all, and that the goals of that course should be, in the name of equity, common, schools become free to recognize differences as social as well as personal virtues. Educational equity should not be confused with a one-size-fits-all model of practice.

I said earlier that the problem of assessing such a program is daunting. It is. Commensurability simplifies life. One set of goals operationalized within a state or district examination that can be hermetically sealed and optically scored to yield numbers from which stanines can be computed really does simplify educational life. I know, after sitting on admissions committees at Stanford's School of Education for more than twenty years, how seductively simple it is to focus on GRE scores and how difficult and time-consuming it is to interpret a student's statement of purpose or even transcripts. When we seriously promote individual differences, we will find it difficult to use the same set of measures to determine what has been achieved. When we care about the journey and the students' experience, as well as the destinations at which they arrive, a fixed multiple-choice test is unlikely to be particularly relevant. When we recognize that learning about culturally rich periods of life requires multiple sources of data, multiple forms of representation, and the use of multiple intelligences, we are inclined to eschew single outcomes. Statistical comparisons may be relevant for some outcomes but surely not for the ones we are likely to care about the most.

Resistances to Change

I would like to conclude with the acknowledgment that the implications for practice I have described are riddled with optimism. My private hope is that the thought can be the parent of the deed. The kinds of practices I have described are, on the whole, more a description of aspiration than a description of fact. So I leave you with questions—questions that ratchet the problem up to what might be considered a political level.

What are the resistances to the kinds of changes I have described? What functions are now served by the forms of practice that now pervade our schools?[8] What makes it so difficult to diversify our programs of study, to alter the structure of our schools, and to use the approaches to research and evaluation in our schools that so many of us have pioneered? These questions invite us to examine what I have called the politics of method (Eisner 1988).

So let me end with another hope. It is the hope that Egon, maybe with our encouragement and help, will be willing to organize another conference next year, one that examines the politics of method and the possibilities of change in our schools. If he does, I know that I, along with all of you, will be among the first in line for tickets.

Notes

1. In some circles, qualitative research is thought to provide no basis for establishing causal relationships. Experiments are considered the paradigm procedure for securing causal knowledge, and qualitative research is considered an essentially exploratory activity until one can secure "hard" data.

2. The distinction between feeling and knowing is deeply ingrained in Western culture. It is also deeply rooted in our educational culture. Relatively few theoreticians dealing with epistemological issues in education underscore the importance of feeling as a source of knowing. The result is a marginalization of subjects deemed "affective." The arts are the first to be assigned to such residual categories. The result, in my view, is a profound misunderstanding of the sources of knowledge.

3. My own institution, Stanford University, does not include grades that students receive in the fine arts in high school when calculating their grade point average for admission to Stanford. This policy is both a symbolic and a practical reminder of the marginality of the arts and the parochial conception of knowledge that still pervades universities.

4. See, for example, the *International Journal for Qualitative Studies in Education.*

5. Membership in the qualitative interest group in AERA has more than doubled since its inception in 1986.

6. Inservice programs operate on the assumption that experienced teachers are well served by listening to professors of education and others teach them, in settings removed from the school, how to perform in their own classrooms. This is akin to a basketball coach providing advice to a team he has never seen play.

7. Sir Herbert Read, British aesthetician, poet, and critic, wrote in *Education Through Art* (1944) that there were two principles that could guide education. One was to make children into what they are not. The other was to help children become what they are. He opted for the latter, stating that fascist societies try to do the former. Self-realization, he believed, was a primary educational goal. Furthermore, when individual differences are cultivated and fostered, the quality of the society itself is increased because of productive diversity. Given Read's observation, one that I share, bringing all children to the same place would be a liability, not an asset, in education.

8. This question has, of course, been raised by many critics of schooling. See, for example, Michael Apple, *Education and Power* (1982), and the works of Henry Giroux.

10

Forms of Understanding and the Future of Educational Research

My address this afternoon is partly the story of a personal odyssey and partly a confessional. It has three parts. The odyssey, the first part, relates to the journey I have taken to try to understand the development of mind and the forms through which its contents are made public. How my ideas about these matters evolved is a story I want to tell. The confessional, the second part, refers to the dilemmas, uncertainties, and conundrums that the ideas that I embrace have caused me. This presidential address is more about quandaries than certitudes. I intend to display my quandaries. My hope is that at least some of what puzzles me will intrigue you. Indeed, I hope it intrigues you enough to want to join me. Finally, in the third part, I want to say what I think the ideas I have explored might mean for the future of educational research, both how it is pursued and how it is presented.

As some of you know, when I was in my twenties, I was a teacher of art and, before that, a painter. I moved from painting to teaching because I discovered that the children with whom I worked, economically disenfranchised African Americans living on Chicago's West Side, became more important to me than the crafting of images; for some reason I came to believe then, as I believe now, that the process of image-making could help children discover a part of themselves that mostly resides beneath their consciousness. Art was a way of displaying to the children and adolescents with whom I worked dimensions of themselves that I desperately wanted them to discover.

It was my interest in children and my need to clarify my vague convictions about the educational potential of art that led me to the University of Chicago and to an initiation into the social sciences, which

116

were at that time the style of intellectual life that defined doctoral study. The Department of Education at Chicago, while steeped in the social sciences, was also intellectually open, and I was given enough slack not only to sustain, but to pursue, my interest in the arts. While no one on the faculty worked in arts education or knew much about it, my intellectual mentors— John Goodlad, Phil Jackson, Joseph Schwab, Ben Bloom, and Bruno Bettelheim—provided support and encouragement. Later I found additional support in the work of Ernst Cassirer, Susanne Langer, Rudolf Arnheim, Michael Polanyi, John Dewey, and Nelson Goodman.

My encounter with the social sciences at Chicago and my long-standing engagement in art, both as a painter and a teacher of art, forced me to confront the tension between my desire to understand and cultivate what is individual and distinctive and my wish to grasp what is patterned and regular.[1] My effort to resolve this tension and my interest in the cognitive character of the arts have been a career-long journey. This journey has been guided by a variety of beliefs.

First among these is the belief that experience is the bedrock upon which meaning is constructed and that experience in significant degree depends on our ability to get in touch with the qualitative world we inhabit. This qualitative world is immediate before it is mediated, presentational before it is representational, sensuous before it is symbolic. This "getting in touch," which is crucial for any artist, I did not regard then nor do I today as a noncognitive, affective event that simply supplies the mind with something to think about. Getting in touch is itself an act of discrimination, a fine-grained, sensitively nuanced selective process in which the mind is fully engaged. I believed then, as I believe now, that the eye is a part of the mind.

Consciousness of the qualitative world as a source of potential experience and the human sensory system as a means through which those potentialities are explored require no sharp distinction between cognition and perception: On the contrary, I came to believe that perception is a cognitive event and that construal, not discovery, is critical.[2] Put another way, I came to believe that humans do not simply have experience; they have a hand in its creation, and the quality of their creation depends upon the ways they employ their minds.

A second idea that has guided my journey is the belief that the use of mind is the most potent means of its development. What we think about matters. What we try to do with what we think about matters. And so it follows, what schools allow children to think about shapes, in ways perhaps more significant than we realize, the kind of minds they come to own. As the English sociologist Basil Bernstein suggests, the curriculum is a mind-altering device (1971). We might extend his observation and say, "Education itself is a mind-making process."

This belief in the constructive character of mind, the critically important role of the senses in its formation, and the contribution of the imagination in defining the limits mind can reach are all consistent with my experience as a painter and as a teacher of art. First, the ability to paint well clearly requires students to de-center their perception, that is, they have to learn how to see relationships among qualities, not just discrete elements.[3] Learning to paint means learning to see how forms fit together, how colors influence each other, how balance and coherence can be achieved. Second, unlike many other school tasks, imagination and individuality are critical to successful production in art. As a teacher of art, I wanted to help students create images that displayed their own personal signature. Individuality of outcome, not conformity to a predetermined common standard, was what I was after. Neither norm-referenced nor criterion-referenced evaluation was an appropriate model for either the aims that mattered or the means through which their realization could be determined.[4] The tasks I pursued in my classroom were both guided by and reinforced by beliefs that only later became more consciously articulated.

One of those beliefs, the third in this journey, has to do with matters of representation. As sensibility is refined, our ability to construct meaning within a domain increases. The refinement of sensibility is no small accomplishment. Hearing, Gilbert Ryle reminds us in *The Concept of Mind* (1949), is an achievement, not simply a task. To *hear* the music, to *see* the landscape, to *feel* the qualities in a bolt of cloth, are not automatic consequences of maturation. Learning how to experience such qualities means learning how to use your mind. But these achievements, as important as they are, are achievements of impression, not expression. Surely there is more. That something more resides in matters of representation.

Representation, as I use the term, is not the mental representation discussed in cognitive science (Shepard 1982, 1990) but, rather, the process of transforming the contents of consciousness into a public form so that they can be stabilized, inspected, edited, and shared with others. Representation is what confers a publicly social dimension to cognition. Since forms of representation differ, the kinds of experiences they make possible also differ. Different kinds of experience lead to different meanings, which, in turn, make different forms of understanding possible.

This argument, with greater elaboration than I am able to provide here, was the essential line in my John Dewey lecture in 1978 (Eisner 1982). This lecture was elaborated and published in book form in *Cognition and Curriculum* in 1982. Howard Gardner's *Frames of Mind*, published in 1983, shares a common interest with *Cognition and Curriculum,* yet they differ in significant ways. Gardner is concerned with describing the multiple ways in which people can be smart. He discusses the ways in which different cultures assign different priorities to different kinds of problem solving. He also explores the developmental history of each type of intelligence. I regard his work as among the most influential that have appeared in the field of education in the last decade. My work focuses on matters of meaning, the kinds of meanings that can be made not only through different forms of representation but also through what I refer to as different *modes of treatment.* Different forms of representation can themselves be treated in different ways[5]—both form and mode matter. I will illustrate this point shortly.

How do these ideas about meaning and forms of representation pertain to schools and to what we teach? What relevance do they have for educational practice? As I see it, the curriculum we use in schools defines the opportunities students will have to learn how to think *within* the media that schools provide.[6] Learning to modulate visual images and learning to logically use language require different forms of thinking. Different forms of thinking lead to different kinds of meaning. By defining the forms of representation that matter within the curriculum, the school significantly influences the kinds of meanings that students can learn to secure and represent.

That meaning is shaped by the form in which it appears is, in many ways, obvious. Humans invented maps to do what narrative could not do as well. The rites and rituals employed in churches and temples, in mosques and in other holy places, are replete with forms of representation that give moment to the occasion. We treat forms in particular ways in order to create the particular meanings we wish to display or experience.

Let's take a look at the way a poem, Tennyson's "Ulysses" (1870, 58), shapes our experience when we hear it read, when we listen to its lines spoken in the context of a political speech, and when we experience it in conjunction with an array of visual images.

"Ulysses" was written by Tennyson over a hundred years ago. It's a poem about a pirate-king who went on an incredible ten-year journey to liberate a Greek queen by the name of Helen who was held captive in the city of Troy. It was Ulysses who devised the trick of using a wooden horse—a Trojan horse—to bring Greek warriors into Troy who then opened the gates of the city to the Greek army. [At this point, I showed a seven-minute video to illustrate points in ways I could not do through text alone.]

The "Ulysses" we find in Teddy Kennedy's speech is a Ulysses intended to celebrate his brother's memory and to inspire his disappointed supporters to carry on in the face of his departure as a presidential candidate. Through language, Tennyson provides the image that allows Kennedy to say, paradoxically, what words cannot say.

We exploit different forms of representation to construct meanings that might otherwise elude us. The most prominent modern example of this function is found in the uses of the computer. The development of software and other forms of computer technology, such as computer-aided design, has expanded our capacity to display in graphic form what cannot be displayed in text or number. By virtue of the synchronic characteristic of visual displays, we are able to comprehend, store, retrieve, and act upon information in ways that visualization facilitates. An image gives us information at once. A narrative provides it over time. Synchronicity and diachronicity have their respective virtues. For example, spreadsheets display visual patterns that words or numbers alone cannot as easily reveal. Ross Perot taught us the powerful lesson that even the simplest visual charts can make plain what political language often obscures. Pie charts, histograms, and other diagrammatic material contribute to our understanding of the relationships we seek to grasp. Outliers are obscured in means and variances. Scattergrams make them visible. The limits of our comprehension, it seems, exceed the limits of our language. Or, as Nelson Goodman (1978) has suggested, there are as many worlds as there are ways to describe them.

Well what's the gist of the argument thus far and what are the problems that perplex me about it? First, the argument. Put as succinctly as I can, it goes like this.

Humans are sentient creatures who live in a qualitative world. The sensory system that humans possess provides the means through which the qualities of that world are experienced. Over time, through development, maturation, and acculturation, the human's ability to experience the qualitative environment increases: Experience is linked to the process of increased sensory differentiation.

Out of experience, concepts are formed. Concepts are imaginative distillations of the essential features of the experienced world. They can be manipulated and modified and they can be used to generate possibilities that, though never encountered directly in the environment itself—infinity and dragons, quarks and goblins, for example—can have pragmatic and aesthetic value. Our conceptual life, shaped by imagination and the qualities of the world experienced, gives rise to the intentions that direct our activities. Intentions are rooted in the imagination. Intentions depend upon our ability to recognize what is, and yet to imagine what might be.

Experience, however, is private. For experience to become public, we must find some means to represent it. Culture makes available to the developing human an array of forms of representation through which the transformation of consciousness into its public equivalent is created. Schools are culture's agencies for selectively developing competencies in the use of these forms. Once public, the content of consciousness is stabilized, and once stabilized, it can be edited, revised, and shared. But representation is not a one-way street. Since experience can never be displayed in the form in which it initially appeared, the act of representation is also an act of invention: The act of representation provides its own unpredictable options, options that can only emerge in the course of action (Collingwood 1958).

The meaning that representation carries is both constrained and made possible by the form of representation we employ. Not everything can be "said" with anything. Poetic meaning requires poetic forms of thought and poetically treated form. Visual art requires forms of thought that address the import of visual imagery. How we think is influenced by what we think about and how we choose or are expected to represent its content. By selectively emphasizing some forms of representation over others, schools shape children's thinking skills and in the process privilege some students and handicap others by virtue of the congruence between their aptitudes and the opportunities to use them in school. In this sense, the school is profoundly political.[7]

As tidy as this conception of the sources of meaning, understanding, and representation appears to me, I am vexed by uncertainties and dilemmas I would like to share with you. Some of these uncertainties are theoretical, some practical. Let's start with the theoretical. Consider the meaning of meaning. We all use the term. It's central to my conception of the aims of education. But just what *meaning* means is not altogether clear. Is it the Peircian (Peirce 1960) triadic relationship between a sign, an interpretant, and a referent, or can meaning be secured in the direct unsymbolized qualitative encounter? What is the role of context in the construction of meaning? And what about language? Does language require referents to be meaningful?

What shall we do with signs whose referents cannot be identified? Shall we regard stories and poems simply as an array of images that language helps us grasp? Are there meanings that language makes possible that are independent of the referents to which the words refer? Are there ideas that are representable only through language? If so, are they also inconceivable without language? What about Einstein's (Holton 1982) reference to the muscular and iconic sources of his understanding, and Poincaré's (Hadamard 1945) allusions to visualization? Or how about Barbara McClintock's (Keller 1983) feeling for the organism? And what about poetic meaning? Don't the meanings of poetry transcend the meaning of words? I worry about such matters because I want to understand the connection between experience and meaning and the contribution that different forms of representation make to each. It seems to me that such matters reside at the heart of any useful theory of education.

Appeals to rationality as an explanation of how meaning is secured are not much of an explanation. In any case, whatever rationality means, I do not want to restrict it to a particular medium of thought. If human rationality can be said to display itself whenever the selection, invention, and organization of elements to form a coherent whole occur, it seems clear that these processes occur in any medium. Why should rational processes be limited to propositional discourse or to number? But then again, why not? And so I return to uncertainty.

Interest in experience, meaning, and understanding ineluctably leads to concerns about knowledge, and so to matters of truth. What shall we do about truth? Should we, as is currently the fashion, give it up altogether—even as a regulative ideal? Frankly, I am reluctant to do so. Should we restrict it to the claims that propositional discourse can make? I think not. To restrict truth to what one can claim is to claim much too little for what we are able to know (Polanyi 1966). As I said earlier, I believe that our discourse defines neither the scope of our rationality nor the varieties of our understanding. But how do we deal with forms of representation whose referents are at best ambiguous? And if we hold as an ideal for truth matters that aspire to the precision of mathematics, don't we wind up with a conception of truth that is limited by what mathematical forms can reveal? Should we, for example, regard the arts as irrelevant to matters of truth? Aren't they, really, simply sources of pleasure and delight, sensory meals for qualitative gourmets?

I believe there is much too much practical wisdom that tells us that the images created by literature, poetry, the visual arts, dance, and music give us insights that inform us in the special ways that only artistically rendered forms make possible. One example of these ways is found in literature. In the following painful passage Elie Wiesel (1969) recounts his experiences in a Nazi death camp:

> Never shall I forget that night, the first night in camp, which has turned my life into one long night, seven times cursed and seven times sealed. Never shall I forget that smoke. Never shall I forget the little faces of the children, whose bodies I saw turned into wreaths of smoke beneath a silent blue sky.
>
> Never shall I forget those flames which consumed my faith forever.
>
> Never shall I forget that nocturnal silence which deprived me, for all eternity, of the desire to live. Never shall I forget those moments which murdered my God and my soul and turned my dreams to dust. Never

shall I forget these things, even if I am condemned to live as long as God Himself. Never. (44)

One way to understand what Elie Wiesel has achieved through the literary treatment of language is to see it through the conceptual frame that Susanne Langer (1976) has created. In this passage, Langer is talking about the cognitive contributions of art. She says:

> A work of art presents feeling for our contemplation, making it visible or audible or in some way perceivable through a symbol, not inferable from a symptom. Artistic form is congruent with the dynamic forms of our direct sensuous, mental, and emotional life; works of art are projections of "felt life," as Henry James called it, into spatial, temporal, and poetic structures. They are images of feeling, that formulate it for our cognition. What is artistically good is whatever articulates and presents feeling to our understanding. (25)

Although intuitively I find Langer's conceptions compelling, I also know that the arts can be used to persuade people to embrace faulty beliefs, beliefs that mislead. Propaganda and advertising are two such examples. Shall we then restrict our conception of truth only to what science can provide? Again, I think not, even though I cannot demonstrate with the kind of assurance I would like the justification for the views that I hold. But what kind of justification do I seek? Perhaps that is the problem.

Some philosophers, such as Richard Rorty (1979), have put truth on the shelf and have replaced it with what he calls "edification." Making the conversation more interesting, Rorty tells us, is what it's all about. As interested as I am in interesting conversation, it, too, is not enough. How do we avoid the verificationist's constipation of conceptual categories on the one hand and the radical relativist's free-for-all, anything-goes, no-holds-barred nihilism on the other? Or are these really untenable alternatives that nobody really believes? Maybe so. But just what is a better basis? And so I continue to struggle.

In talking about experience and its relationship to the forms of representation that we employ, I am not talking about poetry and pictures, literature and dance, mathematics and literal statement simply as alternative means for displaying what we know. I am talking about the forms of understanding, the unique forms of understanding that poetry and pictures, literature and dance, mathematics and literal language make possible.

What is it to say that we have a poetic form of understanding? Or one rooted in vision or in sound? Just what do we learn when we see Teddy Kennedy's profile, hear his Bostonian accent, experience his sense of personal urgency, rise with him as his voice escalates in his moving acknowledgment of his lost candidacy? What do we grasp when we see a young Chinese student in Tiananmen Square engaged in a waltz, head on, with a Soviet tank? What vision of our nation emerges before us when in 1963 we hear Martin Luther King, in the shadow of the Lincoln Memorial, proclaim to the multitude, "I have a dream," or when, 29 years later, we see Rodney King beaten by police in Los Angeles? "What happens to a dream deferred?" Langston Hughes (1958, 123) asks:

> Does it dry up
> Like a raisin in the sun?
> Or fester like a sore—
> And then run?
> Does it stink like rotten meat?
> Or curst and sugar over—
> Like a syrupy sweet?
> Maybe it just sags
> Like a heavy load.
> *Or does it explode?*

If there are different ways to understand the world, and if there are different forms that make such understanding possible, then it would seem to follow that any comprehensive effort to understand the processes and outcomes of schooling would profit from a pluralistic rather than a monolithic approach to research. How can such a pluralism be advanced? What would it mean for the way we go about our work?

I hope that questions of these kinds will become an agenda for our research in the future. The battle that once ensued to secure a place for qualitative research in education has largely been won. Although there are still more than a few places where graduate students encounter resistance, the literature is too full and the practice too widespread to go back to older, tidier times. Now the question turns to just what it is that different forms of representation employed within the context of educational research might help us grasp. Are there varieties of human understanding? What is distinctive about them? Just what *is* poetic insight? What kind of imaginative rationality is made possible through literature? What does the persistent image engender? What sense of life does the fresh metaphor create? Now is the time to search for seas that take us beyond the comforts of old ports.

Let us *suppose* for the time being that the basic notions I have described have merit, that meaning is multiple, and that forms of representation provide the means through which meaning is made. Let us also *suppose* that diversified forms of meaning are related to different forms of understanding and that different forms of understanding have great virtue for knowing how to act in complex circumstances. Given these suppositions, what would the ideas I have been addressing mean for what we do in educational research in the coming few decades? This brings us to the third and final section of my remarks.

If the ideas that I have described were to take hold in the educational research community, we would see an expanding array of research methods being employed in the conduct and display of educational research. In many ways, this diversity has already begun to happen. We now have a growing interest in narrative and in storied approaches to experience. Jerome Bruner's (1990) distinction between paradigmatic and narrative modes of knowing provides a conceptual basis for understanding the differences between scientific and narrativistic ways of dealing with the world.

But stories and narrative by no means exhaust the ways in which the processes of education in and out of schools can be studied or described. Film, video, the multiple displays made possible through computers, and even poetically crafted narrative are waiting in the wings. I believe that we won't have long to wait before they are called to center stage. The exploration of new forms for the presentation of research that this Annual Meeting has made possible is a step in that direction.

The use of visual, narrative, and poetic forms will have consequences for determining who is competent to appraise what they have to say. When research methods are stable and canonized, the rules of the game are relatively clear. With new games, new rules. With new rules, competencies that were appropriate for some forms of research may not necessarily be relevant for others. Furthermore, the ability to make sense of a form of research depends upon one's conception of what counts as research.[8] These conceptions and abilities will also change. What we need to avoid is political polarization as a result of methodological differentiation. Polarization eventually leads to matters of power and control: There is not only a sociology of knowledge; there is also a sociology of method. I hope we can use the future to achieve complementarity rather than methodological hegemony.

Curriculum development as a form of educational research is also likely to be influenced by an expanding vision of the forms of understanding schools can foster. Film, video, narrative, dance, music, the visual arts, as well as more propositionally formulated descriptions of events all have the potential to reveal aspects of the world we want students to understand. Consider what it might mean for the teaching of history.

How we answer the question of whether history is the text historians write or the past historians write about is crucial to our own view of what history is and, therefore, to what is relevant for helping students understand it. If history is text, then text must continue to be central to the teaching of history: To understand history one has to understand text. But if history is the past about which historians write, then any form of representation that sheds light on the past is a relevant, indeed a useful, way to understand history. In this latter view, music, architecture, film, stories, and the like are not only relevant, they are distinctive; each sheds unique light upon the past. But this requires that we know how to make sense of them.

In a study of the ways in which different forms of representation foster the understanding of history, Marcy Singer (1991) found that the use of a wide array of diverse forms to teach history in the context of social studies had two very interesting consequences. First, high school students had a difficult time regarding anything other than text as a source of knowledge about the past. They regarded the textbook as sacrosanct. What is presented was factual truth.

The forms that Singer studied in her research on the teaching of four decades of the twentieth century—the 1920s, 1930s, 1950s, and 1960s—included Charlie Chaplin's *Modern Times,* the film *Rebel Without a Cause,* the music of Scott Joplin, the songs of Pete Seeger, the music of the Beatles, "Eyes on the Prize," *The Autobiography of Malcolm X,* Steinbeck's *The Grapes of Wrath,* the Sacco-Vanzetti painting by Ben Shahn, television's "Leave It to Beaver," Chuck Berry, and the paintings of Jackson Pollack. Yet students did not regard these sources as relevant for understanding history.

At the same time, the very ambiguity—or better yet the openness—of such forms made for the best discussions in class. In retrospect, this is not surprising. After all, what is there to discuss when students confront the certainties of the text? When it comes to forms of representation that invite interpretation, interpretation followed. In *The Principles of Psychology* published in 1890, William James asked for what he called "the reinstatement of the vague to its proper place in our mental life" (Gavin 1986). James recognized then what Singer found about a century later: Ambiguity has a more significant cognitive contribution to make to students than the certain facticity of the text.

The use of a wider array of diverse forms in teaching begs for studies of their consequences. At the same time, the problem of determining consequences is notoriously difficult for several reasons. First, the manifestation of consequences requires giving students the opportunity to display what they have learned in forms of representation congenial to both the content of their learning and the nature of their aptitudes. In addition, to be successful in representing such content, students must be skilled in the medium they wish to use. If students do not possess the skills they need, say of producing a video or a film, of writing a poem or creating a visual narrative, the content they wish to represent is simply not likely to emerge. Representation requires the skills needed to treat a material so that it functions as a medium, something that mediates content.

Second, assuming students do possess such skills, the results of their work will differ. This array of differences will play havoc with traditional conceptions of criterion-referenced evaluation. When goals are prespecified, tasks for students are uniform, and the application of standards is procedurally objective, comparisons among student performances is possible. However, I must tell you, I am not sanguine about meaningfully calibrating to a common scale differences among students who use different forms to display what they have learned. I do not say this to dissuade anyone from pursuing it; it is a direction that should be explored. But I can see complexities emerging as I now see them emerging in the use of portfolios and other forms of authentic assessment. Premises about assessment—such as comparability of student performance—may have to change if practices are to change.[9]

Another potential consequence for educational research relates to the education of doctoral students. As the relevance of different forms of representation for understanding schooling grows, schools of education will be pressed to develop programs that help students learn how to use them. Film, for example, will need to be regarded not only as a way of showing pictures but as a way of understanding some aspects of schooling, teaching, and learning that cannot be understood as well in any other way. Furthermore, the artistic features of film are not merely ornamental but essential to the display of particular messages. Thus, the refinement of both artistic and scientific sensibilities, as the theme of this Annual Meeting implies, is relevant for enlarging human understanding.

Another offshoot of this development deals with the features of acceptable dissertations. In the future they are likely to take on forms that only a few now possess. One of my doctoral students once asked me if Stanford's School of Education would accept a novel as a dissertation. At the time she raised this question, about a decade ago, I could only answer in the negative. Today, I am more optimistic, not because all of my Stanford colleagues share my convictions, but because the climate for exploring new forms of research is more generous today than it was then.

Given the ideas I have been developing, a number of questions emerge. Perhaps the most fundamental of these pertains to the notion that humans have the capacity to formulate different kinds of understanding and that these understandings are intimately related to the forms of representation they encounter or employ and the way in which those forms are treated. Discovering, however, how such forms of understanding are secured and the kinds of meanings they make possible is a core theoretical as well as practical problem. It's one thing to speculate about the validity of an idea. It's another to demonstrate it empirically. What kind of empiricism would be required to identify the different ways in which students come to understand aspects of the world? Are there forms of assessment and approaches to curriculum that would make it possible to know, in advance, the probability that some forms of understanding would be engendered if some forms of representation were employed in the course of teaching and learning? Just what is the relationship between student aptitude and the forms that they have access to? Does the fit between the two facilitate comprehension as we would expect? And what does one do to give students not only the opportunity but the skills to display their understanding? Can we translate what is specific and unique to forms other than those in which such understanding is revealed?

I must confess that I do not have answers to the questions I have just posed. I believe, however, that the questions I have posed are crucial for educational practice and research that does justice to the development of human intellectual capacities.

Another issue pertains to the ways in which the research that is done on such matters can be displayed. We are, of course, habituated to text and number. Our journals are, if anything, encomiums to technical language. What would an entirely new array of presentational forms for research look like? What might we learn about a school or a classroom, a teacher or a student, a form of teaching and a style of learning, through an integration of film, text, photo, and poem?

While envisioning such an integration of forms is difficult, it is the exploration of such possibilities, first imaginatively and then practically, that will enable us to invent an agenda for the future. In some ways, through MTV and other such forms, our students are way ahead of us. Sound and image, more than text and number, are the cornerstones of their experience. What do such possibilities hold for a group of scholars steeped in more conservative traditions? In sum, I am asking us to do what we don't know how to do. I am asking us to recognize the limits of our comfortable past, but not to discard it. As I said, I am asking us to bypass familiar ports and to explore the new seas that we might sail. I think we have already made a wonderful beginning on that journey.

It's not only the conventional canon that's being questioned; it's deeper. It's how we think about mind, the enlargement of human understanding, and what counts as meaningful. From the feminist critique of science by a Sandra Harding (1991) to the reappearance of the Windelbandian distinction between the ideographic and the nomothetic, (von Wright 1971) from the postmodern constructions of a Paul Ricoeur (1981) and a Roland Barth

(1985) to the phenomenological perspectives of a Merleau-Ponty (1962) and a Maxine Greene (1988), the times they are a-changing. And we are also changing.

Virtually everything that I have said pertains to the theoretical matters that continue to puzzle me and to their practical relevance for the conduct of research, the careers of researchers, and the preparation of those who will do research. But I would be remiss if I left this podium leaving the impression that the advancement of research, or the careers of researchers, or the satisfactions that come from the reduction of puzzlement constitute the major aim of the common enterprise in which we are engaged. The major aim, we must not forget, has to do with the African American children with whom I worked on Chicago's West Side at the beginning of my career. It has to do with the improvement of educational practice so that the lives of those who teach and learn are themselves enhanced. Put more succinctly, we do research to understand. We try to understand in order to make our schools better places for both the children and the adults who share their lives there. That aim, from my perspective, needs to remain as frontlets between our eyes. We should fix them as signposts upon our gates. In the end, our work lives its ultimate life in the lives that it enables others to lead. Although we are making headway toward that end, there will continue to be difficulties and uncertainties, frustrations and obstacles. Working at the edge of incompetence takes courage. When the doubts emerge and the safe road beckons, it might be well to remember Tennyson's lines. And so I close my comments with them:

> Tho' much is taken, much abides; and tho'
> We are not now that strength which in old days
> Moved heaven and earth; that which we are, we are;
> One equal temper of heroic hearts
> Made weak by time and fate, but strong in will
> To strive, to seek, to find, and not to yield.

Notes

While I was preparing this address, I benefited from the good advice of several colleagues and friends. I am pleased to acknowledge their contributions here: David Ecker, Howard Gardner, Lisa Goldstein, Alan Peshkin, Richard Snow, and Lesley Taylor.

1. This tension is described as residing within the idiographic and the nomothetic, that is, between efforts to understand the particular and efforts to grasp the general. See von Wright's (1971) *Explanation and Understanding* for further discussion.

2. The cognitive character of perception is given a special force in the writings of Rudolf Arnheim and Ulric Neisser. See Arnheim's (1969) *Visual Thinking* and Neisser's (1976) *Cognition and Reality*. For a philosophical interpretation of the relationship between perception and cognition, see Hanson's (1971) *Observation and Explanation: A Guide to the Philosophy of Science*.

3. The concept of de-centering perception is embedded in the works of Jean Piaget and Rudolf Arnheim. Arnheim calls the focus on particulars in the act of drawing "local solutions," referring to the fact that children are so focused or centered on the object they wish to draw that they neglect its relationship to the context in which it appears.

4. Both norm-referenced and criterion-referenced evaluation are predicated on the need to compare. In norm-referenced evaluation, the comparison is made between one student's performance and the performances of others within some relevant population. In criterion-referenced evaluation, the comparison is made between the student's performance and a known criterion or model. Neither of these conceptions is wholly adequate for evaluation in the arts since in artistic activity a premium is placed upon surprise and the generation of creative solutions that, by definition, are not predictable. Appropriate assessment practice in the arts requires the use of what Robert Stake calls responsive evaluation and what I have referred to as expressive outcomes (see, e.g., Stake 1975, and Eisner 1969).

5. In *Cognition and Curriculum* (Eisner 1982), I identified three ways in which forms of representation can be treated: through mimesis, through expressiveness, and through convention. Mimesis provides an imitation of the world to be represented, as, for example, in onomatopoeia, in efforts at visual realism, and in program music. The expressive treatment of form is found in works whose features evoke responses congruent with the deep structure of what they represent: for example, the images of Edvard Münch, the overtures of Richard Wagner, and the poetry of e. e. cummings. Conventional forms, like the Red Cross or the American flag, reflect social agreements to use the form to refer to "specific" meanings. These meanings cannot, of course, be entirely specified. Nevertheless, there is usually enough congruence within a culture to enable its members to achieve commonality of meaning.

6. In his book *Art as Experience* (1934), John Dewey makes the following point regarding the relationship of mode of thought to medium: "Those who are called artists have for their subject matter the qualities of things of direct experience; 'intellectual' inquiries deal with those qualities at one remove, through the medium of symbols that stand for qualities but are not significant in their immediate presence" (73).

7. The fact that schools both withhold and provide opportunities for students to succeed by virtue of the agenda that they make available to students makes them profoundly political. Students whose aptitudes are not given an opportunity to emerge within the context of schools are often handicapped. Significantly, universities often discount or disregard the grades that students receive in the fine arts when considering a candidate for admission. Even when schools make certain kinds of performances possible for students, and even when those performances are graded by the schools, there is no assurance that the quality of student performance will be taken into account by tertiary institutions. This practice, utterly unconscionable from my perspective, has a profound influence on what college-bound students believe they can afford to study in school.

8. One of the most significant shifts that is likely to occur in the educational research community is the broadening of its conception of what counts as educational research. This increased breadth is not a license for "anything goes," but a recognition that the roads to understanding are many and that a narrow view of method is likely to lead to a limited understanding of how schools work.

9. Educational evaluation and measurement have been predicated on the need to compare students with each other or with a known criterion. As I indicated earlier, such a premise is not a necessary condition for any kind of evaluation. As our premises change so that we are open to forms that are distinctive, we will be in a much better position to develop evaluation practices that recognize the cultivation of productive idiosyncrasy as an important educational outcome and thus to honor it in assessment.

11

Reshaping Assessment in Education

If there ever was a time in which the calls were clearer or more strident for new, more authentic approaches to educational assessment, I cannot remember when they occurred. Yet, despite its salience, the term *assessment* is more an aspiration than a concept that has a socially confirmed technical meaning. The older term, *evaluation,* while not particularly ancient in the literature of U.S. education, is no longer as popular as it once was; *assessment* has given it a gentle but firm nudge.

Before discussing assessment, explaining why it has emerged, and proposing some of the new criteria it ought to meet, it will be useful to examine the historical and ideological ground upon which the older version we call educational evaluation emerged. Once we have examined the terrain, we should have a better picture of the significance of current efforts to create new forms of educational assessment.

The early attempts to create a science of the social emerged during the Enlightenment. During the late seventeenth and eighteenth centuries, scholars such as Condorcet and Condillac (Berlin 1986) attempted to grasp the order of nature by studying it through the scientific methods advanced by Galileo and his followers. The spirit that animated Galileo, Condorcet, Condillac, Newton, and later Auguste Comte, was a conviction that the world could be studied through procedures that not only revealed its regularities, but brought them under a theoretical net that would satisfy the human's need to know. No longer beyond our control, humans could come to understand how the world actually operated, beliefs about its features could be empirically tested and, in some cases, nature itself could be brought under control (Toulmin 1990).

The psychological laboratories developed in Germany by Fechner and Wundt and in England by Galton in the latter part of the nineteenth century represented efforts to apply to the study of human beings the methods that had been applied to nature; humans were surely a part of nature and if nature could be understood, why not humans? American psychology in general, and American educational psychology in particular, were rooted in European soil and the ideas that guided their growth were essentially the same: to come to understand how nature works and through such knowledge to control its operations. Our aim in the West was *not* to create a partnership.

These ideals are themselves based on several core beliefs. First was the belief that nature was orderly; it possessed a pattern and this pattern could be identified. Second was the faith that rational procedures, epitomized by science, could be used to discover those natural regularities. Third was the belief that theoretical ideas about the regularities of nature could be constructed and that the truth of these ideas could be determined. Fourth was an admiration for the virtues of quantification. Mathematics had an order and possessed a precision that would diminish both subjectivity and the presence of untestable speculation. It lent itself to the dominant conception of rationality permeating the science of the social and, in addition, the data it provided could be treated by the tools emerging from the newly developing field of statistics. Measurement, rationality, theoretical explanation, and eventually prediction and control were the hallmarks of the emerging science. The overall aim, rooted in the Enlightenment, was to create an objectively detached, true description of the world as it really is.

American educators, and particularly American educational psychologists, saw promise in these methods for, with them, educational practice itself could become a scientifically guided activity (Jonçich 1968). For the first time, educational practice could be grounded in true understandings of how humans learn and educational policy could be formulated by appealing to scientific knowledge. One of the most vivid manifestations of such beliefs is found in that practice invented by Frederick Taylor called "scientific management" and, in education, its progeny, the "efficiency movement," with its stopwatch efforts to measure human performance and its prescriptions to teachers on how teaching could be made more efficient (Callahan 1962). It also manifested itself in the eugenics movement with its efforts to apply scientific principles to social policy. And it emerged in the powerful scientific legacy that Edward L. Thorndike left to American education (Jonçich 1968).

American educators found in Thorndike a useful ally for, unlike his contemporary, Sigmund Freud, Thorndike was interested in learning and his research and theories concerning learning had practical implications for both teachers and writers of textbooks. Thorndike's notions of frequency, recency, and intensity were guiding ideals for pedagogical practice and his theory of identical elements, namely, the belief that transfer of learning occurs only in so far as the elements in one situation were identical to those in the other (Thorndike 1910), became lawlike in their significance in the training of teachers.

It is not surprising that the new field of education, just out of its infancy, should look to science to provide what is intellectually respectable. The first normal schools in America were founded in the 1850s and they needed more than an apprenticeship model to secure intellectual legitimacy. The science of the social was there to provide it. The work that was done in Europe by Wundt and others provided the intellectual grounding for what American pedagogues needed.

The scientific conception of method and knowledge that was initiated in Europe and developed in America during the early part of this century has profoundly influenced how we think about education today. Much of this influence was carried by the test and measurement movement, a movement given special impetus with Robert Yerkes' (1929) work on the Alpha and Beta tests. The Alpha and Beta tests were commissioned by the Army to identify levels of literacy among enlisted men during the First World War and to select those who were suitable for officers' training school. These group tests helped demonstrate the practical utility and social relevance of the social sciences. In fact, they represented a conception of testing and evaluation that is only now beginning to change.

There is no doubt that educational measurement has become a highly refined and sophisticated field. It has not only its own distinctive history, it has its own journals, its own training programs and, if Educational Testing Service (ETS) is any example, its own industry. The creation of standardized achievement tests and the use of mark-sensed answer sheets and optical scanners have made it possible for the American public to get a quick (if often illusory) fix on the state of schooling. Given the efficiency of new scoring methods, the public's desire to know how schools are doing, and the virtual absence of competing indicators, achievement testing has become one of the most visible and influential manifestations of scientific technology at work in education.

Yet as efficient as the optical scanner is, it became clear during the educational reform efforts of the 1960s that standardized achievement tests could not adequately assess the outcomes of the new curricula. The curriculum reform movement of the 1960s represented an effort not only to catch up with achievements in space of the then Soviet Union, but to rethink what was being taught in schools and to achieve aims that had not previously been conceptualized. These aims were formidable. For the first time, we wanted students to learn how to think like scientists, not just to ingest the products of scientific inquiry (Bruner 1961). We wanted students to understand the structure of mathematics, not just be competent at computation.

Furthermore, the creation of new curricula was not a single undertaking; even the best of our seemingly good ideas might not fly in third-grade classrooms. We recognized that we needed to evaluate not only what students learn, but the program that was intended to enable them to do so. Scriven's (1967) terms *formative* and *summative evaluation,* as much as any, became the new banners of the day. Evaluation, not merely testing, came into its own. Educational evaluation had a mission broader than testing. It was concerned not simply with the measurement of student achievement, but with the quality of curriculum content, with the character of the activities in which students were engaged, with the ease with which teachers could gain access to curriculum materials, with the attractiveness of the curriculum's format, and with multiple outcomes, not only single ones. In short, the curriculum reform movement gave rise to a richer, more complex conception of evaluation than the one tacit in the practices of educational measurement. Evaluation was conceptualized as a part of a complex picture of the practice of education. With this enlarged focus, there was a subtle but significant shift in epistemology. This shift is perhaps best represented in Schwab's (1969) seminal article on the "practical." The shift was from regarding evaluation as a predominantly knowledge-seeking activity to a decision-making one. Once evaluation was conceptualized as an important element within the complex of educational practice, it was expected to contribute to the enhancement of practice. Yet practical activities are not so much focused on trying to determine what is true, as in making good decisions. To treat curriculum, teaching, and evaluation as practical activities is to shift not only focus, but also the kind of knowledge considered relevant: The meaning of knowledge slowly, but ineluctably, became related to what Aristotle (McKeon 1941) called *phronesis* or, more simply, *practical* as distinct from *theoretical* knowledge. It was not concerned with identifying immutable patterns in nature, but providing context-dependent tentative information useful for making defensible decisions.

At about the same time as the U.S. curriculum reform movement was in high gear (the late 1960s), another development emerged that also had a significant long-term effect on our views of assessment. The development I refer to is the empirical, qualitative, interpretive study of what goes on in schools and classrooms. Willard Waller (1932), a sociologist who worked in the 1930s, is often credited with making the first modern study of teaching in the public schools. But in more recent years, Philip Jackson's *Life in Classrooms* (1968) must be regarded as one of the most influential. Jackson's study is the result of over a year of observations of how teachers taught. It is rich in description, insightful, beautifully written, compelling. At about the same time, there appeared Louis Smith and William Geoffrey's *The Complexities of an Urban Classroom* (1968). A beginning had been made. Returning to schools to find out what was going on, something Schwab had urged, became important—even stylish.

These early ventures revealed empirically what people like John Dewey had known and said years earlier. In *Experience and Education* (1938), Dewey remarked that "One of the greatest of educational fallacies is that the student only learns what he is being taught." What visitors to classrooms discovered for themselves is that classroom life, not to mention life in schools as a whole, is complex, unpredictable and much less tidy than the systematizers and scientific managers had imagined. The early twentieth-century ideal of achieving scientific efficiency in the management of classrooms and teaching by following standardized procedures designed to eliminate wasted motion seemed quaint, indeed at odds with the unpredictable character of eight- or even eighteen-year-olds. The game was considerably more complicated.

To give order to such complexity some disciplined set of procedures had to be found. Enter ethnography. It is not difficult to understand why ethnography should be attractive as a way of studying educational practice. First, for those committed to the development of a scientific understanding of education, ethnography, as a branch on cultural anthropology, is within the family of the social sciences: the stretch is not wrenching. It is like moving from an Episcopalian or Anglican congregation to a Methodist one. Second, ethnography, to paraphrase Clifford Geertz (1973), is about the inscription of cultural meaning. Inscription stabilizes thought and makes it available for inspection and correction. Such an aim seems appropriate to many of those who wish to understand schools. Third, ethnographic practices have almost as long a history as psychology. Although these practices seem much more tidy to outsiders than they actually are, the scientifically minded believed that ethnography could be employed to discover the basic patterns of classroom life and to unearth systematically its deep structure. Ethnographic-like accounts of schools and classrooms have, of course, emerged in not only Jackson's and Smith's work but in the work of Rist (1972), Erickson (1982), Barone (1983), Lightfoot (1983), Wolcott (1984), Peshkin (1986), and others. Indeed, many of the graduate courses offered in schools of education designed to teach students how to use qualitative methods in educational research employ ethnographers as teachers.

I will not now describe the strengths and limitations of ethnography as a way of studying and assessing educational practice. Both its strengths and limitations are many and they are significant. My main aim is to trace the ideological shifts in the study, evaluation, and improvement of education. We began with the aspiration to develop a science of the social, one that relied on mathematical accounts to describe natural regularities in the life of human beings. We moved to scientific management, represented in the efficiency movement, next to the technology of testing intended to measure the educational productivity of schools and teachers. We then noted the shift from the reliable measurement of student achievement to a broader interest in evaluation as a way of understanding and enhancing educational practice, including the improvement of school curricula. From there we moved to the study of schools and classrooms as social educational organizations through procedures resembling ethnography.

While no description of the past ever has as much fidelity to actual events as the writer makes out, I believe the journey I have described so far adumbrates the general contours of the trip that has been taken and sets the stage for an examination of our current situation. It is this situation, the emergence of new conceptions of educational assessment, to which I will now turn my attention.

The Recent Past and the Current Scene

To begin, one might reasonably ask why the broader conception of educational evaluation which was stimulated by the curriculum reform movement of the 1960s did not take hold and continue. Why are we now turning to an interest in what is called assessment, indeed not only assessment, but *authentic assessment* (Wiggens 1989)? What happened between the end of the curriculum reform movement and the current interest in finding new and better ways to determine what students are learning?

What happened was the American public's growing concern about the quality of American schools. During the 1970s, it became increasingly clear that Scholastic Aptitude Test (SAT) scores were dropping (Harnischfeger and Wiley 1975) and the public was hearing from the armed forces that recruits could not read well enough to use the manuals prepared for the equipment with which they were to work. "Bonehead English" was oversubscribed, even in prestigious universities having selective admission policies, and the private sector complained that the recent high school graduates that they were hiring needed to be retrained: the schools had failed them.

As a result of such concerns, the remedy, at least to the American public and to government policy makers, seemed clear. Establish minimum standards for local school districts, design achievement tests to measure what students had learned, and monitor the system carefully. In a word, the operative term became *accountability.* Accountability was largely defined in terms of testing. Achievement testing became the means through which schools would become accountable to a concerned public. The decade between the mid-1970s and the mid-1980s was a decade that returned to the past. "Back to the basics" was the watchword.

The broad view of educational evaluation that emerged with the curriculum reform movement of the 1960s could not withstand the criticisms stimulated by declining SAT scores, dissatisfied employers and the United States inferior international position in mathematics achievement. Neither the public nor policy makers were happy about the state of U.S. education: it was time to get tough. The demand for higher standards and demonstrated achievement began to soften in the mid-1980s. It became clear to some that educational standards are not raised by mandating assessment practices or urging tougher tests, but by increasing the quality of what is offered in schools and by refining the quality of teaching that mediated it. The problem is *not* one of correct policy formation. Policies are relatively easy to formulate and often easier to mandate. *The problem is one of practice.* Good teaching and substantive curricula cannot be mandated; they have to be grown.

Furthermore, assessment (the new term) needed to be more generous, more complex, more closely aligned with life than with individual performance measured in an antiseptic context using sanitized instruments that were untouched by human hands. The model needed to be changed and the term *assessment* symbolized this ambition. In sum, the modern birth of educational evaluation as a field associated with the curriculum reform movement was not strong enough to withstand the public's need to get down to brass tacks, to go back to the basics, to measure, to monitor, to mandate. A decade later, however, we find ourselves exploring new routes to excellence, partly because we have recognized that mandates do not work, partly because we have come to realize that the measurement of outcomes on instruments that have little predictive or concurrent validity is not an effective way to improve schools, and partly because we have become aware that unless we can create assessment procedures that have more educational validity than those we have been using, change is unlikely.

Some Functions of Assessment

The exploration and development of the new approaches to assessment had made some things quite clear. Assessment, like educational evaluation, is not one, but several things. It performs different functions and needs to be regarded in light of the educational functions it is intended to perform. For example, one function of assessment is a kind of educational temperature-taking. The U.S. National Assessment of Educational Progress performs a temperature-taking function. Its purpose is not to provide information about the performance of individual students or even individual school districts, but to describe the educational health of the century. It does this by using a multiple matrix sampling technique that makes it possible to report to the U.S. public the performance of nine-, thirteen-, and seven-teen-year-olds by sex and region of the country on tasks that are not limited to the specific content taught in schools.

A second function of assessment is a gatekeeping function. The SAT is designed to measure individual students' aptitudes for work in college. Although colleges and universities claim that SAT scores do not determine who they admit, SAT scores *do* influence admission decisions. Other gatekeeping functions are served by bar examinations, medical board ex-aminations, and many final course examinations that are used to determine who passes and who does not. A third function of assessment is to determine whether course objectives have been attained. In this, its classical use, assessment in schools is sometimes used for gatekeeping functions and sometimes to help teachers provide remedial help to students who need it.

A fourth function of assessment is to provide feedback to teachers on the quality of their professional work. Teaching is a complex and subtle art. What makes a lesson fly or flop may be due to the way in which information is provided, the way a teacher defines tasks for students, or by the way in which a teacher responds to students' questions. Many of the subtle qualities of teaching that matter, the teacher cannot or does not notice. The assess-ment of teaching can help a teacher become more reflective about his or her own performance so that it can be improved.

A fifth function of assessment focuses on the quality of the program that is being provided. Although the least prominent of assessment function, this function is arguably one of the most important. What is the *quality* of the educational diet provided? What is the *character* of the activities in which students are engaged? What is the *sequential nature of the events* in the program as it unfolds over time? How *attractive* are the materials students and teachers use? All of the foregoing are questions designed to reveal the quality of the program as such. If the program's quality is poor to begin with, the quality of teaching does not matter much: if it's not worth teaching, it's not worth teaching well.

In a sense, all of the foregoing functions (and there are others I have not identified) can be reduced to the assessment of the program that is provided, the quality of teaching, and outcomes that result from the inter-action of the first two. Program evaluations, teacher evaluation, and student evaluation are the major areas of focus for any form of educational assessment. And one important realization that has emerged in the past few years is that different forms of evaluation or assessment are required for different functions. To help teachers understand how they perform requires a form of assessment that is fundamentally different from an approach designed to describe the general contours of student outcomes. This realization is significant for it contributes to the pluralism in method and knowledge that has been developing in U.S. educational research since the late 1960s. This growing pluralism is likely to open up the field of assessment still further and will dramatically increase the array of data describing educational practice and its consequences. Ironically, the richness of this array is likely to complicate rather than to simplify our understanding of schooling. For simple conclusions, one wants simple data or data arrayed on a common metric. When neither the data are simple nor the metric common, complexity is virtually inevitable.

Features of the New Assessment in Education

Given the level of interest in authentic assessment, what features might such an assessment possess? What criteria might be appropriate for guiding those designing new approaches to assessment in education? What follows are eight criteria that seem to me to be appropriate for creating and appraising new assessment practices in education.

> *The tasks used to assess what students know and can do need to reflect the tasks they will encounter in the world outside schools, not merely those limited to the schools themselves*

One of the peculiar features of student evaluation as it occurs through the process of achievement testing is its remoteness from the kinds of tasks people engage in outside school. Where, except in school and in the most exceptional situations outside school, are people asked to fill in anything like mark-sensed answer sheets? On what occasions are they asked to provide bits and pieces of information regarding specific content-oriented questions? In what encounters outside school must they sift through a series of short-answer questions and select among alternatives to find a single correct answer? I am sure that it is possible to identify such occasions (taking an examination for a driver's license, for example) but they are notable by their rarity. But even more than their rarity is the fact that what really counts as a measure of what students have learned in school is not what they can do in the context of school classrooms, but in the context of life outside schools. The purpose of schooling is not to ensure excellence of schools, but to increase the student's ability to solve problems that are not limited to school tasks and, even more generally, to deepen and expand the meanings students can construe in daily living.

This aspiration, a long-held aim of progressive educators, is now referred to by some cognitive psychologists as *situated learning* (Greeno 1989), by others as *grounded knowing* (Oliver 1990). Situated learning refers to the realization that context matters and that test items that have little resemblance to life as normally led may yield scores that have little predictive value with respect to that life. A student might know how to calculate equations on algebra tests and not know how to deal with quantitative problems in a nonalgebraic context. Furthermore, what a student can do is not necessarily an index of what a student will do, and it is what a student will do that matters in life. The new assessment practices will need to provide tasks that resemble in significant ways the challenges that people encounter in the course of ordinary living. This will require an entirely different frame of reference for the construction of assessment tasks than the frame we now employ.

The tasks used to assess students should reveal how students go about solving a problem, not only the solutions they formulate

Most tests in schools, particularly so-called objective tests, provide no information about the way in which students arrive at their answers. Alternative answers are provided by the test maker and the student's task is to select, not construct, a response. As a result, it is impossible to determine the quality of reasoning or the process of thinking, the answers considered and rejected, the hypotheses formulated, or the explanations entertained in scoring the student's answer. Although there are some achievement tests that do allow scorers to track the sequence of choices a student has made in the course of a solution, most preclude such information. Understanding how a student arrived at an answer provides a basis through which teachers might be better able to modify their programs or alter their teaching strategies. Knowing what a student considered on the way to a solution also implies knowing what a student neglected and areas of neglect can be as important in furthering the development of problem-solving skills as determining whether the answer is correct. Indeed, it is quite possible for a student to arrive at a correct answer for entirely irrelevant reasons.

The business of constructing tasks that make it possible to make valid observations or inferences about the course of reflection in problem solving is not easy, yet it is the process of reasoning that is essential to any conception of education concerned with increasing the transfer of learning and with the process of generalization. Learning how to learn, as the slogan goes, is a fundamental educational aim and since learning is a verb, seeing it unfold, both haltingly and smoothly, is a prime aim of diagnostically useful assessment and, therefore, an important criterion for creating or appraising new assessment practices.

Assessment tasks should reflect the values of the intellectual community from which the tasks are derived

In *The Process of Education,* Jerome Bruner (1961) comments that "Any subject can be taught in an intellectually respectable way to any child at any age." Putting hyperbole aside, the ideas within subject fields or disciplines as they are called are a part of an intellectual community. They are a part of a specialized discourse. It is also true that ideas in the course of both teaching and assessment can be severed from their intellectual moorings and trivialized in the process of assessment. Notwithstanding the aspiration to enable students to recognize the relationship between ideas learned in the context of a discipline and the social and personal uses to which those ideas may be put, ideas, concepts, and images are a part of a larger intellectual constellation. One of the significant achievements of intellectual life is appreciating their place in that constellation. This achievement is, in large measure, an *aesthetic* achievement. Like the appreciation of a pattern, ideas in their intellectual context are hooked to a network of related ideas. In a sense, they form an intellectual tapestry. In the context of teaching, not all ideas are located in such a tapestry. When students are not taught or do not learn to see ideas as a part of a fabric, a changing fabric, ideas become, as Whitehead commented, "inert".

The challenge to assessment is to somehow create tasks that give students opportunities to display their understanding of the vital and connected features of the ideas, concepts, and images they have explored. In short, the aim is to help students demonstrate that they have grasped ideas as a part of a larger field and as historically situated elements within a community of discourse. The virtues of such learning are twofold. First, it increases both meaning and retention because it allows connections between intellectual networks and thus reduces the meaningless fragmentation of bits and pieces of information. Second, as more and more of the puzzle pieces come together to provide a coherent picture of the domain to which ideas are related, the probability is increased that learning will have aesthetic features.

One of the marks of expertise is the possession of highly differentiated schemata in some domain (Eisner 1991). Both differentiation, which implies the ability to notice differences in qualities, and schema, which implies some form or gestalt, give the expert the ability to see what others with less expertise miss and allow the expert to retain through a coherent schematic structure a set of tools with which to perceive, examine, and comprehend the features of some domain. Whether we can, in fact, construct the kinds of assessment practices that will reveal the existence of such intellectual competencies remains to be seen, but the aspiration to do so is more hopeful than an unwillingness to appreciate the intellectual and educational importance of such an ambition.

Assessment tasks need not be limited to solo performance

Many of the most important tasks we undertake require group efforts. There is a tradition in the United States that puts a premium on individual accomplishments. Rugged individualism is a part of the national heritage. Yet many of the most important adult tasks that we encounter are tasks that require participation and cooperation with members of a group. If one of the important functions of schools is to assist the young in acquiring some of the skills needed for life in the adult community, it makes no sense to censor or proscribe tasks that best reflect the features of that life. This means that curricula will need to be designed so group tasks become part of the norms of acceptable classroom activity just as they are now a part of the norms of adult activity. It means also that the assessment of group performance and the contributions of individuals to that performance become a part of our assessment agenda. In many ways, this aspiration flies in the face of the dominant image we have of valid assessment: an individual student working on an individual test protecting his or her answers from the eyes of fellow students. We celebrate the individual, sometimes at a cost that might very well be both too high and inappropriate.

Determining the contribution of individual performance to group achievement has a long history in games such as baseball, football, and basketball. There is no comparable history in the realm of academic life in schools. Our tendency has been to measure individual achievement and to locate such achievement in relation to the achievement of others. Indeed, the grading and marking practices in U.S. schools, which are based on the normal curve, put students in competition with fellow students: One student's A is another's B. We define excellence as a scarce resource, hence confer it upon only a few.

In recent years criterion-referenced tests have been designed to ameliorate the norm-referenced assumptions of the tests we have used for so long, but even criterion-referenced tests are designed to measure individual, not group achievement of program goals. The new assessment will, I think, have to provide a place for assessing growth on group tasks and school programs will need to be designed to enable students to learn how to contribute to the realization of group goals.

New assessment tasks should make possible more than one acceptable solution to a problem and more than one acceptable answer to a question

One of the pervasive beliefs in the methodology of educational research is the need for objectivity. Objectivity refers both to ontological objectivity, that state in which one's perception or understanding of the world is isomorphic with the world itself, and procedural objectivity, that method that allows little or no personal judgment or interpretation to enter the operations through which the world is described (Eisner 1991). The former, within the beliefs of a constructivist account, is inherently untenable. The latter is attainable if instruments are available that can be applied without recourse to judgment. The use of the optical scanner for the scoring of test performance exemplifies a procedurally objective approach to the rating of performance.

Procedural objectivity became virtuous because of the fear that personal judgment, and therefore subjectivity, would enter into what ought to be an entirely objective account of a state of affairs. I will not here discuss the implications and issues pertaining to this belief, except to point out that such a view of methodological virtue constrains in significant ways what can be asked of a student and the kinds of responses that can be considered legitimate. The multiple-choice test, like the true and false test before it, stands as an ecomium to procedural objectivity. Ironically, single correct answers and single correct solutions are not the norm of intellectual life, nor are they the norm of daily life. The problems that people confront in their intellectual endeavors, like the problems they confront in ordinary living, are replete with reasonable alternative solutions. To design tests that convey the message that most, or even all, correct answers and solutions are singular is to convey a message at odds with what people confront when they engage in serious inquiry.

The implication of the foregoing is the need to design tasks that permit and credit alternative ways of responding. This will, of course, create a labor-intensive assessment task; the optical scanner is not a likely tool in considering a novel solution or appraising the cogency of an explanation. It is in the provision of tasks that make such options possible that we begin to approximate the twin ideals of practical relevance and intellectual authenticity. For large-scale temperature-taking assessment tasks, the use of such procedures may be limited or even inappropriate, but when we want to know how or if a student is able to address problems, issues, or questions for which alternatives are not only possible but desirable, the use of such assessment practices is mandatory.

In addition to the foregoing benefits, tasks that present or even require alternative responses provide important pedagogical cues to students and guidance to teachers regarding what is educationally important. Students want to know what they will be held accountable for, as do teachers. Assessment procedures, more than teacher testimony, eloquently testify to what really matters. In this sense, the use of assessment procedures that put a positive value on alternative answers and solutions may not only provide information about students' thinking, but may help alter the pedagogical priorities of classroom life.

Assessment tasks should have curricular relevance, but not be limited to the curriculum as taught

Conventional approaches to evaluation emphasize the view that for a test to have content validity it needs to reflect the content to which students have been exposed. There surely is wisdom in such an approach. It would be unfair to hold teachers or students accountable for content that had not been taught. Yet, the relevance of tests to curriculum can be carried to an extreme. One of the major aims of education is to enable students to use what they have learned in settings other than the ones in which they were taught. This aim puts a premium on the transfer of learning but, even more, it emphasizes the importance of enabling students to modify or adapt a set of ideas or skills to materials and tasks that have a resemblance to but not an identity with what was taught or studied. In other words, it is important for students to come away from their studies with a set of modifiable tools; the content they were taught will rarely be encountered in the form in which it was learned.

The implication, therefore, of this criterion is the need to design assessment practices that, while relevant to the curriculum, are not limited to it. That is, assessment tasks should make it possible for students to display intelligent adaptation of the ideas they presumably learned.

In constructing such tasks, there is a need for subtle types of judgment. How closely related should a set of problems be to the kind of problems students encountered in their classroom? Should a student who studied the structure and function of grasshoppers in a biology class be expected to employ those concepts on living creatures other than insects? What about human organisms? How far is fair?

Merely recapitulating content taught in schools is, at best, a test of memory but, even when it is more than this, it might not display the range of transfer that is desirable. Hence, the construction of tasks that reveal the student's ability to use at the level of principle what has been learned is of critical importance in the new assessment. Put another way, assessment tasks that assess only what has been taught are too meager. Those that assess more than is reasonable are unfair. The key term *reasonable* is what is central to the construction of such assessment tasks. Reasonableness requires judgment.

Assessment tasks should require students to display a sensitivity to configurations or wholes, not simply to discrete elements

The conduct of inquiry is seldom a series of single certain steps toward some unambiguous destination, except, of course, in its textbook version. In the real world, inquiry proceeds haltingly, uncertain about both means and ends, and displays the flexibility and the concern for pattern which enables the intelligent inquirer to create ideas or products that possess that elusive but precious quality we call coherence. It is the coherence or elegance of a solution that experts value. The sense of rightness of fit, as Goodman (1978) calls it, is one of the most compelling indicators of our rationality. What does such an ability mean for assessment and how might it be displayed?

Although I do not have crisp answers to these questions, some seem to me to be promising. Creating tasks that require students to engage in larger problematic situations than are typically characterized by most standard achievement test questions might make it possible to observe their decision making in process and to interrupt that process at strategic moments in order to secure an explanation, as well as they can provide it, for the choices they have made and the strategies they have employed. The aim of such an exercise is to create the conditions through which the student's ability to de-centrate perception and problem solving can be noted. It is to provide the kind of information to teachers that will enable them to assist students in widening the array of data they consider when working through a problem.

In artistic tasks, such skills are of the utmost importance. A student in a life-drawing class must not only pay attention to the contour of an arm, but to its relationship to the body of which it is a part. But even more, the body or figure as a whole must be carefully related to the entire paper on which it is drawn. In other words, attention not only to the figure but to the ground is critical if one is to create a coherent or satisfying drawing. Similar features hold in other forms of problem solving, and understanding the extent to which they can be adequately addressed is an important aspect of the student's educational development.

Assessment tasks should permit the student to select a form of representation he or she chooses to use to display what has been learned

One of the major assumptions used in group achievement tests is that all of the students taking the test should encounter the same items. The reason for this assumption is clear. When the items are identical, comparison between students is possible. Statistical procedures can be used to select appropriate test items and the bell-shaped curve can remain an ideal for distributing students' performance.

What this means in practice is that not only will the items be common across students, but also the form of their response. The multiple-choice test provides a common set of questions and a common array of alternative possible answers. A group of students who have taken the test can have their scores arrayed within a distribution that approximates a normal curve.

When one of the major aims of testing is to sort students out, such a procedure has certain utility. In a sense if one wants to identify winners in a race, it makes sense to have runners start at the same place, and if this is not possible (and it is not in academic contexts) they should at least run on the same track. But if one's view of the function of assessment is to determine the unique ways in which students interpret or apply what they have learned, then a common set of test items and a common set of response alternatives might not be appropriate. In new approaches to assessment, students will not only be given opportunities to construct their own responses to what they have learned, they will also be given opportunities to select the medium through which what they have learned can be made public. This means, for example, that after a unit of study in history or the social studies some students might elect to create a ballad, or a poem, or write a short story. After a study in biology some students might elect to construct a three-dimensional model of evolution or write a speculative piece on the future of evolution.

Such options for students will surely create problems for assessors. Incommensurability among responses will certainly be pervasive. Each student's work will need to be appraised on its own terms. A common cookie-cutter criterion will no longer be appropriate. Despite these difficulties, such a practice, at least as a part of the new assessment, will symbolize to students that personal proclivities matter, that productive idiosyncrasies count, and that individual interpretation and creativity are values the school cares about.

It is well to remember that in the "real world," outside professional specialization, individuals *do* create their own responses and their own preferred form in reacting to experience. After a trip to Paris, some people write poetry, others paint pictures, some show the photographs that they have taken and talk about their experience. It is precisely in the diversity of response to "common experience" that our cultural lives are enriched. The celebration of such diversity is congruent with the creation of a civilization in which what is unique about individuals flavors the common weal. The invention and use of new conceptions of assessment have important roles to play in the realization of that ideal.

As assessment leads to increasingly fine-grained, interpretive appraisals, it is less amenable to reductive measurement and comparison of student learning, experience, and performance. Can the public appetite for discrete certainty in assessment be satisfied by interpretive assessment practices? What vision of education must a public hold to accept less discrete indicators? Can a rationally oriented meritocracy embrace such a vision? Will a functionally differentiated conception of assessment increase the acceptability of approaches to assessment that are more personalistic in focus? If it does, will the reductionistic testing practices that now prevail marginalize the newer assessment as parents and others in the community continue to seek "the bottom line"?

I can only hope that with responsible and articulate interpretation, authentic assessment will be understood and valued by the public at large. If it is, assessment will not only contribute to better schooling for children, it will contribute to a broader, more generous conception of education itself.

12

What Artistically Crafted Research Can Help Us Understand About Schools

In my presidential address to AERA in 1993, I spoke about the potential of different forms of representation to uniquely influence our experience and, thus, to alter the ways in which we come to understand the world. I argued that visual forms—maps, pictures, bar charts, for example—which are synchronic in character afford us an "all-at-onceness" in our perception that reveals what would be hard to grasp in diachronic forms such as language and number. Conversely, language and number make it possible to conceive of relationships and to achieve types of precision that are difficult, even impossible, to envision or describe in images.

What I did not address in that presentation was the fact that forms of representation are, at base, merely resources that have the *potential* to inform. Whether they do or not depends upon how they are used. How a form is crafted depends upon artistry. The artistic treatment of any form of representation is a way of creating an impact, of making ideas and images clear, of having an effect on those who "read" the form.

We typically regard the artistic treatment of form as belonging to those works we call *art:* the images found in painting, sculpture, film, and video for example; or the forms of patterned sound we call music, or the dynamic forms of dance, or the linguistic forms we call literature and poetry. Artistically crafted research is usually thought of as research that uses one or more of these forms as a major means of communication.

While embedding artistry in what we normally think of as art is understandable, artistry is not restricted to what we usually think of as art. Put simply, the arts have no monopoly on art. There is art in science just as surely as there is art in art. This article is intended to describe briefly both the artistry in art and the artistry in science, particularly social science. My observations are guided by certain key questions: What is artistic in art? What is artistic in social science? Where is such artistry located? Does artistry in social science inform in special ways? If so, what can research having artistic features help us to understand about schools?

The phrase "artistry in art," at first glance, seems both tautological and self-evident. But just what artistry is—or more generally what art is—is far from self-evident. In fact, aestheticians have been trying to define it for years. Should art be conceived of as a special form of qualitative experience, as John Dewey (1934) suggests, or as the communication of emotion, as Leo Tolstoy (1899) suggests, or as a particular form of cognition, as suggested by Ernst Cassirer (1961), Susanne Langer (1960), and Nelson Goodman (1976)? Or should we think of art as significant form, as suggested by Roger Fry (1947) and Clive Bell (1958), or, if these theories of art will not do, as the creation of forms that replicate the organic features of nature, as Herbert Read (1958) proposed in his writing on art?

I cannot within the limits of this paper examine the implications for researchers of each of these views of art. What I will do is describe some of the general features of art and then what I believe the artistic treatment of research entails. Finally, I will say what functions such research might perform in helping us to understand schools.

To provide a context for my analysis, I wish to make some preliminary remarks about the meaning of "art." First, we can mean by art things like painting, sculpture, music, or dance, regardless of how they are executed. In this general conception art is a category that encompasses certain traditional kinds of work, regardless of its quality. Second, we can mean by art those works within this and related categories that possess certain valued features, features that we prize. In this conception, art is more than a description; it is a normative ideal that only certain works approximate. Third, we can mean by art the process of bringing something into existence. In this view, art is related to creation.

The first conception describes a form of representation, the second describes a product that displays certain kinds of excellence, and the third conception focuses on the process of "arting." Here I shall be concerned mainly with the second conception, namely the features that works of art possess. Three features are especially important.

The first of these is that artistically crafted works of art often make aspects of the world vivid and generate a sense of empathy. Artistically crafted novels, poems, films, paintings, and photographs have the capacity to awaken us from our stock responses and to create the kind of "wide-awakeness" that Maxine Greene (1978) talks about. Sometimes this is done through focal attention to telling detail and at other times through a process of defamiliarization: the artist recontextualizes the familiar so that it takes on a new significance. Marcel Duchamp's exhibition of a urinal which he titled "Fountain" is a case in point, but so are the works of surrealists and the abstractions of a Helen Frankenthaler or a Mark Rothko. Through their work our awareness of previously unseen qualities is heightened.

But while wide-awakeness is almost always a virtue, artistically crafted work also has the capacity to put us in the shoes of those we do not know and thus to foster empathic understanding: Dorothea Lang's photographs of the great depression, Charlie Chaplin's *Modern Times,* and now Steven Spielberg's *Schindler's List.* Or consider Washington, D.C.'s Holocaust Museum. As a work of art it was designed to serve epistemic as well as moral and political interests: In that museum we get a sense of how it felt even though we were not there.

Most of these examples are taken from the visual arts. But what about examples of artistically rendered works of art that pertain to schools, to teaching, and to learning? We do not have far to look. Literary works abound from *Goodbye, Mr. Chips* to *Oliver Twist,* from *Dead Poets' Society* to *The Autobiography of Malcolm X,* from Frederick Wiseman's *High School,* to *The Prime of Miss Jean Brodie.*

The works I have cited are not normally thought of as examples of research; they are regarded as personal creations sprinkled liberally with metaphor and displaying points of view that are vague and subjective. But this distinction between research and nonresearch is too sharp. There are works in the social sciences that have artistic features: Sarah Lawrence Lightfoot's *The Good High School,* or Jonathan Kozol's *Death at an Early Age* and *Savage Inequalities.* If we move a bit out of education as such we find Oscar Lewis' *The Children of Sanchez.* The creation of composite characters in ethnographic studies, the selective process that goes on in building a story, and attention to plot and character in the writing of history represent a far cry from a disinterested reporting of the so-called facts. In such works, we are dealing with constructions, and where there is construction artistry is always possible, even in doing research.

I think the question regarding what counts as research is a question of critical importance. I believe the answer turns on our conception of understanding. As I see it, the primary tactical aim of research is to advance understanding. The works I have cited help us to understand because their creators have understood and had the skills and imagination to transform their understanding into forms that help us to notice what we have learned not to see. They provide an image fresh to behold, and in so doing provide a complement to the colorless abstraction of theory with renderings that are palpable. The consciousness and insight they provide make understanding possible. Perhaps we should expand our conception of research as well as our conception of what helps us come to comprehend.

A second feature of artistically crafted works of art is their capacity to generate awareness of particularity—but not only particularity. Language as it is normally used is categorical; it describes classes but does not typically address individuality. What artistically crafted work does is to create a paradox of revealing what is universal by examining what is particular. This is especially evident in literature and drama. Consider the images we encounter in these forms. To what extent do books and plays provide prototypes we use subsequently to frame our perceptions? How many people like Mr. Chips have you met—or like Don Juan, Scarlett O'Hara, Willy Loman, Mr. Sammler? In one way or another, we have all known some. All of these fictional characters, all of these make-believe "case studies," generalize. We recognize their real-life counterparts because we have read the novel or seen the play. Artistry bites and leaves an iconic residue which we use to appropriate the world. In a sense, art does not imitate nature; nature comes to imitate art. Eventually, the forms of art, like the forms of science, become structures through which our understanding is organized.

Third, artistically crafted work achieves many of its effects by virtue of the relationships that artists compose within the work. Collectively these relationships display a sense of coherence, a holding together that is so well integrated that a discussion of "parts" of the work seems awkward. In organic systems there are no parts, at least not independent ones. The perception of this coherence is at the root of aesthetic experience. But coherence not only contributes to aesthetic experience, it is critical for credibility. A fragmented narrative or a report that is incoherent is incredible.

So it might be said that art does several things. First, works of art make the obscure vivid and make empathy possible. Second, they direct our attention to individuality and locate in the particular what is general or universal. Third, they possess a sense of wholeness, a coherence, a kind of organic unity that makes both aesthetic experience and credibility possible.

I turn now to artistry in social science. Although as a former painter my roots are in the visual arts and although a substantial part of my intellectual effort has been devoted to the seemingly hopeless task of making a decent place for the arts in our schools, I have increasingly come to recognize that the qualities that I value in what we normally call works of art are also to be found in works of science. As I said, inartistic science, certainly inartistic social science, is likely to be as feckless as inartistic "art." The artistic qualities I have identified are also important features of social science research.

However, in addition to these features I would argue that the formulation of the researchable situation is itself an artistic achievement—an achievement in *constructive neglect.* What the perceptive educational researcher does, in part, is to know what *not* to attend to. It is this construal of the situation, this act of *making* sense through selective perception, that is among the first artistic acts in the research process.

But neglect only tells you what to leave out. The researcher also has a positive contribution to make: the problem must be formulated, it must be focused, it must display insight. Leaving things out is half the story; making things clear is the other half.

Another artistic feature in science might be called *imaginative extrapolation.* Imaginative extrapolation involves using what one sees to generate theoretical interpretations that give the particular situation a fresh significance. Facts never speak for themselves, and when unrelated to a broader theoretical structure they are likely to be little more than bits and pieces that do not add up. Imaginative extrapolation provides the material through which new perspectives are made available, facts are made meaningful, and coherence is made possible.

Finally, there is the process of being *artistically engaged.* I believe that this process rests upon the ability to negotiate the tension between control and surrender, between giving in to the insistent demands of the world and yielding to the chaos of the unconscious. The space between the world and the unconscious is what Lawrence Kubie (1961) refers to as the "preconscious." Using that space productively is of paramount importance in the shaping of incisive and aesthetically revealing work, regardless of the domain in which it is done.

The conclusion I draw from this brief analysis is that artistically crafted research can inform practicing educators and scholars in ways that are both powerful and illuminating. Research with no coherent story, no vivid images, and no sense of the particular is unlikely to stick. Coherence, imagery, and particularity are the fruits of artistic thinking.

Hence artistically crafted research helps us to understand much of what is most important about schools. By its concern with particularity it can help us to recognize what individual teachers actually do when they teach. Without such knowledge, we tend to treat teachers as if they were redwoods: "when you've seen one, you've seen them all." When such beliefs prevail, efforts at school reform are likely to fail. By its concern with what is unique, it can help us to appreciate the distinctive qualities of individual students, thus avoiding the anonymity that numbers invariably confer. By its concern for empathic knowing it can help us to know what it feels like to be in a particular classroom or school, and what it means to succeed or fail. By its concern for coherence it can offer us a narrative that helps us to make sense of what would otherwise be incoherent complexity. By being responsive to the subtle and significant, it reminds us that not everything can take the impress of the literal and measurable. Such contributions to our understanding of schools are far from trivial.

But equally important is the notion that artistically crafted research includes more than simply the use of representational forms we typically refer to as art: social science generally can be regarded as an art form and, I believe, at its best, it ought to be. The bottom line, therefore, is that the education of researchers, in a very deep sense, should be regarded as the education of artists. Artists need skill, discipline, imagination, sensibility, and insight, and so do those doing social science research.

It is ironic that qualities as fundamental and powerful as those that constitute art have been so neglected in the discourse of research methodology.[1] We academics have made such a sharp differentiation between art and science that we believe social science has nothing at all to do with art. This view not only reveals a parochial conception of art, it reveals a distorted view of science. It is a view that does not serve educational research well.

Perhaps the growing interest in the cognitive contributions of the arts heralds a prologue. Perhaps we are, at last, entering a time in the educational research community when educational researchers will regard the arts not only as a fundamental part of schooling, but as a basic feature of excellent social science. I, for one, certainly hope so.

Notes

This is a slightly revised version of a paper presented at the Annual Meeting of the American Educational Research Association, New Orleans, April 1994.

1. I reviewed the tables of contents and the indices of ten major American books on both quantitative and qualitative research methods and not one included artistry as a reference.

THE PRACTICE AND REFORM OF SCHOOLS

Educational reform has been a constant companion to the practice of education in the United States. However, during the past quarter century, it has received unusual impetus. In the seventies the behavioral objectives movement emerged as a way to clarify our educational aims and therefore to increase the precision and power of educational practice. The 1970s also brought with it the accountability movement, an effort to use achievement tests to demonstrate to communities the educational productivity of the schools. In the 1980s *A Nation at Risk* emerged, a program of educational reform that was built upon a terrifying view that American schools were so dismal that they were undermining our culture. In the nineties, Goals 2000 emerged to once again call for measurable standards for the 100,000-plus schools in the United States, subject by subject, and to implement those standards through tests built around a common national education agenda. Although there was talk of "systemic reform," more often than not the focus was on one putative solution after another. Some of these solutions were contrary to other aims that were embraced with equal enthusiasm. For example, there has been much talk about the importance of integrating fields of study in order to make curriculum meaningful to students, yet current national reform efforts are treated on a subject-by-subject basis. There is much talk about school-based management and the importance of professionalism in teaching, yet a national prescription for the content and aims of schools appears to compromise teacher autonomy by withholding choice from them on the very aspects of curriculum that matter most: its aims.

The desire to find administratively efficient solutions to complex educational problems is understandable. Yet more often than not those "solutions" result in feckless outcomes. In our zeal for improvement, schooling is often underanalyzed, oversimplified, and underfunded. The pursuit of "what works" leads to nonsolutions.

Part 4 presents a conception of the ecology of schooling, a conception rooted in biology that regards human behavior as adaptive and institutions

155

as organisms that must cope with the vicissitudes of their environments. The use of a biological metaphor is intentional. It suggests that adaptability and interaction are a fundamental part of the ways in which organizations function and that teachers and administrators usually make intelligent adaptations to the institutional press they encounter. The improvement of schools will require not only attention to its aims, but to the structure of the institution itself, to the content and organization of the curriculum, to the quality of teaching that's provided, and to the ways in which the performance of students and teachers are appraised. All of these factors need to be brought into a productive alliance if we are to create the kind of conditions that optimize teaching and which can generate the kind of environment that will give us the kind of schools we need.

13

Educational Reform and the Ecology of Schools

The aspiration to reform schools has been a recurrent theme in American education. This aspiration frequently is stimulated by changes outside the United States. For example, the successful launching of *Sputnik I* on October 4, 1957, was sufficiently traumatic to our sense of national security to motivate the Congress of the United States to provide funds for the development of curricula in science and mathematics in order to "catch up with the Russians." During the 1960s over $100,000,000 was spent in building new programs in these fields and in retraining teachers. Despite all the effort and all the money, there is little that now remains in American schools that reflects the aspirations of the curriculum reform movement of the 1960s: Few of the curricula are to be found. *Sputnik I* motivated many, but its educational residue is difficult to find.

Since *Sputnik I,* American schools have been subjected to numerous reform efforts. The latest was initiated at a presidentially sponsored education summit on April 18, 1991, a summit attended by the nation's governors, by the U. S. Secretary of Education, and by educators holding positions of high office, to announce Bush's new plans for educational reform. Yet only a few years earlier another president supported another effort at educational reform. *A Nation at Risk,* a document that enjoyed the highest level of visibility of any American educational policy paper published during this century, caught not only the attention but the enthusiasm of almost everyone (USA Research 1984). Despite these reform efforts, the major features of schools remain largely as they were. What went wrong? Is there anything to learn from past efforts that might make current efforts more successful? This article first describes some of the conditions that make change in school difficult and then presents a potentially useful framework for developing a more effective agenda for school reform.

Schools as Robust Institutions

One thing is clear: It is much easier to change educational policy than to change the ways in which schools function. Schools are robust institutions whose very robustness provides a source of social stability (Cuban 1990). But what is it about schools that makes them so stable? Consider the following nine factors.

Internalized Images of Teachers' Roles

The images of what teachers do in classrooms, how they teach and organize children and tasks, are acquired very early in a child's life. In one sense, teaching is the only profession in which professional socialization begins at age five or six—when children begin school. In no other field do children have as much systematic opportunity to learn what a professional does in his or her work. Indeed, many children spend more time with their teachers than with their parents. This fact of early professional socialization should not be underestimated. Many young adults choose teaching because of their image of teachers and this image is not unrelated to what they believe being a teacher entails. Images of teaching and ways of being a teacher are internalized early in a child's life and bringing about significant changes in the ways in which teachers function requires replacing old images with new, more adequate ones. When a university teacher education program tries to promulgate a new image of teaching, but sends its young, would-be teachers back to schools that are essentially like the ones in which they were socialized, the prospects for replacing the old ideals in the all too familiar contexts in which new teachers work is dimmed: The new wine is changed when it is poured into the old bottle.

Attachment to Familiar Pedagogical Routine

Being a teacher, if it requires any set of skills and understandings, requires the ability to manage a group of children so that the class remains coherent and intact; nothing can be done if the class as such is in a state of disarray. But matters of management are only one part of the equation. The other is having something to teach. Teachers acquire a useful pedagogical repertoire by virtue of their experience in classrooms and that repertoire includes some degree of mastery of both the content they wish to teach and the methods and tactics through which to teach it (Berliner 1986). This repertoire is extremely important to teachers, for it provides them with a source of security and enables them to cope with pedagogical demands efficiently. If a teacher does not know what to teach or is insecure about a subject, attention must be paid to matters of content. This can exacerbate both problems of management and problems of pedagogy. It is difficult to be pedagogically graceful when you are lost in unfamiliar territory. Teachers are often reluctant to relinquish teaching repertoires that provide an important source of security for them. New content areas might require new pedagogical routines. Given the overload that teachers typically experience in school—large numbers of students and many courses or subjects to teach—economy of effort is an important value (Flinders 1987). Familiar teaching repertoires provide economy of effort; hence changes in schools that require new content and new repertoires are likely to be met with passive resistance by experienced teachers who have defined for themselves an array of routines they can efficiently employ. To make matters even less promising for school reform, few efforts at reform in the United States have provided time for teachers to develop mastery of new content or the skills required for new forms of teaching. Typically, new expectations for teachers are "add-ons" to already overloaded curricula and very demanding teaching schedules.

Rigid and Enduring Standards for Appropriate Behavior

A third source of school stability resides in the persistence of school norms. Every social occasion from the birthday party to the funeral service is pervaded by social norms that prescribe implicitly, if not always explicitly, ways to be in the world. Schools are no different. What teachers are supposed to be, how children are supposed to behave, what constitutes an appropriate and fair set of expectations for a subject, are defined by the norms of schooling. These norms have been described by Dreeben (1968), Jackson (1968), Lortie (1975), Lightfoot (1983), Powell (Powell, Farrar, and Cohen 1985), and Eisner (1985), and decades earlier by Waller (1932). In the past two decades educational scholars on the political Left such as Apple (1982) and Giroux (1989) have also examined the ways in which the pervasive and sometimes covert norms of schooling shape attitudes, create inequities, and often reproduce the inequities of the society at large. Undoubtedly some of their observations are correct, but my point here is not so much to make a statement about what Bourdieu (1977) has called "cultural reproduction" as to make it plain that if schools are to seriously address matters of intellectual development, the cultivation of sensibility, and the refinement of the imagination, changes must be made in educational priorities. Such changes will require institutional norms different from those now salient in schools.

Norms, after all, reflect values. They adumbrate what we care about. Trying to convert schools from academic institutions—institutions that attempt to transmit what is already known—into intellectual ones—institutions that prize inquiry for its own sake—will require a change in what schools prize. Most efforts at school reform fail to address this challenge. The tack taken in most educational policy papers is typically superficial and the language is technical. The problem is often thought to be solvable by curriculum "installation"; we are to "install" a new curriculum and then "align it" with other curricula. We typically employ a language of change that reveals a shallow and mechanistic conception of what real change requires. Policy makers cannot install new norms in schools any more than they can install new teaching methods. Both need careful cultivation and nurture. By persisting in using inappropriate mechanical metaphors for thinking about the process of school reform, we persist in misconceptualizing the problem and undermining genuine change.

Teacher Isolation

A fourth factor that thwarts school reform is the fact that in the United States, we have structured schools and defined teaching roles in ways that make improved teaching performance difficult to achieve. Consider the ways in which teachers are insulated and isolated from their colleagues. Teaching, by and large, in both elementary and secondary schools is a lonely activity. It is not that teachers have no contact with people; after all, they are with students all day. The point is that they have very little contact with other adults in the context of their classrooms. Some school districts in the United States and some enlightened policies provide teachers with aides and with special assistance by certified professionals, but these human resources are relatively rare. Most teachers spend most of their time in their own classrooms, closed environments, with twenty-five to thirty-five children or adolescents. Of course, there are occasions—lunchtime and the occasional staff meeting, for example—where teachers see each other, but seldom in the context of teaching. Even teachers who have worked in the same school for twenty years are likely to have never seen their colleagues teach.

The result of professional isolation is the difficulty that teachers encounter in learning what they themselves do in their own classrooms when they teach. Classrooms, unlike the rooms in which ballerinas practice their craft, have no mirrors. The only mirrors available to teachers are those they find in their students' eyes, and these mirrors are too small. Hence the teacher, whether elementary or secondary, must learn on his or her own, usually by reflecting on how things went. Such personal reflection is subject to two forms of ignorance, one type remediable, the other not.

The two types of ignorance I speak of are primary and secondary ignorance. Primary ignorance about teaching, or about anything else for that matter, is when you do not know something but you *know* that you do not know it. In such a situation, you can do something about it. Secondary ignorance is when you do not know something but do *not know* you do not know it. In this case, you can do nothing about the problem. The professional isolation of teachers fosters secondary ignorance. How can a teacher learn that he or she is talking too much, not providing sufficient time for student reflection, raising low-order questions, or is simply boring students? Teachers unaware of such features of their own performance are in no position to change them. Educational reform efforts that depend on new and better approaches to teaching yet make it difficult for teachers to learn about their own teaching are destined to have a poor prognosis for success. Despite what seems obvious, we have designed schools both physically and organizationally to restrict the teacher's access to other professionals. Discretionary time for teachers is limited and although the school principal could make the time to provide teachers with useful feedback, he or she often does not have the inclination or the skills or is so preoccupied with other matters of lesser importance that attention to the improvement of teaching becomes marginalized. As a result, it is not unusual for teachers to feel that no one really cares about the quality of their work (Eisner 1985).

Inadequacies of Inservice Education

Inservice education is the major means used in the United States to further the quality of teaching. But inservice education typically means that teachers will attend meetings or conferences to hear experts (often university professors who have had little contact with schools) provide advice on the newest developments in teaching mathematics, social studies, or the language arts. The assumption is that once teachers are exposed to such wisdom, they will implement the practices suggested in their own classrooms. The inservice seminar is one in which the advice-giver typically has never seen the teachers who comprise the audience. The advice-giver does not know the teachers' strengths or their weaknesses. The situation is much like a voice coach giving advice to a singer whom he or she has never heard sing. General recommendations go only so far.

Thus, we try to improve teaching by asking teachers to leave their classrooms so that they can travel to distant locations in order to get general advice from people who have never seen them teach. One does not need to be a specialist in learning theory to know that for complex forms of human action, general advice is of limited utility. Feedback needs to be specific and focused on the actor in context. What we do, however, is to decontextualize in-service education and, as a result, weaken its potential usefulness.

My remarks should not be interpreted to mean that inservice programs for teachers cannot be useful, but that inservice education without some direct observation of teachers in the context of their own classrooms is not likely to be adequate. In this case, as in so many others, we have greatly underestimated what it will take to improve what teachers actually do in their own classrooms.

Conservative Expectations for the Function of Schools

Another factor that contributes to the robust quality of schools and their resistance to change is that the expectations of both students and parents regarding the function of schools and the forms of practice that are appropriate are usually conservative. What does a good teacher do? What kinds of questions are appropriate for students to ask? How much freedom should teachers provide? What kinds of problems and projects should students be asked to engage in? How should students be evaluated? Should they have any role in their own assessment? Answers to each of the foregoing questions are related to expectations of what schools, classrooms, and teachers should be. The expectations of parents and students are often quite traditional on such matters.

The call for "back to basics"—a return to the educational practices of the past—is regarded by many as the way to save American schools from mediocrity or worse. Familiar practices are not threatening; the past almost always has a rosy glow. Practices that violate tradition are often regarded as subversive of high-quality education. School reform efforts that challenge tradition can be expected to encounter difficulties, especially from the segment of the population that has done well in socioeconomic terms and has the tendency to believe that the kind of schooling that facilitated their success is precisely the kind their own children should receive.

Expectations by students for practices with which they are familiar go beyond general forms of teaching practice; they include expectations for the way in which specific subjects should be taught. For example, students whose experience in art classes has not included learning about the history of art or writing about the qualities of particular works of art may regard such practices as distasteful; for many students reading and writing have no place in an art class. A program in social studies that requires group cooperation on project-centered work can be regarded as inappropriate by students whose concept of social studies is one that is devoted exclusively to individual tasks. Parents whose experience in learning mathematics emphasized drill and practice may regard an arithmetic program oriented toward the practical applications of arithmetic as less intellectual and less rigorous. The point here is that educational consumers can exercise a conservative function in the effort at educational reform. It is difficult for schools to exceed in aim, form, and content what the public is willing to accept.

Distance Between Educational Reformers and Teachers Implementing Change

Reform efforts in American education are almost always from the top down. For whatever reason, educational policy makers mandate change, often through national or state reports or through new educational legislation that sends the message of changed policies to those "on the front line." The tacit assumption is that once new policies are formulated, a stream of change will begin to flow with little further assistance. When assistance is provided it sometimes comes in the form of new policy papers, curriculum guides, and district conferences. Typically, the structural conditions of schools stay the same. Teachers remain on the receiving end of policy and have little hand in its formation.

The attraction of providing teachers with a hand in shaping educational policy is quite limited if one believes educational practice, at its best, will be uniform across school districts and geographic regions. If one's model of ideal educational practice is one of standardized practice, the way in which an efficient manufacturing plant might function, giving $2\frac{1}{2}$ million American teachers the opportunity to determine what is best for their own school or school district can appear chaotic or even nihilistic. Thus, there is a real tension in the process of school reform. At one end there is the desire to create a uniform and "equitable" program for children and adolescents, regardless of who they are or where they live. This requires centralized decision making. At the other end is the realization that unless teachers feel some commitment to change, they are unlikely to change. To feel such commitment it is important for teachers to have the opportunity to participate in shaping the change process.

Many veteran teachers, those who have seen educational reforms come and go, are skeptical about new reforms and respond with passive resistance:

They simply ride out the new policies. This can be done without much difficulty for two reasons. First, educational reform policies come and go about every five or six years, more visible in the media than in the classroom. Second, once the classroom door is closed, the ways in which teachers teach is essentially a private affair. Elementary school principals rarely monitor teaching practice closely, and at the secondary level, they do not have the subject-matter expertise in a wide variety of fields to do so.

The growing desire to engage teachers in the change process has led to the notion of "teacher empowerment." In general, the idea is that, as important stakeholders in what schools do, teachers need to have authority to plan and monitor the quality of the educational process in their schools. The effort, in a sense, is to democratize educational reform by giving teachers a say-so in what happens. This say-so includes defining curricular goals and content, improving teaching practice, and developing ways to assess what children experience during the school day. In some cases, it includes decision making about budget allocations through a process called site-based management.

A practice related to this general thrust of teacher improvement is called *action research*. Action research is intended to encourage teachers to collaborate with other teachers and, at times, with university professors in order to undertake research in their own school or classroom (Atkin 1989). The aim of the enterprise is to stimulate professional reflection by encouraging teachers to take a more reflective intellectual role in understanding and improving their own teaching practice.

It is not yet clear just how many teachers are interested in being "empowered." It is not yet clear how many teachers want to do educational research. It is not yet clear how many teachers are interested in assuming larger responsibilities such as the formulation of educational policy. Many teachers gain their deepest satisfaction in their own classroom. The classroom is their professional home and they are not particularly interested in collaboration or in doing educational research. As I indicated earlier, conceptions of the teacher's role are acquired early in development and teachers are often comfortable with these conceptions. If a bird has been in a cage for a decade and suddenly finds the door open, it should not be too surprising if the bird does not wish to leave. The familiar is often more comfortable than the uncertainty of the unknown.

Empowering teachers is more complex than I have suggested. When innovative reform policies are formulated or new aims or programs presented, they are often prescribed *in addition* to what teachers are already doing; they are add-ons. Given that the teacher's day is already quite demanding, it should come as no surprise that taking on added responsibilities for the formulation of policy or for monitoring the school should be regarded by some as an extra burden. Put more bluntly, it is unrealistic to expect overworked teachers who have very little discretionary time in the school day to be more active in their school without relief from some of their current responsibilities. To provide relief will require restructuring. Restructuring is likely to require money, something that is in scarce supply in many school districts. As a result, much of the activity in the context of school reform is more at the level of rhetoric than at the level of practice.

As educational reformers have become increasingly aware of the difficulty of bringing about significant change in the ways in which schools function, they have talked about the restructuring of schools (Restructuring California Education 1988). For this term, which to me generates an image of fundamental rather than superficial change, there are almost as many meanings as there are writers. In my discussions with school principals and school superintendents, "restructuring" meant to them changing the ways in which funds were allocated rather than reconceptualizing the organization, content, and aims of schools. Conceptualized in terms of financial resource allocation, the power of the concept was neutralized.

Another complexity regarding teacher empowerment involves the question of authority and responsibility. If teachers are given the authority to change local educational policy in their schools, will they assume responsibility for the consequences of those policies? If so, how will those consequences be determined? What will be the responsibilities of the school district's superintendent and the district's central office staff? Just what is the appropriate balance between authority and responsibility and who is responsible for what when responsibility and authority are localized?

These questions are not yet resolved. The recent interest in giving teachers a genuine role in the reform of schools is seen by many (including me) as salutary, but how lines of authority and responsibility are to be drawn is far from clear. Can genuine school improvement occur without commitment from teachers? It seems unlikely. Just how can such commitment be developed? These questions are on the current agenda of school reform in the United States.

Artificial Barrier Between Disciplines and Between Teachers

An eighth factor that impedes school reform pertains to the ways in which the school itself is organized. One of the most problematic features in the organization of schools is the fact that they are *structurally fragmented*, especially at the secondary level. By structurally fragmented I refer to the fact that curricula are divided and organized into distinct subject matters that make it difficult for students to make connections between the subjects they study (Eisner 1985). In the United States, secondary school students will typically enroll in four to six subjects each semester. As a result, teachers must teach within narrow time blocks. They teach four to seven classes each day, see 130 to 180 students each day; students must move every fifty minutes to another teacher who teaches them another subject. There is no occupation in American society in which workers must change jobs every fifty minutes, move to another location, and work under the direction of a different supervisor. Yet this is precisely what we ask of adolescents, hoping, at the same time, to provide them with a coherent educational program.

Structural fragmentation also pertains to the fact that the form of school organization that we have created isolates teachers. And as I have already indicated, isolation makes it difficult for teachers to receive critical and supportive feedback about their work. Teachers experience little colleagueship in the context of the classroom, and of course it is in the context of a classroom that the real business of education is played out. Unless there is significant change in the way in which teachers and students live and work together, any significant change in schools is illusory.

Because the forms of school organization are cultural rather than natural entities, they need not be regarded as being of necessity; that is, they can be other than the way they are. Moses did not receive instructions about school organization on Mount Sinai, at least as far as I know. Yet we persist in maintaining school structures that might not be in the best interests of either teachers or students. I can tell you that the organizational structure and the curricular requirements of the secondary school I attended forty years ago are quite like the organizational structure and curricular requirements secondary school students encounter today. How much structural and curricular overlap is there between the secondary school you attended and today's secondary schools?

Feckless Piecemeal Efforts at Reform

The last factor that impedes significant educational reform is the piecemeal and superficial way in which reformers think about educational reform. Minor efforts at change are eventually swamped by the factors in the school that do not change. Robust systems can withstand minor incursions. Thus the need, I believe, is to think about school reform ecologically, or at least systemically. Aspects of schooling that remain constant militate against those features of schooling that are being changed. For example, efforts to help teachers learn how to teach inductively are not likely to succeed if the evaluation system the school employs rewards other types of teaching. Efforts to encourage teachers to engage in reflective teaching are likely to be feckless if teachers have no time during the school day for reflection. Efforts to create intellectual coherence in the student's understanding are likely to fail if the form that the curriculum takes makes coherence impossible. Improvement in teaching is unlikely as long as teachers get no useful feedback on the work they actually do in their own classrooms.

It is important in educational reform to think big even if one must start small. There needs, I believe, to be an overall conception of what schools are as forms of shared communal life as well as persuasive and attractive visions of what such shared living might become. The next section describes a means for securing a better understanding of what schools are as living organisms. The last section provides a model or framework that identifies important candidates for educational change.

Schools as Living Systems

The place to begin school reform is in the effort to understand the ways that schools actually function, what it is they teach both implicitly and explicitly, and how they reward the people who spend so much of their lives there. Unfortunately, the effects of efforts at school reform are based on the results of standardized achievement testing and the results of such testing say little about the processes that lead to them. We cannot know much about the educational quality of schools simply by examining test scores. We need a finer, more refined screen, one that focuses on the processes as well as the outcomes of schooling.

Much recent research in the United States has focused on the quality and process of schooling (Goodlad 1984; Sizer 1984; Powell, Farrar, and Cohen 1985; Eisner 1985). Some of these studies have used ethnographic research methods or modifications of such methods (Wolcott 1984). Some studies have been rooted in critical approaches (Willis 1977) and others in methods derived from the arts and humanities (Lightfoot 1983). As a result of this work a number of salient features of schools, many of which are quite common across a variety of schools, have been identified: structural fragmentation, teacher isolation, didactic teaching, treaties between teachers and students, the particular ways in which effective teachers and school administrators relate to students, the emphasis on extrinsic rewards, and the like. How salient are these features? Are there important differences? How can we know?

The only way I know to discover the salient and significant features of schools is to look. The implications of what is found will depend on what is found and on the educational values that give direction to the schools themselves.

To look at schools as I have suggested is not enough. Anyone can look. The trick is to see. Seeing requires an enlightened eye. It requires schemata through which different genres of teaching can be appreciated (Eisner 1991). It is a mistake to assume that all good teaching has identical characteristics, that one size fits all. Thus, to see what happens in classrooms requires a willingness and a set of sensibilities and schemata that can pick up the distinctive features of particular types of teaching. These types of teaching are not simply generic. They emerge within the constraints and possibilities of particular subject matters—*what* one teaches counts. As Stodolsky (1988) says, "the subject matters." Even more than this, any given subject matter—history, for example, or mathematics—can have a wide variety of aims and methods. Perceiving school processes requires an understanding of the types of teaching possible within the subject-matter field and an awareness of the varieties of quality that can be manifested within each.

This article is not the place to describe in detail the forms of perception and description of life in schools I have in mind. Readers interested in what I have called "educational connoisseurship" and "educational criticism" can find the approach described in a variety of articles and particularly in my latest book (Eisner 1991). The point is that school reform should begin with a decent understanding of the schools themselves, not with old memories of schooling held by middle-aged men and women working in institutions far removed from schools. A major part of the current investment in school reform should be aimed, in my opinion, at trying to understand such processes as how teaching takes place in particular fields, what constitutes the implicit as well as the explicit norms of the school, the sense that students make of what they study, the aims that teachers say are important and the relationship of those aims to what they do in their classrooms. It should also deal with the intellectual quality of what is taught and the procedures that are used in the classroom to motivate and reward students and teachers. The aim of such inquiry is to secure an organic, cultural picture of schools as places to be. The basic questions direct attention to the value of what goes on in them. Such questions are easy to raise but difficult to answer, yet unless they are raised educational reform is likely to be predicated on very partial forms of understanding of what schools are like for teachers and students.

As I have indicated, the kind of study I am suggesting is one that is organic or cultural. To study schools in this way is likely to require an approach to educational research that is *qualitative* in character. It is an approach that pays attention to the processes of schooling and to the context in which those processes occur. I know of no way to find out what schools are like except by going to schools themselves to see, to describe, to interpret, and to evaluate what is occurring. Such an understanding can provide a foundation for reform that addresses what is genuinely important in education.

Five Major Dimensions of School Reform

In the final section of this article, I identify five dimensions of schooling that I believe must be considered in order to think comprehensively about the reform of schools. I call these dimensions the *intentional*, the *structural*, the *curricular*, the *pedagogical*, and the *evaluative*.

My thesis is that meaningful and educationally significant school reform will require attention to each of these dimensions. Attention to one direction without attention to the others is not likely to lead to change. Where change does occur, it is likely to be temporary and superficial.

The intentional refers to what it is that schools are intended to accomplish. What really counts in schools? Defining intentions pertains to both the general aims of schooling and the aims of the particular subject matters being taught. Consider, for example, intentions that are typically *not* given high priority in schools or in reform efforts: fostering a desire to continue learning what schools teach, the development of curiosity, stimulating the ability to think metaphorically, creating a caring attitude toward others, the development of productive idiosyncrasy, the ability to define one's own goals and the ability to pursue them, the ability to raise perceptive questions about what one has studied. An argument for each of these intentions could be made that is cogent and relevant to the world in which children live. If such intentions were taken seriously, their ramifications for educational practice would be considerable. My point here is not to advocate such intentions (although I do not reject them) but rather to illustrate the idea that the conventional intentions schools serve are not necessarily the most important ones. What is important will depend on an argued set of educational values and an understanding of the students and society schools serve.

Most efforts at school reform operate on the assumption that the important outcomes of schooling, indeed the primary indices of educational success, are high levels of academic achievement as measured by standardized achievement tests. Just what do scores on academic achievement tests predict? They predict scores on other academic achievement tests. But schools, I would argue, do not exist for the sake of high levels of performance in the context of schools, but in the context of life outside of the school.

The significant dependent variables in education are located in the kinds of interests, voluntary activities, levels of thinking and problem solving, that students engage in when they are not in school. In other words, the real test of successful schooling is not what students do in school, but what they do outside of it.

If such intentions were genuinely central in our educational planning, we would probably make other arrangements for teaching, curriculum, and evaluation than those we now employ. Significantly new intentions are likely to require new ways of leading educational lives.

The structural aspects of schooling pertain to the ways in which we have organized subjects, time, and roles. I have already alluded to the fact that we structure subjects by type. We use what Bernstein (1971) has called a collection-type curriculum. Each subject is bounded and kept distinct from others. This boundedness is reinforced by how time is allocated, what is taught, and in some secondary schools, where on the school campus a subject matter department is located. In some schools there is a section of the school devoted exclusively to the sciences, another to the fine arts, another to business and computer studies. We emphasize separateness and reinforce that separateness through a departmentalized structure.

Departmentalization might be, in the long run, the most rational way to structure schools, but it is not the only way. My aim here is not to advocate a particular change, but to problematize the structures we have lived with for so long that we come to think about them as natural entities rather than as the results of decisions that could have been otherwise. Is a departmentalized structure the best way to organize schools? It depends on a set of educational values and an exploration of alternative modes of organization. In the United States very few efforts at school reform—open schooling being a vivid exception—have tried to restructure schools. The curriculum reform movement of the 1960s attempted to create curricula designed to fit into existing school structures. Can new messages change the school or will the school change the messages?

The structure of the school also influences the way in which roles are defined. In American schools there are basically two roles for adults: teacher and principal. The teacher spends his or her day with children or adolescents. The principal seldom is responsible for teaching functions and has far more discretionary time than do teachers. If a teacher wants to secure more professional life-space, he or she must leave teaching and become a school administrator. Once such a decision is made, for all practical purposes, there is no return to the classroom—as the caterpillar, once it becomes a butterfly, remains a butterfly until it dies.

Working as an educator in a school need not be limited to two roles, nor must these roles be conceived of as "permanent." Schools can be structured so that teachers who are interested can devote some years or parts of some years to curriculum development, to the design of better evaluation methods for their school, to serving as mentors to beginning teachers. Teachers could create liaisons with community agencies such as museums, hospitals, cultural centers, retirement homes, in order to secure services that could enhance and enrich school programs. Teachers could devote time to research in their own school and assist parents with children who are having difficulty in school. There is a host of possible roles that could make important generic contributions to a school's way of life, but for these contributions to be made, educators need to create school structures that permit them to be developed. American schools, with few exceptions, are structured to inhibit these roles rather than to encourage their formation. The paradigms we have internalized about the nature of schooling—the way time is allocated, the way subjects are defined, the way in which roles are specified—are so strong that efforts at reform are typically conceptualized to fit into the constraints of those structures, thus defining the parameters within which reform efforts are to occur.

The curricular is the third dimension that needs attention in any effort to create genuinely significant educational reform. Decisions about curriculum can be made about several of its features. Among the most important are those about the content that is to be provided, about the kind of activities that are to be used to help students experience that content, and the way in which the curriculum itself is to be organized. As I have indicated, most efforts at curriculum reform in the United States have left the organization of curriculum intact: Separate subjects separately taught has been the dominant mode of organization, although at the elementary level such organization is less prevalent than at the middle or secondary school levels. Yet in spite of frequent admonitions by educational scholars to reduce curriculum fragmentation (Eisner 1985; Sizer 1984), the separation of subject matters persists and is supported by the infrastructure of professional education: testing programs, university admissions criteria, teacher training programs, specialization among subject-matter teachers. This collection-type form of curriculum organization (Bernstein 1971) is not the only way in which curriculum can be organized. Whether it is the most appropriate form, given the potential costs of other forms of organization, depends upon our educational intentions. If integration of learning is desired, separation may indeed be problematic. Again, my point here is not to argue for a specific form of curriculum reorganization as much as to urge the careful rethinking of the organization that now prevails.

What is taught in the first place is of primary importance. One way to increase the probability that something *will not be learned* is to ensure that it *will not be taught,* that is, to make a subject matter a part of a *null curriculum* (Eisner 1985). The fine arts are often relegated to this position. For many citizens the arts are someone else's pleasures. Large and important legacies of culture go unseen, unheard, unread, and as a result, unloved. Schools perpetuate this state of ignorance by withholding from the young important parts of their cultural legacy. The list could be expanded.

Regarding the activities that allow students to grasp or experience what is taught in schools, according to Goodlad (1984), the lecture still dominates at the secondary school level. Students typically have few opportunities to formulate their own questions and to pursue them. They are expected to do what the teacher requests; their role is in the application of means rather than the formulation of ends. They become, says Apple (1982), deskilled, unable to formulate the aims and goals they seek to attain.

The provision of opportunities for students to define at least some of their purposes is arguably an important educational aim and the ability to do so an important educational achievement. To what extent does it occur? Genuine reform of schools will require attention not only to intentions and school structure, but to the content, tasks, and forms of organization of the school curriculum. Which aspects of curricula should receive attention will depend on what is now occurring in schools; the only way to know that is to go to the schools to see.

The fourth dimension needing attention in genuine school reform is *the pedagogical* aspects of educational practice. If the curriculum is the systole of education, teaching is the diastole. No curriculum teaches itself and how it is mediated is crucial. In fact, I find it useful to distinguish between the *intended* curriculum and the *operational* curriculum (Eisner 1985). What we plan to teach—materials, outlines, projective activities and goals—constitutes the intended curriculum. The operational curriculum is the curriculum that is played out in the context of classroom life. In this process pedagogy plays a crucial role. When programs call for new teaching skills that teachers do not possess—inductive teaching, for example—teachers understandably use the skills they possess and these may not be adequate to the task.

No intended curriculum can be followed by teachers as a script; the classroom is too uncertain a place for recipes. The professional teacher needs to use the curriculum as a resource, as an amplifier of his or her own ability. Different teachers need different amounts of guidance and specificity. Thus, the pedagogical is a central aspect of school reform. Unless classroom practices change, changes on paper, whether in policy or in curriculum, are not likely to be of much consequence for students.

How can students of education know about the ways in which teaching occurs? What are the strengths teachers possess and what are their weaknesses? Are there important educational consequences on both sides of the ledger? These questions are, of course, easy to pose but difficult to answer. At minimum, qualitative studies of classroom life must be undertaken. Such studies could provide the basis on which effective change strategies could be initiated and could provide a focus for efforts aimed at pedagogical issues. *Both* curriculum and pedagogy need to be seen in context and both need attention for strengthening school reform.

Finally, the fifth dimension needing attention in school reform is *the evaluative.* It makes no sense whatsoever to write policy papers about educational reform and to prepare syllabi and curriculum guides for teachers that advocate a new direction for educational practice and continue to assess the outcomes of schooling on instruments that reflect older, more traditional views. Yet, this is what we often do. Consider the proposition that good schools increase individuality and cultivate productive idiosyncracy. Consider the idea that good schools increase differences among students, not diminish them. If we truly embraced these views, how would we go about evaluating the educational effectiveness of schools? Would commensurability remain an important criterion? What kinds of opportunities could be provided to students to develop what they have learned? To what extent would we use closed-ended examinations?

High-stake assessment procedures symbolically and practically represent what "higher-ups" care about and performance on such procedures significantly affects both the options students have and the professional reputation of teachers. How outcomes are evaluated is a major agent influencing what teachers and school administrators pay attention to. Thus, the redesign of assessment instruments so that they provide information about what teachers and others care about most from an educational perspective is a fundamental aspect of school reform. Schools cannot move in one direction and assess teachers and students using procedures that represent values in quite another direction.

Evaluation, however, should not be conceived of exclusively in terms of outcome assessment. Evaluation, it seems to me, should be regarded as an educational medium. The processes of teaching and the quality of what is taught, as well as their outcomes, are the proper subject matter of an adequate approach to educational evaluation. If the quality of the content being taught is poor, it does not matter much if the quality of teaching is good. Indeed, if the content being taught is pernicious, excellence in teaching is a vice.

Evaluation is an aspect of professional educational practice that should be regarded as one of the major means through which educators can secure information they can use to enhance the quality of their work. Evaluation ought to be an ongoing part of the process of education, one that contributes to its enhancement, not simply a means for scoring students and teachers.

These factors, the *intentional,* the *structural,* the *curricular,* the *pedagogical,* and the *evaluative,* are all important and interacting dimensions of schooling. Collectively they constitute a kind of ecology of schooling. To bring about reform in schools that is more than superficial and short-term requires attention to all of them.

To consider these dimensions not simply as an academic enterprise but as an activity leading to an agenda that can be acted on is the tough test of educational reform efforts. In some way that agenda has to be set. In setting this agenda teachers will need to be involved, as well as school administrators who themselves are not afraid of new forms of practice. The details of this agenda—the role, for example, that universities might play in school reform—cannot be addressed in this article. Yet unless the plan for school reform is comprehensive, it is likely to leave little residue in the long run. We sometimes say in the United States that educational reform is like a pendulum swing—we go back and forth. Pendulums are objects that move without going anyplace. Recognizing the ecological character of schools and facing up to the magnitude of the task of educational reform are important beginning efforts in dismounting from the pendulum.

14

Standards for American Schools
Help or Hindrance?

Efforts to reform American schools are not exactly a novel enterprise. When the Soviet Union sent Sputnik circling the globe in 1957 the U. S. Congress looked to the schools to recover what we had thought we had: leadership in space. The curriculum reform movement of the 1960s was intended, in part, to help us regain our technological superiority in the Cold War. In the 1970s "accountability" became the central concept around which our education reform efforts turned. If only we could identify the expected outcomes of instruction and invent means to describe their presence, school administrators and teachers could be held accountable for the quality of their work.

In April 1983, *A Nation at Risk* was published. In its memorable opening passage the impact of the schools on U.S. society was likened to a foreign invasion. By the late 1980s *A Nation at Risk,* one of the most prominent reform publications of the century, seemed to have faded, and its passing set the stage for America 2000—the reform agenda of the Bush Administration, now signed on to by the Clinton Administration. America 2000 was intended to do what the curriculum reform movement of the 1960s, the accountability movement of the 1970s, and *A Nation at Risk* and the "excellence movement" of the 1980s had been unable to accomplish.

We now have in Goals 2000 (the Clinton version of America 2000) an approach to education reform that uses standards as the linchpin of its efforts. Standards are being formulated for the certification of teachers, for the content of curricula, and for the outcomes of teaching. Virtually every subject-matter field in education has formulated or is in the process of formulating or revising national standards that describe what students should know and be able to do.

If anyone detects a slight echo of the past in today's reform efforts, let me assure you that you are not alone. We seem to latch on to approaches to reform that are replays of past efforts that themselves failed to come to grips with what it is that makes school practices so robust and resistant to change.

Consider, for example, the concept of standards. The term is attractive. Who among us, at first blush at least, would claim that schools—or any other institution for that matter—should be without them? Standards imply high expectations, rigor, things of substance. To be without standards is not to know what to expect or how to determine if expectations have been realized—or so it seems.

Yet once we get past the illusions that the concept invites—once we think hard about the meaning of the term—the picture becomes more complex. To begin with, the meaning of the term is not as self-evident as many seem to believe. A standard meal, for example, is a meal that I think we would agree is nothing to rave about—and the same could be said of a standard hotel room or a standard reply to a question. A standard can also be a banner, something that trumpets one's identity and commitment. A standard can represent a value that people have cared enough about to die for. Standards can also refer to units of measure. The National Bureau of Standards employs standards to measure the quality of manufactured products. Electrical appliances, for example, must achieve a certain standard to get the UL seal of approval.

Which conception of standards do we embrace in the reform movement? Surely we do not mean by standards a typical level of performance, since that is what we already have without an iota of intervention. As for standards that represent beliefs or values, we already have mission statements and position papers in abundance, but they do not have the level of specificity that reformers believe is needed for standards to be useful.

The third conception of standards—as units of measure that make it possible to quantify the performance of students, teachers, and schools— seems closer to what we have in mind. We live in a culture that admires technology and efficiency and believes in the possibility of objectivity. The idea of measurement provides us with a procedure that is closely associated with such values. Measurement makes it possible to describe quantity in ways that allow as little space as possible for subjectivity.[1] For example, the objectivity of an objective test is not a function of the way in which the test items were selected, but of the way in which the test is scored. Objective tests can be scored by machine, with no need for judgment.

Standards in education, as we now idealize them, are to have such features. They are to be objective and, whenever possible, measurable. Once a technology of assessment is invented that will objectively quantify the relationship of student performance to a measurable ideal, we will be able to determine without ambiguity the discrepancy between the former and the latter, and thus we will have a meaningful standard.

Those who have been working in education for twenty or so years or who know the history of American education will also know that the vision I have just described is a recapitulation of older ideals. I refer to the curriculum reform movement of the 1960s. It was an important event in the history of American education, but it was not the only significant movement of that period. You will also remember that it was in the 1960s that American educators became infatuated with "behavioral objectives." Everyone was to have them. The idea then, like the notion of standards today, was to define our educational goals operationally in terms that were sufficiently specific to determine without ambiguity whether or not the student had achieved them.

The specifics of the procedures, given prominence by Robert Mager's 1962 book, *Preparing Instructional Objectives,* required that student behavior be identified, that the conditions in which it was to be displayed be described, and that a criterion be specified that made it possible to measure the student's behavior in relation to the criterion. For Mager a behavioral objective might be stated as follows: "At the end of the instructional period, when asked to do so, the student will be able to write a 200-word essay with no more than two spelling errors, one error in punctuation, and no errors in grammar."

It all seemed very neat. What people discovered as they tried to implement the idea was that to have behaviorally defined instructional objectives that met the criteria that Mager specified required the construction of *hundreds* of specific objectives. Heaven knows, school districts tried. But it soon became apparent that teachers would be bogged down with such a load. And even so ardent a supporter of behavioral objectives as James Popham (1972) eventually realized that teachers would be better off with just a few such objectives. The quest for certainty, which high-level specificity and precision implied, was soon recognized as counterproductive.

Those who know the history of American education will also know that the desire to specify outcomes and to prescribe the most efficient means for achieving them was itself the dominant strain of what has come to be called the "efficiency movement" in education (Callahan 1962). The efficiency movement, which began in 1913 and lasted until the early 1930s, was designed to apply the principles of scientific management to schools.

Its progenitor, Frederick Taylor, the inventor of time-and-motion study, was a management consultant hired by industrialists to make their plants more efficient and hence more profitable. By specifying in detail the desired outcomes of a worker's efforts and by eliminating "wasted motion," output would increase, profits would soar, wages would rise, and everyone would benefit.

American school administrators thought that in Taylor's approach to the management of industrial plants they had found a surefire method for producing efficient schools. Moreover, Taylor's approach was based on "science." The prescription of expected outcomes, of the manner of performance, and of the content in which competence is to be displayed is a not-too-distant cousin of the teacher performance standards and curriculum content standards that accompany today's discussions of standards for student performance.

School administrators caught up in the efficiency movement gradually learned that the basic conception and the expectations that flowed from it—namely, that one could mechanize and routinize teaching and learning—did not work. Even if it were possible to give teachers scripts for their performance, it was not possible to give students scripts. There was no "one best method," and there was no way to "teacher-proof" instruction.

My point thus far is that what we are seeing in American education today is a well-intentioned but conceptually shallow effort to improve our schools. My point thus far is to make it plain that the current effort in which we are enmeshed is no novelty; we have been here before. My point thus far is to suggest that successful efforts at school reform will entail a substantially deeper analysis of schools and their relationships to communities and teachers than has thus far been undertaken.

To try to do justice to the aspirations of the national education reform movement, I will try to make a sympathetic presentation of its arguments. I start with the acknowledgment that there is a sense of sweet reason to the arguments that the reformers have made. After all, with standards we will know where we are headed. We can return rigor to schooling; we can inform students, parents, and teachers of what we expect; we can have a common basis for appraising student performance; and we can, at last, employ a potent lever for education reform. Without standards, we are condemned to an unbroken journey into an abyss of mediocrity; we will remain a nation at risk.

In addition, the task of formulating standards is salutary for teachers and others involved in curriculum planning. By establishing national goals for each subject that schools teach, we will be able to achieve professional consensus that will give us a unified and educationally solid view of what students are expected to learn. By trying to define standards for each field, a single vision of a subject will be created, teachers will have an opportunity to profit from the goals and standards formulated by their peers, and ambiguity will be diminished because teachers will know not only the direction their efforts are to take, but also the specific destinations toward which their students are headed. Furthermore, teachers will have something of a timetable to help determine not only whether, but when, they have arrived.

As if they had just taken a cold shower, a population of sometimes lethargic and burned-out teachers will be reawakened and will become alert. Our nation will, at last, have a national educational agenda, something that it has never possessed. Ultimately, such resources and the approach to education that those resources reflect will help us regain our competitive edge in a global economy. Parents will be satisfied, students will know what is expected of them, and the business community will have the employees it needs for America to become number one by the year 2000, not only in science and in math but in other fields as well. Our students and our schools will go for and get the gold at the educational Olympics in which we are competing. Our schools will become "world class."

An attractive vision? It seems so, yet a number of questions arise. You will recall that the standards about which reformers speak are national standards. The organizations—and there are dozens—that are engaged in formulating standards are doing so for the nation as a whole, not for some specific locality. Put another way, in a nation in which 45 million students in 50 states go to approximately 108,000 schools overseen by some 15,000 school boards and in which 2.5 million teachers teach, there is the presumption that it makes good educational sense for there to be uniform expectations with respect to goals, content, and levels of student achievement. I regard this assumption as questionable on at least two counts.

First, the educational uses of subjects are not singular. The social studies can be used to help students understand history, to help create a socially active citizenry, or to help students recognize the connection between culture and ideas. Biology can be used to help students learn to think like biologists, to understand the balance of nature, to appreciate the limits of science in establishing social policy, or to gain an appreciation of life. The language arts can be used to develop poetic forms of thought, to learn to appreciate great works of literary art, to acquire the mechanics of written and spoken language, to learn to appreciate forms of life that require literary rather than literal understanding. Mathematics can be taught to help students learn to compute, to understand the structure of mathematics, to solve mathematical problems, to cultivate forms of mathematical cognition, and to help students appreciate the beauty of structures in space. Where is it written that every subject has to be taught for the same reasons to 45 million students? Despite the effort to achieve professional consensus about the educational agendas of specific subjects, the virtue of uniformity is, to my mind, questionable.

Uniformity in curriculum content is a virtue *if* one's aim is to be able to compare students in one part of the country with students in others. Uniformity is a virtue when the aspiration is to compare the performance of American students with students in Korea, Japan, and Germany. But why should we wish to make such comparisons? To give up the idea that there needs to be one standard for all students in each field of study is not to give up the aspiration to seek high levels of educational quality in both pedagogical practices and educational outcomes. Together, the desire to compare and the recognition of individuality create one of the dilemmas of a social meritocracy: the richness of a culture rests not only on the prospect of cultivating a set of common commitments, but also on the prospect of cultivating those individual talents through which the culture at large is enriched.

A second problematic feature of the aspiration to adopt a common set of standards for all is a failure to recognize differences among the students with whom we work. I am well aware of the fact that deleterious self-fulfilling prophecies can be generated when the judgments educators make about individuals are based on a limited appreciation of the potentialities of the students. This is a danger that requires our constant vigilance. However, the reality of differences—in region, in aptitude, in interests, and in goals—suggests that it is reasonable that there be differences in programs.

The framers of the U.S. Constitution implicitly recognized the need for the localities they called states to develop educational programs that addressed the values and features of the populations in those states. We do not need the U.S. equivalent of a French Ministry of Education, prescribing a one-size-fits-all program. Ironically, at a time when the culture at large is recognizing the uniqueness of us all and cultivating our productive differences, the education reform movement, in its anxiety about quality, wants to rein in our diversity, to reduce local discretion, and to give everybody the same target at which to aim.

Thus, with respect to aspiration, I think there are fundamental problems with the concept of standards as applied to the nation as a whole. But there are other problems as well, and these problems relate to the concept of standards as it applies to the process of education and to what we know about normal patterns of human development.

You will remember that I referred to standards as units of measure that make possible the "objective" description of quantitative relationships.

But there are qualitative standards as well. To have a *qualitative* standard you must create or select an icon, prototype, or what is sometimes called a benchmark against which the performance or products of students are matched. To have a *quantitative* standard you must specify the number or percentage of correct answers needed to pass a test or the number of allowable errors in a performance or product and to use that specification as the standard.

In each case, there is a fixed and relatively unambiguous unit of measurement. In the qualitative case, the task for both judge and performer is one of matching a performance with a model. This kind of matching is precisely what occurs in the Olympics. Olympic judges know what a particular dive should look like, and they compare a diver's performance to the model. The diver, too, knows what the model looks like and does his or her best to replicate the model.

With respect to the quantitative case, the application of a standard occurs in two different ways. The first has to do with determining the correctness of any individual response. An item response is judged correct if the appropriate bubble is filled in, or if the appropriate selection is made, or if some other indication is given that the student has hit a prespecified mark. The prespecified correct response serves as a standard for each item. Once these item responses are summed, a determination is made as to whether the total number of correct responses meets a second standard, the standard specified as a passing grade by the test-maker or by some policy-making body.

Notice that in both cases innovation in response is not called for. The diver replicates a known model. The test-maker determines whether a student's score is acceptable, not by exercising judgment, but by counting which bubbles have been filled in and comparing the number of correct responses to a fixed predetermined standard.

There are, we must acknowledge, a number of important tasks that students must learn in school in which innovation is not useful. Learning how to spell correctly means knowing how to replicate the known. The same holds true for much of what is taught in early arithmetic and in the language arts. There are many important tasks and skills that students need to learn—i.e., conventions—that are necessary for doing more important work and that educational programs should help them learn. The more important work that I speak of is the work that makes it possible for students to think imaginatively about problems that matter to them, tasks that give them the opportunity to affix their own personal signature to their work, occasions to explore ideas and questions that have no correct answers, and projects in which they can reason and express their own ideas.

Learning to replicate known conventions is an important part of the *tactical outcomes* of education, but it is not adequate for achieving the *strategic aspirations* that we hold. These strategic aspirations require curricula and assessment policies that invite students to exercise judgment and to create outcomes that are not identical with those of their peers. Again, the cultivation of productive idiosyncrasy ought to be one of the aims that matter in American schools, and, to my way of thinking, we ought to build programs that make the realization of such an outcome possible, even if it means that we will not find it easy to compare students. When we seek to measure such outcomes, we will not be able to use a fixed standard for scoring the work students have produced. We will have to rely on that most exquisite of human capacities—judgment.

Paradoxically, many of the groups that have been working diligently to formulate standards are not really formulating standards at all. They are formulating goals. Consider the following, all of which purport to be standards.

- "Accomplished teachers work with families to achieve common goals for the education of their children" (Board for Professional Teaching Standards, 1994).
- "Construct Personal Meaning from Nontraditional Dramatic Performances" (National Standards for Arts Education, 1994).
- "How Progressives and Others Addressed Problems of Industrial Capitalism, Urbanizations, and Political Corruption" (United States History: Exploring the American Experience, 1994).
- "Folklore and Other Cultural Contributions from Various Regions of the United States and How They Help to Form a National Heritage" (United States History: Exploring the American Experience, 1994).

Such broad, general statements are aspirations that can function as criteria with which to interrogate the work students produce. But criteria are not the same as standards. John Dewey described the difference in *Art as Experience,* one of his most important books, which is largely unread by educators. In a telling chapter on the relationship of art criticism to perception, written when he was 75 years old, Dewey said that, in assessing works of art, standards are inappropriate: criteria are needed. Standards fix expectations; criteria are guidelines that enable one to search more efficiently for the qualities that might matter in any individual work. Describing the features of a standard, Dewey wrote:

> There are three characteristics of a standard. It is a particular physical thing existing under specified physical conditions; it is *not* a value. The

yard is a yardstick, and the meter is a bar deposited in Paris. In the second place, standards are measures of definite things, of lengths, weights, capacities. The things measured are not values, although it is of great social value to be able to measure them, since the properties of things in the way of size, volume, weight, are important for commercial exchange. Finally, as standards of measure, standards define things with respect to quantity. (1934, 307)

Later, he went on to argue:

Yet it does not follow because of absence of an uniform and publicly determined external object [a standard], that objective criticism of art is impossible. What follows is that criticism is judgment: that like every judgment it involves a venture, a hypothetical element: that it is directed to qualities which are nevertheless qualities of an *object*; and that it is concerned with an individual object, not with making comparisons by means of an external preestablished rule between different things. (308)

To say that by the end of a course students will be able to write a convincing essay on the competing interests of environmentalists and industrialists that marshals good arguments supported by relevant facts is to identify criteria that can be used to appraise the essay; it is not to provide a standard for measuring it. Regarding the meaning of criteria, Dewey wrote:

If there are no standards for works of art and hence none for criticism (in the sense in which there are standards of measurement), there are nevertheless criteria in judgment. . . . But such criteria are not rules or prescriptions. They are the result of an endeavor to find out what a work of art is as an experience, the kind of experience which constitutes it. (309)

One might wonder whether it is appropriate to think about the appraisal of work produced by students at the elementary and secondary school level as being comparable to the assessment of works of art. Aren't artworks objects in a different category? Criteria may be appropriate for paintings and poetry, but schoolwork requires the application of standards.

As plausible as this might seem at first glance, things are not so simple. The creation of conditions that allow students to display their creative and reasoning abilities in ways that are unique to their temperaments, their experience, and their aims is of fundamental importance in any educational enterprise—in contrast to one concerned with training. And because such features are important, it is criteria that must be salient in our assessment.

Standards are appropriate for some kinds of tasks, but, as I argued above, those tasks are instrumental to larger and more important educational aims.

We really don't need to erect a complex school system to teach the young how to read utility bills, how to do simple computation, or how to spell; they will learn those skills on their own. What we do need to teach them is how to engage in higher-order thinking, how to pose telling questions, how to solve complex problems that have more than one answer. When the concept of standards becomes salient in our discourse about educational expectations, it colors our view of what education can be and dilutes our conception of education's potential. Language matters, and the language of standards is by and large a limiting rather than a liberating language.

The qualities that define inventive work of any kind are qualities that by definition have both unique and useful features. The particular form those features take and what it is that makes them useful are not necessarily predictable, but sensitive critics—and sensitive teachers—are able to discover such properties in the work. Teachers who know the students they teach recognize the unique qualities in students' comments, in their paintings, in the essays they write, in the ways in which they relate to their peers. The challenge in teaching is to provide the conditions that will foster the growth of those personal characteristics that are socially important and, at the same time, personally satisfying to the student. The aim of education is not to train an army that marches to the same drummer, at the same pace, toward the same destination. Such an aim may be appropriate for totalitarian societies, but it is incompatible with democratic ideals.

If one used only philosophical grounds to raise questions about the appropriateness of uniform national standards for students in American schools, there would still be questions enough to give one pause. But there are developmental grounds as well. The graded American public school system was built on an organizational theory that has little to do with the developmental characteristics of growing children. In the mid-nineteenth century we thought it made very good sense for the school to be organized into grades and for there to be a body of content assigned to each grade (Goodlad and Anderson 1987). Each grade was to be related to a specific age. The task of the student was to master the content taught at that grade as a precondition for promotion to the next grade. At the end of an eight- or twelve-year period, it was assumed that, if the school and the teacher had done their jobs, everyone would come out at roughly the same place.

If you examine the patterns of human development for children from age five to age eighteen, you will find that, as children grow older, their rate of development is increasingly variable. Thus the range of variation among children of the same age increases with time.

For example, for ordinary, nonhomogeneous classes, the average range of reading achievement is roughly equal to the grade level: at the second grade there is, on average, a two-year spread in reading achievement. Some second graders are reading at the first-grade level, and others are reading at the third-grade level. At the fourth grade the spread is about four years, and at the sixth grade, about six years. In the seventh grade the range is about seven years: some children are reading at the fourth-grade level, and some are reading at the tenth-grade level.

What this means is that children develop at their own distinctive pace. The tidy structure that was invented in the nineteenth century to rationalize school organization may look wonderful on paper, but it belies what we know about the course of human development. Because we still operate with a developmentally insensitive organizational structure in our schools, the appeal of uniform standards by grade level or by outcome seems reasonable. It is not. Variability, not uniformity, is the hallmark of the human condition.

I do not want to overstate the idea. To be sure, humans are like all other humans, humans are like some other humans, and humans are like no other humans. All three claims are true. But we have become so preoccupied with remedying the perceived weaknesses of American schools that we have underestimated the diversity and hence the complexity that exists.

The varieties of unappreciated complexity are large. Let me suggest only a few. When evaluating students in the context of the classroom, the teacher—the person who has the widest variety of information about any particular student—takes into consideration much more than the specific features of a student's particular product. The age, grade, and developmental level of the student; the amount of progress a student has made; the degree of effort that the student has expended; the amount of experience a student has had in a domain are all educationally relevant considerations that professionally competent teachers take into account in making judgments about a student's progress. Experienced teachers know in their bones that the student's work constitutes only one item in an array of educational values and that these values sometimes compete. There are times when it may be more important educationally for a teacher to publicly acknowledge the quality of a student's work than to criticize it, even when that work is below the class average.

Beyond the details of the classroom, there are more general questions having to do with the bases on which educational standards are formulated. Should educational standards be derived from the average level of performance of students in a school, in a school district, in a state, in a nation, *in the world*? How much talk have we heard of "*world class*" standards?

If national policy dictates that there will be uniform national standards for student performance, will there also be uniform national standards for the resources available to schools? To teachers? To administrators? Will the differences in performance between students living in well-heeled, upper-class suburbs and those living on the cusp of poverty in the nation's inner cities demonstrate the existing inequities in American education? Will they not merely confirm what we already know?

The socioeconomic level of the students and the resources available to them and their teachers in a school or school district do make a difference. If those urging standards on us believe that the use of standards will demonstrate inequities—and hence serve to alleviate them—why haven't these already painfully vivid inequities been effective in creating more equitable schools?

And, one might wonder, what would happen to standards in education if by some magic all students achieved them? Surely the standards would be considered too low. At first blush this doesn't sound like a bad thing. Shouldn't the bar always be higher than we can reach? Sounds reasonable. Yet such a view of the function of standards will ineluctably create groups of winners and losers. Can our education system flourish without losers? Is it possible for us to frame conceptions of education and society that rest on more generous assumptions? And consider the opposite. What will we do with those students who fail to meet the standards? Then what?

Perhaps one of the most important consequences of the preoccupation with national standards in education is that it distracts us from the deeper, seemingly intractable problems that beset our schools. It distracts us from paying attention to the importance of building a culture of schooling that is genuinely intellectual in character, that values questions and ideas at least as much as getting right answers. It distracts us from trying to understand how we can provide teachers the kind of professional opportunities that will afford the best among them opportunities to continue to grow through a lifetime of work. It distracts us from attending to the inevitable array of interactions between teaching, curriculum, evaluation, school organization, and the often deleterious expectations and pressures from universities.

How should these matters be addressed? Can schools and teachers and administrators afford the kind of risk-taking and exploratory activity that genuine inquiry in education requires?

Vitality within any organization is more likely when there are opportunities to pursue fresh possibilities, to exercise imagination, to try things out, and to relinquish the quest for certainty in either pedagogical method or educational outcome. Indeed, one of the important aims of education is to free the mind from the confines of certainty. Satisfaction, our children must learn, can come from the uncertainty of the journey, not just from the clarity of the destination.

I am not sure that American society is willing at this time to embrace so soft a set of values as I have described. We have become a tough-minded lot. We believe that we can solve the problems of crime by reopening the doors to the gas chambers and by building more prisons. But it's never been that simple. Nor is solving the problems of schooling as simple as having national education standards.

And so I believe that we must invite our communities to join us in a conversation that deepens our understanding of the educational process and advances our appreciation of its possibilities. Genuine education reform is not about shallow efforts that inevitably fade into oblivion. It is about vision, conversation, and action designed to create a genuine and evolving educational culture. I hope we can resist the lure of slogans and the glitter of bandwagons and begin to talk seriously about education. That is one conversation in which we must play a leading role.

Notes

1. The presence of subjectivity in scientific work has long been regarded as a source of bias. Most measurement procedures aspire to what is called "procedural objectivity," which represents a process in which the exercise of judgment is minimized. A competent 10-year-old can do as well as a Nobel Prize winner in measuring a room. Tasks that can be accomplished without appealing to human judgment can also be done by machine. Optical scanners can score multiple test forms more quickly and more accurately than humans. Some idealizations of science aspire to a pristine quantitative descriptive state that does not depend on human judgment or interpretation at all. For an extended discussion of the concept of "procedural objectivity," see Elliot W. Eisner, *The Enlightened Eye: Qualitative Inquiry and the Enhancement of Educational Practice* (New York: Macmillan, 1991).

15

What a Professor Learned in the Third Grade

It is a truism in the social sciences that the ways in which we have been socialized influence the ways in which we see the world. Our views of schooling and what we believe constitutes responsible and effective teaching are the result of our socialization, both professional and personal. My socialization has been fed by two major streams. The first is my experience in the arts, at first as a painter and later as a collector of arts. What I cherish and what I look for have been shaped by what I have learned how to see and what I have come to value. These values and this seeing are not limited to the fine arts; they pervade the way I lead—or try to lead—my life. Thus, for example, the kind of experience that a process or an object makes possible, whether in a museum, a concert hall, or a classroom, is important to me. In a sense, for me, the journey is the reward.

The second stream feeding my socialization has been the social sciences. I regard the concepts and theories that social scientists invent as *structures of appropriation*. They are devices through which focus is secured and certain kinds of meaning obtained. In this sense, artists and scientists share a common mission: to create structures—qualitative and theoretical forms—through which the world is viewed. Indeed, following Nelson Goodman (1978), I would say that it is through these structures of appropriation that our worlds are made.

My experience in the arts has led me to eschew abstract formalisms in so highly nuanced an enterprise as teaching. It has led me to emphasize the centrality of perception in cognition, for it is through perception that consciousness is born, and it is through consciousness of the qualities that we attend to, whether in a classroom or a concert hall, that our understanding is enlarged.

The practical consequence of these foregoing experiences has been, for me, the development of an approach to the study of schooling that, on the one hand, roots itself firmly in the humanities, in the literary, and in the qualitative and, on the other, uses concepts and theories from the social sciences to try to account for what has been given an account of. My general aim has been to try to expand and to legitimate a broader, more catholic approach to educational inquiry. This approach does not aspire toward the ethnographic. I am not an anthropologist. I am an educator. Its closest relatives are to be found in the humanities, particularly in the practices of connoisseurship and criticism. My aim is to exploit the capacity of perception to see what matters in educational settings and to use whatever language, in all its forms, can deliver to make vivid what an enlightened eye has seen (Eisner 1991). These aims are realized through what I have called *educational* connoisseurship and *educational* criticism. They require going into schools to see firsthand how schooling is played out, a practice that now, in the 1990s, is much more common than it was in the 1970s. My return to school—the third grade—was an effort to get closer to the phenomena than the comforts of a university office at Stanford make possible.

I provide this context because it is so critically important in the kind of work this orientation to research makes possible.

Two Third Grades in Stanford's Shadow

The two schools in which my observations were made are located in a well-to-do suburb near Stanford University. The parents of many, although by no means most, of the pupils are employed by the university. But virtually all the parents, as one can detect by the prevalence of the word *Stanford* emblazoned on their maroon sweatshirts, would like their children to succeed academically and to attend a prestigious university. The school district is one that is considered successful by any standard measure of academic performance. Its students rank in the 95th percentile or higher within the state on academic measures and have done so for decades. The parents attend school board meetings in numbers far larger than what is considered typical for a community of this size, and their expectations for school performance are very high indeed.

The two schools in which I observed are single-story structures, well supplied, orderly; an atmosphere of affluence and material comfort pervades these institutions. One school, built in the late 1960s, was originally designed for open education, an innovation at the time, but in more educationally conservative periods returned to traditional forms of school organization: the flexible folding doors that were once opened are now closed, and each teacher works in his or her own space with a group of elementary-aged children ranging in class size from about twenty-one to thirty.

What we have, therefore, are two well-appointed schools serving a student population consisting of academically motivated children coming from homes of high-aspiring parents, many of whom work for a prestigious research university. It is not a typical American school district.

I chose the two classrooms in this school district because I wanted to observe educational practice in what might be regarded as "the best of circumstances." I wanted to see teachers who were regarded by their peers and by building principals as particularly strong; indeed, among the very best. I intended to interview several teachers before making a selection, but it became clear after I had talked to the first two that interviewing others would be unnecessary. Their intelligence and commitment were hard to miss, even during a single interview session.

I describe these institutions and the characteristics of the teachers I observed in order to emphasize the "special" nature of the setting and the people. I do not know whether the teaching patterns I saw would be effective with other, less fortunate children, although I think they would. In any case, I believe that there is much to learn from excellent teachers, regardless of the context.

Just what did I learn from my three-month sojourn? Some of what I learned may appear prosaic. It is. But there is a profound difference between knowing something in the abstract and knowing it through direct experience. Consider, for example, the idea that all children are different. To professors of education, that notion is about as prosaic as can be, but seeing the ways in which a group of eight-year-olds can differ in size, temperament, maturity, interests, energy level, and personal style is quite another matter. Their presence makes plain the vacuity of the concept "the average eight-year-old." Direct experience underscores the personal idiosyncrasies of students that any elementary school teacher must deal with. It makes vivid the truth of Goethe's observation that between the universal and the particular, the particular always prevails. Teachers cannot deal with abstractions or averages when they teach. Their knowledge of individuals is crucial in enabling them to make appropriate assignments, to provide comfort and support, to impose sanctions, to define limits to behavior, to remind individual students of obligations, to encourage participation, and to foster attitudes of cooperation. It is awareness of individual children that makes it possible for teachers to encourage the development of nascent but valuable interests and the expression of well-developed talents. Spending three months in the third grade seeing these individual and irrepressible personalities in living color makes clear the pallor of textbook renditions of human development. Such renditions might well serve the interests of psychologists, but they do not portray the human realities that elementary school teachers must face.

A second thing that I learned was the ingenious ways in which teachers create a common culture, almost a special language through which the coherence of the group is maintained and the teacher's own energy level conserved. This language emerges in the kinds of signals and routines that teachers employ to get children's attention, to initiate a familiar set of activities, to bring a teaching episode to a close. The way of life that teachers share with children is complex, and modi vivendi need to be created that will make smooth transitions within the school day possible. The forms that these transitions take and the cues that teachers use are well known to students, so well known that they need not be articulated. For the visitor, however, they need to be learned. For example, one teacher used a simple but ingenious method for collecting student papers. Each of her students was assigned a number, and by counting off a set of numbers, tests or papers to be graded were turned in alphabetically. Certain mailboxes were available for students to hand in or pick up their work. Certain people in the classroom performed particular tasks, and these tasks were rotated on specific days. Certain groups—or tribes, as they were called in one class—were formed to enable students to work together, and membership in each tribe changed during the course of the year. This made it possible for students to have opportunities to learn to work with everyone in the class. A whole complex set of arrangements was designed to facilitate the achievement of the academic and social aspirations of both teachers and students. None of these routines, as far as I could tell, was hyperrationalized, overbureaucratized, or mechanical. They were a comfortable, ongoing part of a way of life that the students shared with each other and with their teacher.

Do those kinds of activities and arrangements fall under the heading of "teaching"? Does teaching include the design of these arrangements? Are people teaching when they invent the conditions through which students take responsibility for the distribution of papers and materials, when they manage and monitor cleanup, when they assume responsibility for equipment? I think that teaching encompasses these tasks as well as the conventional conception of instruction. What does the saliency of such task demands imply for research on teaching? These tasks in teaching are not simply manifestations of subject matter knowledge or pedagogical skills related to instruction. They are pedagogical all right, but pedagogical in terms of social arrangements.

A third feature that I saw was the diversity—indeed, the rhythm—among the curriculum activities that these teachers employed. The class day has some clear structured divisions. One portion of the day is devoted to whole-group activities, another to small-group instruction, and another to individual student work, defined by these eight-year-old students but pursued within general constraints defined by the teacher. These arrangements create changes in tempo. Like a ballet, the day is choreographed; indeed, one teacher analogized her work to the work of a director of a play—the entire sequence of acts needed to be planned and matters of tempo and timing considered in order to avoid tedium.

One of the ways in which tedium is avoided is by creating classrooms that have an open structure. Children are free to move about and to talk with each other, except on those occasions in which there is whole-class activity that requires the participation of everyone—the use of the overhead projector to teach spelling, for example. Indeed, conversations among children are encouraged by their seating arrangements: groups of three or four eight-year-olds sit together, face to face. One teacher encouraged students to whisper the answers that they had arrived at to their neighbors, a kind of personal sharing.

What also avoids tedium is the practice of self-regulation that the classrooms' open structure makes possible. Since children do not need permission from the teacher to move about, and since they can speak at will to other classmates, just how much moving and talking they do is something that they themselves learn to control. This structure is complemented by a procedure that both teachers employ in planning their activities.

Some classroom activities engage children in tasks in which the content or skill to be learned is highly rule-governed. The teacher's aim is to get the children to learn the material in a socially correct form. Learning to spell, learning to punctuate, and learning to do multiplication tables are examples of tasks in which innovation in outcome is not a particular virtue. Creative spellers are not sought by teachers, regardless of the innovative forms of cognition that might lead a child to spell a word in a particular way. As important as understanding is in mathematics, accuracy in computation is still a primary virtue. There are many tasks in schools, perhaps most, in which children are expected to acquire the skills of impression, that is, learning how to take something in. In a sense, the aim is to internalize social conventions.

There are other tasks, particularly in the fine arts, including creative writing, in which the child's internal life can be given leave to take flight.

Here the end in view is not to internalize social conventions but to enable children to place their own stamp on their work, hopefully a stamp that has soared on the wings of imagination. These are the skills of expression. These two emphases in task features are also a part of the tempo that these two teachers orchestrate. Some tasks demand strict adherence to socially pre-scribed norms and outcomes, while other tasks put a premium on letting one's mind take flight. Whether eight years old or eighty, humans need such variety. We need to be able to do our accounting when we must, but we also need to walk in the forest, to move into our private worlds, and to listen to the Brandenburg Concertos.

These teachers do not rationalize their curricular choices as I have just described, but they make them nevertheless. They recognize that they are planners of a day, implementers of a program, creators of tasks that engage twenty-five children in a set of activities that will maintain their interest over the course of a day. They do this five days a week, forty weeks a year.

I would like to say a word about the teachers' temperaments. Above all, at the elementary school level, the teacher is the major shaper of the form of shared social life that students experience. How affection is pro-vided, the particular ways in which limits are enforced, the amount of flexibility that children experience, the clarity with which tasks are assigned, the pace and mood of the day are profoundly influenced by the head of the household—the classroom teacher. At the secondary level, departmentaliza-tion mitigates such effects, since students encounter five or six teachers each day, but at the elementary level, the class teacher is clearly the major force pervading the classroom. These personal factors may be among the most difficult to influence, yet they are, in my experience, among the most important in establishing classroom tone. What children learn from their teacher as a person that does not emerge on the standardized achievement tests used to assess the outcomes of schooling may be among the most important things that they learn in school. They are clearly among the most important things that children will remember when they are asked to recall the teachers that influenced their lives.

Another factor that became clear to me during my observation was the extent to which children pick up instructional cues, not only when they are given to them directly but also as they are overheard or seen when given to other children. By the time they are eight, children are well practiced at exploiting a vast array of sources for orienting themselves to their environ-ment. Thus, the teacher who teaches one child is often teaching the entire class. In this sense, individualized instruction is seldom individualized.

Another thing that I learned about classrooms is the extent to which these teachers think pedagogically about almost everything. What I mean is that they exploit every reasonable opportunity to get children to draw their own conclusions. Questions raised by children are seldom answered directly; instead, they are followed by another question from the teacher or by suggestions about where to look for answers. The teachers pedagogical routines are, it seems to me, almost on automatic pilot in responding this way, just as they appear to be on automatic pilot in using positive comments to "correct" student behavior. During the three months that I spent in these classes, I heard or saw practically no significant forms of negative reinforcement used by either teacher, a feat that demands my utmost admiration. This should not be interpreted to mean that children do not know when the teacher is not pleased—they do know. What I mean is that the overt use of aversive comments or acts by the teachers is virtually nonexistent when they interact with their students.

Part of the reason for the saliency of positive reinforcement emanates from the inclination among teachers, particularly at the elementary school level in California, to be concerned about matters of self-esteem. These concerns have created a climate that has led to the practices that I have described. Whether such practices are in the child's best interests in the long run depends on what one believes to contribute to effective forms of socialization and the norms of the society in which the child lives.

The maintenance of a class as a cohesive group is a form of pedagogical achievement. These teachers employed a variety of techniques to maintain such cohesiveness. One such technique is to deal explicitly with details so that nothing is left to chance or to assumption; it cannot be assumed that children will know what adults have taken for granted. Another is to ask children themselves to review what they are supposed to do—this provides them with a kind of advance organizer and a reminder of what is to take place. Others are to review plans for the school day at the day's beginning and post the sequence of events on the blackboard and to bring the class together from time to time to review where things stand. What is clear is that these procedures are intended to keep movement and coherence present. The teacher is indeed a planner, a producer, and a director. The most apt metaphor may be that of a chef. Like a chef, the teacher has to know how to use a wide variety of ingredients, how to put them together, what level of flame is required, and when it is necessary to get back to the pots to keep them from boiling over. At times, the teacher must innovate when ingredients are unavailable. All of this must be done with a sense of orchestration to keep the whole enterprise moving forward and working well.

These features by no means exhaust what I learned from the two third-grade classrooms that I observed. I have neither the time nor the space to describe the ways in which these teachers convey the seriousness of their work to students, how they help them understand that the work they do is important. I cannot describe the physical forms of affection that they provide to their children, nor can I describe the extent to which these particular children have internalized the norms of achievement or how much the small victories—spelling a word correctly or being called on to assume a small responsibility—that to an adult seem trivial, mean to these children. I cannot describe the degree to which these teachers are psychologically fed by their students or the energy that they expend in planning and executing plans in their classrooms. I cannot comment on the degree of administrative acumen required to keep what is often a four-ring circus functioning in full gear and without a hitch. These achievements are part of what I judge to be the fine professional performance of the elementary school teachers I observed in the schools I visited. The parts of these teaching skills that pertain to subject matter knowledge are important to be sure but, I believe, minor in importance compared to the teachers' personal and organizational skills. Immersion in these elementary school classrooms relegates most university teaching demands to the minor leagues.

Expectations for Future Research on Teaching

Given the particularity, the phenomenological density, and the dynamic complexity of what these two third-grade teachers do in the course of their workday, what is it that we can reasonably expect research on teaching to provide? In what ways can research on teaching increase the effectiveness of teachers and help them become more professionally responsible? There are, I believe, five major options that we can consider. The first of these—the creation of a science of teaching—was thought to be a realistic aim for educational research by the father of educational psychology in America. I speak, of course, of E. L. Thorndike. Thorndike believed that a "complete science of psychology" was possible and that eventually we would have a tested technology of practice that would efficiently and effectively enable teachers to achieve their most lofty educational aims. Writing in the first issue of *Educational Psychology,* published in 1910, he said:

> A complete science of psychology would tell every fact about everyone's intellect and character and behavior, would tell the cause of every change in human nature, would tell the result which every educational force— every act of every person that changed any other or the agent himself— would have. It would aid us to use human beings for the world's welfare with the same surety of the result that we now have when we use falling

bodies or chemical elements. In proportion as we get such a science we shall become masters of our own souls as we now are master of heat and light. Progress toward such a science is being made. (Thorndike 1910, 6)

There are few people today who share the level of optimism that Thorndike expressed in 1910. No one whom I know believes that even in principle it will be possible to provide teachers with specific procedures for teaching specific subjects to particular children. The prospects of "getting teaching down to a science," by which I mean a procedure that can be systematically employed to yield highly predictable results, time after time, are considered extremely dim by virtually everyone.

If the aspiration for pedagogical algorithms is a wrongheaded hope for research on teaching, what expectations appear more reasonable? One is the expectation that research on teaching will provide empirically derived generalizations about variables related to teaching effectiveness and to matters associated with it. Such generalizations might be derived from correlational studies or from experiments designed to lead to generalizations about causality. I leave aside issues related to the logical status of generalizations derived from experiments whose validity depends on the existence of conditions present in the initial experimental design. Those criteria are typically too difficult to meet as a standard for justifying the use of such generalizations. It is seldom clear whether the classrooms to which the generalizations are to be applied sufficiently approximate the classrooms in which the initial studies were made: the so-called application of research conclusions to practice is made primarily on the basis of analogical reasoning, not statistical inference or deduction. But again, putting such matters aside, what can we expect reasonable and robust generalizations to provide to those who work in particular classrooms, located in particular schools, in particular parts of the country?

One thing seems reasonably clear. The farther away one is from the particular setting in which the individual teacher works, the more useful the generalization appears to be. That is, when we think about third graders in general, we find it more congenial to invoke generalizations about third graders. But it is equally clear that individual teachers do not work with third graders in general. They work with little Tommy Johnson or with overweight Katy Epstein. Tommy's mother and father have just decided to divorce after several years of arguing and bickering, and Tommy is uncertain and frightened about his future. Katy, however, comes from a secure home but suffers from the pressures exerted by academically anxious parents. Katy's problem is fear of failure. She, too, is uncertain and insecure, but for different reasons and in different ways. Teachers do not deal with the abstractions that university professors and government policy makers typically address; they deal with Tommy and Katy. Effective and responsible teaching might be quite different for each of these children. Thus, generalizations are at best guidelines, rules of thumb, so to speak, that a teacher might want to consider if there is time to do so and if the generalization is thought to be relevant.

When we come to the uses of generalization, two complications are encountered. The first has been suggested by Gage (1978) in his book *The Scientific Basis of the Art of Teaching*. Gage recognizes that generalizations—that is, statements about consistent and robust relationships among variables—can be usefully employed in the context of teaching *if* the variables that are relevant for making a teaching decision are few. But when variables become numerous—more than three or four, as they always are in classrooms—artistry must take over. Gage writes:

> Scientific method can contribute relationships between variables taken two at a time and even, in the form of interactions, three or perhaps four or more at a time. Beyond say four, the usefulness of what science can give the teacher begins to weaken, because teachers cannot apply, at least not without help and not on the run, the more complex interactions. At this point, the teacher as an artist must step in and make clinical, or artistic, judgments about the best ways to teach. In short, the scientific base for the art of teaching will consist of two-variable relationships and lower-order interactions. The higher-order interactions between four and more variables must be handled by the teacher as artist. (20)

The artistry that Gage describes is infused in the teacher's judgment of what *this* situation at *this* time calls for. Paradoxically, as more generalizations are created through research on teaching, more rather than less artistry will be demanded from the teacher. One aspect of such artistry is great particularity in perception, what I call connoisseurship (Eisner 1991).

One possible response to this paradox is to expect that one day something like a limited array of powerful macrogeneralizations derived from the empirical study of teaching will be created. This limited array will diminish the burden on teachers because a few generalizations will do the work of many. Aside from the improbable quality of such an expectation, the drift of research on teaching is currently toward the rediscovery of the importance of subject matter in teaching. This creates an even greater need for particularity. Although Charles Hubbard Judd wrote a book in 1915 on the psychology of school subjects, the aim of research on teaching through the 1970s was to try to understand teaching as a process that was content-free; that is, a process that could be improved and understood without reference to what was being taught. Shulman's (1987) work on teaching and Stodolsky's (1988) book *The Subject Matters* are predicated on the view that the subject does, indeed, matter.

Once the subject enters our research paradigm, we are in a position to partition generalizations about teaching. Once this partitioning is done, generalizations take on validity as they pertain to the teaching of something. In one sense, we have fewer generalizations, but in another sense, we have more. We can expect that some generalizations will hold for some subjects but not for others.

But the problem is not so simple. What one is teaching is not identical to something called a subject matter. As Schwab pointed out in 1969, there are a dozen versions of the social studies and five orientations to mathematics, and the fine arts can be taught from a wide variety of perspectives for a diverse set of ends. To paraphrase Gertrude Stein, a subject is not a subject is not a subject. Once we recognize the plurality of approaches to the teaching of any subject—and by approaches, I mean what is aimed at, what constitutes appropriate content, and how this content should or should not be related to other fields—generalizations, too, must become more numerous. Again, even greater particularity. The question of what a relevant generalization is for teaching children to memorize the multiplication tables fades into oblivion if memorization is no longer considered an important aim in mathematics education. In other words, conceptualizing teaching within a subject matter requires far more than identifying a body of content. It requires situating that content within an educational context, and this means, among other things, understanding its educational function.

The point of my analysis is not to reject the search for generalizations—we need them in all walks of life, not merely in trying to achieve effective and responsible teaching—but rather to illuminate the complexity with which we are dealing and to increase our appreciation of those fine teachers who by dint of artistry in teaching somehow manage to be both effective and responsible.

One comment with respect to the art of teaching: whether we refer to what teachers do when they effectively handle classroom complexities as intuitive, as employing the wisdom of practice, or as engaging in the craft or art of teaching, it is clear that such aspects of the teacher's performance are of critical importance. It is especially ironic, therefore, that in none of the three handbooks of research on teaching is there any index entry on the art of teaching. The latest handbook (Wittrock 1986), for example, has 880 main index entries, and although there is indeed an entry pertaining to art, it refers to the teaching of art, not to the art of teaching. The virtual absence of attention to artistry in teaching dramatizes a critical aspect of the teacher's work that needs attention and at the same time reveals something about the assumptions with which we work.

Another area of expectations for research on teaching is its potential role in guiding the teacher's perception and interpretation of classroom events. All research on teaching or on any other aspect of educational practice is rooted in schemata of one kind or another that parse practice in particular ways. Schemata gain their power both from the windows that they provide and from the walls that they create to obstruct our vision. Put less metaphorically, schemata define what will count as relevant while at the same time they neglect other potentially important candidates for perception. These reciprocal functions—concealing and revealing—make particular classroom phenomena vivid. Wait time, for example, becomes an important candidate for attention as this aspect of the teacher's behavior is noticed and labeled. Time on task becomes important for the same reason. Researchers on teaching notice what they believe matters and assign it a name. Once named, it can be shared; once shared, it can become a part of our cognitive lexicon, a device that we use to look for the named qualities.

One virtue of schemata is that they can be used flexibly. One vice is that schemata are often used with little attention to the particular context in which the teacher functions. For example, increasing wait time is usually regarded as beneficial for students, but surely there are significant exceptions to that general expectation. How long to wait depends on the contextual conditions in which longer or shorter wait times are appropriate. These conditions are not a part of the schema, nor are they a part of the generalization about wait time or time on task. We could not deal with the vast number of subgeneralizations that specified the contingencies under which different amounts of time were appropriate. To assume that more time is better is a bit too simple.

The same caveats apply to time on task. Optimal conditions for learning might very well require *time off task*. Furthermore, whether time on task is a virtue depends, at least, on the kind of task one is on: Relief from an assigned academic task might be exactly what students need. When schemata are treated as decontextualized rules, their potential utility for improving learning is diluted.

The point of the foregoing is that even when structures as potentially flexible as schemata are used, individual pedagogical judgments must still be made. Such judgments depend on context sensitivity. Thus, the boon in using schemata in teaching—which we must inevitably employ in any case—is their contribution to focus. The bane is their potential for limiting our sight. But even when schematas are numerous and refined and our awareness of relevant classroom phenomena large, no set of schemata, regardless of how large, can encompass the particular configuration of phenomena or the competing educational values that a teacher must reconcile. The reconciliation of two competing goods that at a particular pedagogical moment may be mutually exclusive is not an uncommon pedagogical task: do I call on Harry and give him a momentary place in the sun even though I suspect that his response will lead the discussion astray, or do I neglect Harry and call on Mary, who is likely to keep the discussion on track but who at this moment does not need a place in the sun?

There is one other complication that I wish to mention regarding the use of schemata in teaching. When talking about teaching, there is a tendency to regard schemata as structures through which meditative processes called decision making occur. In fact, some educational researchers have likened this process to a kind of hypothesis testing, a form of scientific experiment. While the forms of reflection implied by an extended form of decision making might be appropriate for those domains of teaching that Jackson (1986) refers to as preactive, interactive teaching, the kind of teaching that occurs when teachers are working directly with students seldom provides time for reflective deliberation. As Clark (1990), Schoen (1983), and others have pointed out, much of what teachers do in *the context of action* has an immediacy about it that differs qualitatively from the type of reflection exercised in *the context of planning*. I believe that in the context of action, the perception of qualities displayed by students is immediate. In some ways, as is the case with the highly skilled soccer player, there is no time for extended deliberation. The action must be instantaneous and on target. My observations of teachers suggest to me that not only do they possess a variety of schemata for seeing what is important, an observation that Berliner (1986) has emphasized in his work on the expert pedagogue, but they also have a broad repertoire of moves with which to quickly and gracefully act on the situation that they see. If my observations about schemata are plausible, we can ask how schemata become a part of the iconic structures that make the identification of particular classroom conditions recognizable. How does one move from linguistically portrayed schemata to their application?

I believe that this application occurs by one's acquisition of referents for the schematic structures that one learns. For example, the words *retroactive inhibition* cannot be meaningful without an image of what the words themselves point to, and one cannot secure such an image without some form of association, either through a direct empirical connection or through language sufficiently vivid to enable the reader to envision what the words mean. Extended further, this line of argument suggests that the possession of what Broudy (1987) has called a rich *allusionary base* is at the root of expert perception and that it is through this perceptual expertise that action follows. That is why, I think, someone can possess expertise without possessing a set of technical linguistic terms with which to label the conditions or qualities on which the expert acts. Following Michael Polyani (1967), we do seem to know more than we can tell.

There are two other options that we can consider for expectations pertaining to the potential contributions of research on teaching: its diagnostic potential and its usefulness in constructively undermining simplistic conceptions of causal relationships in teaching, conceptions that lead to dysfunctional prescriptions for teachers. I address each briefly.

The ways in which schemata and generalizations from research on teaching might be used to enhance practice are embedded in some of the issues that I have already addressed. To the extent to which research provides practice-relevant schemata for seeing and explaining what teachers and children do in classrooms, these schemata call to our attention what we might look for and how we might interpret what we see. As long as the caveats that I have provided are taken into account, the creation of new schemata that help us see what is occurring in classrooms is a nontrivial aspect of school improvement. Images related to terms such as *turn taking, set induction, advance organizers, null curriculum,* and *forms of representation,* as well as *time on task* and *wait time,* are tools in our perceptual arsenal. They are resources for noticing what we might not otherwise see. What they cannot do is provide prescriptions for practitioners in a form indifferent to the context in which practitioners work. In short, the conceptual devices that researchers use to study teaching can function as "perceptual maps" for seeing, but they ought not to become recipes for performance or criteria for evaluating the value of the terrain.

I emphasize this point because in the United States, there is a strong tendency, particularly in bureaucracies, to create lists of so-called research-proven teaching behaviors for use in evaluating teachers. The states of Georgia, Texas, and Florida justify their use of such lists by citing research studies. Such practices commit the *fallacy of constituency*—that is, they operate on the belief that the presence of discrete constituent elements constitutes a successful whole. What constitutes a successful whole, given a particular set of values, depends on how the constituent elements are composed, not their mere presence. The fact that Mozart used a particular number of F-sharps and B-flats in his Jupiter Symphony is no assurance whatsoever that if we used the same number, our own symphony would be as wonderful as his. In human affairs, both the configuration of elements and attention to nuance are critical. The schemata that research on teaching provides can enable us to notice those configurations and to see those nuances in the individual teaching performance of particular teachers.

The last research option that I will identify is an orthogenic one. Research on teaching can undermine simplistic conceptions of what effective teaching consists of when it does justice to the complexity of a complex act and when it provides a more replete analogue of what is involved in teaching. Research on teaching has debilitating effects when it oversimplifies and reduces the complexity of teaching and when it decontextualizes research conclusions and uses them to prescribe "what works" or "what research tells us."

My comments about using research findings to tell teachers what they should be doing should not be interpreted to mean that research findings cannot provide teachers with useful leads or ideas. Rather, my comments are aimed at prescriptions about what teachers should do in their own classrooms that are made by both researchers on teaching and bureaucrats in the field of education without considering, as they seldom can from their offices in universities and bureaucracies, what the context is. We hear, for example, from one researcher (Rosenshine 1976) that to teach skills efficiently, teachers should follow a particular sequence of steps. We hear from other students of teaching (Hunter 1982) that six enumerated processes are what teachers should engage in. We hear from still others that good teachers do such and such or that such and such elements are what effective teaching consists of. How many model prescriptions are there? Mastery teaching, cooperative learning, individualized instruction, the Madeline Hunter method, inductive teaching—one could go on and on. The sheer number of prescriptions is sufficient to engender more than a little skepticism among experienced teachers whose experience tells them that, as we say in the United States, there is more than one way to skin a cat.

The major focus of my remarks so far has been on the practices and forms of cognition that teachers employ when they teach, what teachers do in the course of their work as it unfolds in their classrooms. The theme of this volume, however, is effective and responsible teaching. The improvement of teaching that the terms *effective* and *responsible* suggest will require more than insightful generalizations about correlated variables, refined forms of perception, or new and more practice-sensitive schemata with which teachers might think about what they do when they teach. It will require attention to the institutional conditions in which teachers and students work and the effects of those conditions on how they function in schools. It is to this final topic that I now turn.

The Context of Teaching

To convey to prospective teachers, or even to experienced ones, the fruits of research in the expectation that such knowledge will alter what they do in their classroom is too simple. The primary feature of human behavior is its adaptive nature. We accommodate ourselves to the demands of the environment when we cannot change it. Schools are places that are difficult to change. What kinds of adaptations must secondary school teachers make to the fact that they must teach a different class every fifty minutes? What does such a structural requirement impose on students? Is there any other occupation that you can think of in which every fifty minutes a person changes jobs, moves to another location, and works under the direction of a new supervisor? This is precisely what we ask adolescent students to do, and this request has implications for what teachers do.

Consider the issue of feedback to teachers about their teaching. In most schools, teachers are afforded very little discretionary time: they are with students almost all day. This virtual absence of discretionary time makes it almost impossible under typical school conditions for teachers to observe their colleagues teaching. Since teaching is, in part, a skilled form of human performance, and since complex skills profit from coaching, where is the coaching of teaching provided for in schools? In U. S. public schools it is rare, although there is one place where it is even rarer: U. S. universities. Thus, time for planning is difficult for teachers to secure, and useful, sympathetic, and critical feedback is largely unavailable. Principals, those whom we might expect to provide it, are often preoccupied with other, less important matters.

One resource used to assist teachers is what is called inservice education. This practice consists of having teachers attend conferences or institutes to listen to experts talk about what they ought to do in their own classrooms. The problem, however, is that the experts (often university professors who have not been in schools for years) have never seen the teachers whom they advise teach. How does one know what advice to give? Do we expect voice coaches to give advice to singers whom they have never heard sing? How does one discern individual teachers' strengths and weaknesses? Is it realistic to expect that teachers will be able to apply what they have been told by visiting experts, or will their well-internalized teaching routines and the conventional norms and structural conditions that permeate their schools override the innovations that are being recommended to them?

Is it realistic to expect teachers to engage in the time-consuming features of inductive teaching when they are going to be held responsible for covering the curriculum? Is it reasonable to expect teachers to emphasize higher-order questioning when the norm-referenced tests that their students will take emphasize recall? Can teachers be expected to make intellectual connections between what they teach and what their colleagues teach when they work in a departmentalized school structure that makes it difficult to know what their colleagues teach? My point here is that the infrastructure of schools creates a powerful set of conditions to which most teachers adapt. There are some teachers, to be sure, who manage to overcome the organizational conditions imposed on them, but most teachers adapt to such conditions or leave teaching. One way to leave teaching is to find work outside the field of education. Another is to become a school administrator.

The constraints of the organizational structures that I have described include some of the aspects of schooling that affect teaching performance, but clearly not all of them. For example, there are also the conditions that Dreeben (1968) identifies in his book *On What Is Learned in School.* Dreeben's major point is that schools are agencies intended to facilitate the child's transition from dependency on adults in the context of the home to the acquisition of the social competencies needed to function as an adult in society. Schools, Dreeben argues, teach much that is not and cannot be taught pedagogically. The so-called hidden curriculum is a program that shapes learning because of the ways in which schooling is structured. Organizing children into homogeneous age groups, for example, increases the sense of competition among them. Emphasizing the norms of competition and achievement makes assistance to others a form of cheating. Learning the norm of universalism is fostered by being treated as a unit within a category. This is very much a part of what it means to be a student in school. Learning to accept, even prize, grades given by others for tasks that others assign, even though the tasks may be neither satisfying nor meaningful, is another lesson that schools teach.

Many of these lessons, once learned, are in fact conducive to socialization toward adulthood. In this sense, schools are indeed effective teachers. Whether they are responsible teachers depends on one's views of the norms that schools emphasize as well as one's views of the norms salient in the society. Successful socialization to norms that are themselves intellectually problematic is not a good way to define responsible teaching.

My point here is that the improvement of teaching is not likely to occur unless the conditions of schooling change. It is utopian to believe that large-scale improvement in teaching performance is likely in a social organization that itself teaches students lessons that are questionable and that constrains what teachers, at their best, wish to do. Making it possible for teachers to be educationally effective and morally responsible will require more than research on teaching. It will also require attention to the organizational and social structure of the school. Thus, the mission of those who wish to improve teaching must include the creation of schools that make fostering the growth of teachers almost as important as fostering the growth of students. From this perspective, the major locus of teacher education is not the university, the teacher training college, or textbooks and research journals. It is the school itself. We have yet to take this task seriously. Until we do, I have little confidence that small, piecemeal efforts will have the impact that we desire. What is called for is not only a theory of teaching but *a theory of schooling,* one that will situate the teacher and the process of teaching within a social configuration. Such a theory will not only help us understand why teachers do what they do; it will help us create the kind of schools that children will come to love.

16

Preparing Teachers for the Twenty-first Century

There are few subjects in the educational literature that have received more attention than the preparation of teachers. Virtually all of this literature is pervaded by the belief that central to the education of children is the competence of teachers, a belief that is as intuitively right as it is unsurprising. What is surprising is the inattention paid to the idea that what constitutes competence in teaching is intimately connected with the kind of education that we think students should receive. Put another way, what we want teachers to be able to do is related to the aspirations we hold for our children. And what aspirations do we hold for our children? What kind of outcomes do we seek? What kind of people do we hope they will become?

In the United States such questions do not have uniform and tidy answers. Nor is there public consensus—beyond the so-called basics—concerning priorities, direction, and manner in education. In many ways this lack of consensus is a strength rather than a weakness. Diversity in education breeds social complexity and social complexity can lead to a richness in culture that uniformity can never provide. What democratic cultures need is unity in diversity; both are necessary. In holding this view concerning the virtues of pluralism in education, I believe I am in a professional minority. There is in the United States a major effort now under way to create a national consensus on the goals and standards for American schools.[1] Indeed, many believe that American schools are not as good as they should be because as a nation we have not had national goals or standards for our schools. Once such goals and standards are formulated then systemic processes can be employed to achieve them. As a result, our students will become competitive with students in other countries.

206

This position concerning the need for common national outcomes and national means through which those outcomes can be measured has a comfortable, rational ring to it. The conventional means-ends model of educational planning seems to make all kinds of good sense. Uniform national goals and assessment reduce complexity and make monitoring and management possible—or so it is believed. At the same time, I would remind us that there is no single correct conception of the pedagogical purposes of any subject matter. History and chemistry, mathematics and the arts, geography and economics can all be taught for different purposes. And legitimately so. Furthermore, there is substantial variability regarding the characteristics of the populations the schools serve. These differences pertain to matters of ethnicity and to class differences, to differences in traditions, to differences in locale and climate, and to differences concerning the expectations that parents in particular and the community in general have for students. Historically, such diversity was considered a strength in America, not a weakness. But since schools in the United States have been judged to be weak according to international test comparisons of student performance, the tendency has been to tighten up, to reduce local discretion, and to prescribe what it is that teachers should accomplish.

My aim, however, is not to describe national reform policies in education in the United States but rather to examine the kind of education that teachers might receive to help students to deal with the vicissitudes of the century before them. I shall have three major topics. The first pertains to the uses and limits of theory, the second to the school as an educative environment for teachers, and the third to the ecological character of schools. I turn now to the uses and limits of theory.

Educators, particularly those working in universities, have traditionally felt uneasy about their status as scholars within the university community. Among the fields taught within universities, the field of education does not enjoy a high status. Partly because of this feeling of low status, educators have tried to legitimate their place in the university community by creating a respectable basis for practice. This basis is and has been a scientific one, the idea being that if educational researchers were able to emulate the work of their higher status colleagues in the natural sciences, their status would rise and teachers could distance themselves from the belief that their work was "merely" a craft. If educational researchers could develop sophisticated scientific theories of teaching and learning, of curriculum planning and evaluation, of school organization and the design of instructional materials, it would be possible not only to produce systematic ways to increase professional effectiveness, but to achieve academic respect as well.

During the past quarter century, it has become increasingly clear that theory as a guide for teaching has its limits.[2] No single theory, indeed no combination of theories in the social sciences, can ever be adequate for dealing with the highly contextualized and particularistic decisions that must be made by individual teachers in specific classrooms. Theories portray idealized relationships.[3] These relationships are statistical relationships and are always less complex than the specific contexts and decisions teachers have to make and the particular contexts within which they must work. Furthermore, theory, by definition, is both conscious and linguistic. When someone has a theory of something, someone has a conception that can be described in propositional form. But as we have come to realize, there is much that we know how to do for which we have tacit rather than theoretical knowledge. (Polanyi 1967) Tacit knowledge is intuitive; it is personal; it is experiential in character; it is often qualitative in form. It is a form of knowledge that often is secured in the context of action; it is knowledge that depends upon having direct experience with the phenomena, and which enables one to make effective decisions "in flight." These decisions may not have a theoretical justification but nevertheless may be educationally effective and intuitively right.

This new realization in education concerning the importance of tacit knowledge—new being a quarter of a century in length—has increasingly turned the attention of educational researchers to the use of narrative, such as teacher stories about teaching, as a way of understanding what teachers know when they act. Why narrative? Because stories get at forms of understanding that cannot be reduced to measurement or to scientific explanation.

In his writing on the meaning of meaning, Jerome Bruner (1990) makes a distinction between two ways of knowing: paradigmatic knowledge and narrative understanding. Narrative understanding is fostered through stories while paradigmatic knowledge is generated through scientific explanations. Bruner's distinction is related to the German terms *Naturwissenschaften* and *Geisteswissenschaften;* the former is scientific, the latter humanistic. As a result of this pluralization of knowledge, literary and artistically crafted narratives have become increasingly important both as sources of understanding teaching by researchers and as resources that teachers might use to improve their own teaching. The following books are examples of this kind of narrative approach to understanding: *Untaught Lessons* (Jackson 1992); *Teachers as Curriculum Planners* (Connelly and Clandinen 1988), *The Call of Stories* (Cole 1989); *The Enlightened Eye* (Eisner 1991), and *Transformative Curriculum* (Henderson in press). There are scores of other books, but these are representative.

The implications of this reconceptualization of the sources of human understanding are profound. In the past, researchers aspired to develop educational theories that would prescribe teaching practices. For decades in America the aim of educational researchers and school administrators was to find the one best method (Tyack 1974). Time and motion studies and scientific management are examples (Callahan 1962). Another example is related to the model used in agriculture. In this model the research biologist who worked in the university produced the knowledge, an extension agent brought this knowledge to the farmer, the farmer implemented the recommendations made by the extension agent and, as a result, greater yield per acre was achieved. That model was used for years as the way to conduct and disseminate educational research. Teachers were thought to be like farmers who waited for technical input from their higher-up colleagues working in universities.

I am happy to say that we have begun to discard such naive conceptions of change. Newer and more adequate views place greater responsibility on the teacher as someone who needs to make good decisions in the context of action. These views recognize the limits of theory in guiding teaching and emphasize the importance of what some have called "insider" knowledge (Atkin 1989).

When I speak of the limits of theory I do not want to convey the idea that theory has no place in the preparation of teachers or that traditional research forms have no place in education. This is not the case at all. What I do wish to emphasize is that theory has limitations and can never replace sensitive, in-context judgment; theory is a tool to use, not a rule to follow. The hunt for the one best method was always a mistake. There is no single best way to teach. Furthermore, what constitutes excellence in teaching depends on some of the considerations I mentioned at the outset of my remarks, that is, on what vision of education one has and what conception of culture one wishes to realize. That is why the visions and values of the community are so important.

Thus, the first point I wish to make pertains to the relatively new realization that we are not likely to have a psychophysics of teaching. Teaching always occurs in highly contextual situations; there is not now nor will there be a replacement for the teacher who understands which course of action and which decision is most appropriate in *this* particular circumstance at *this* particular time. Put another way, artistry and intuition are enormously important aspects of all forms of teaching and teachers need the space and encouragement to use both in their work (Eisner 1991).

The development of such insight and the cultivation of such artistry bring me to the second consideration in the preparation of teachers. How is it that one can develop artistry and insight in teachers? It is all very good to say that we should rely on stories, on narrative, on personal experience, but how should teachers be prepared and where should this preparation occur?

Teacher preparation has historically been located within normal schools and, since the turn of the century in the United States, increasingly in universities. Students who finished secondary school and wanted to be teachers went to normal schools, others went to universities and entered teacher education programs. Although we have very few normal schools left in the United States, the pattern is largely the same. Students wishing to become teachers enroll in undergraduate programs in universities, take courses in education either before or after they graduate, do student teaching, and then apply for state certification as a teacher. Teacher education is seen as the responsibility of the university. Teacher education programs are accredited by state and regional accrediting agencies and a field devoted essentially to the preparation of teachers at the preservice level has become very strong.

The idea that teacher education is and should be primarily a function of the university is a strong and widely held belief in almost all countries. Yet, I want to argue that the major locus of teacher education is not the university—it is the primary and secondary school.

What we have tried to do in the university is to prepare young people from nineteen to twenty-one years of age to be teachers. Teacher education programs have been and are designed to certify competence, while the state issues the license. Once teachers begin to teach, they have an opportunity, from time to time, to have something called inservice education. Inservice education usually means that someone who has a specialization in some area of education will talk to teachers about how to improve their own work. It is almost always the case that the person providing such advice has never seen the teachers to whom he or she speaks teach, a practice that is like hiring a football coach who had never seen the team play advise a team of players on how to play. What we would find strange in football we do in education.

The conception of teacher education that I am putting forward differs radically from standard preservice or inservice education. The conception I am advancing conceives of the school itself as a major locus for the professional development of the professional staff—and this includes the principal of the school as well. For this conception to occur in practice, a number of very significant changes need to be made. Some of these changes are conceptual, others are practical. First, it must be recognized that learning to teach is a lifelong professional activity, not something that one completes in a teacher training program; teacher training programs provide an initiation into teaching, not a culmination. Second, it must be recognized that what matters most in learning to teach is the twenty-five years that someone spends in school as a teacher, not the year and a half that someone spends in the university learning to teach. Third, it must be recognized that in order to get better at the complex and subtle art of teaching, one needs to have constructive feedback on one's work. Fourth, it must be recognized that for useful feedback to occur, two other conditions must be present. First, there needs to be in each school a professional norm in which getting better at teaching is a part of what it means to be a teacher in that school. Second, there needs to be an organizational structure that makes it possible for other teachers to see how their colleagues teach. The reason this is important is because it is very difficult to be adequately self-reflective about one's own performance as a teacher. We are too close to ourselves to really grasp what we do when we work with students or deal with others. What I think we need to do is to create a professional climate in schools in which teachers learn how to see and critique teaching. This can be done initially through the critique of videotapes of teachers at work and later through the live observation and feedback one gets about one's own teaching from colleagues.[4]

When one considers that even the best of performers—Luciano Pavarotti, for example—use coaches and critics to help them learn how they are performing, it does not seem to me to be far-fetched that schools provide a similar form of feedback to those engaged in the complex and subtle art of teaching.

To do this well, of course, will require that those who provide such feedback be perceptive about the complexities of classroom life and of teaching performance. This in itself is a formidable challenge. Yet, it is a challenge that can be addressed. What I have called *educational connoisseurship* (Eisner 1991) in my own writing about educational research is the act of learning how to see and understand how teachers teach and what students learn in classrooms. It is an appreciative art, similar in some respects to learning how to see a football game, a polo match, a play, or how to really hear music. Connoisseurship is a learnable skill having to do with the appreciation of subtle and complex forms of performance. Connoisseurship provides the basis for what follows. What follows educational connoisseurship is what I call *educational criticism*.

When I use the term criticism I do not mean saying nasty things about how people behave. I am talking about providing constructive feedback on performance. There are critics of literature, art critics, music critics, dance critics, film critics, critics of architecture, food critics, and social critics. All of these critics are concerned with making judgments and conveying those judgments to others either through speech or text. The aim of criticism is to expand our awareness of what we might not have noticed. For teachers to become aware of how they are functioning, they need the assistance of those who are able to see and share with them what they see going on.

Incidentally, such feedback to teachers by teachers is not only useful for those who receive the feedback, it is also useful for those doing the observation. Often the teacher doing the observation learns as much about teaching as the person who receives information from the observer. Thus, the second point that I wish to make is that in conceiving of the school as the primary locus of teacher education, I am talking about a school that has professional norms that support the practice of educational criticism and that possesses an organizational structure that makes it possible for teachers to see and to talk with each other about their work.

In most cases, we have structured schools in ways that isolate teachers from other adults and that do not provide much assistance. In fact, if we wanted to design schools that made it difficult for teachers to learn about their own work, we could not do better than what we have done. The current conditions of schools will have to change in order to genuinely prepare teachers for the coming century. This will require a major change in our conception of who is responsible for teacher education.

In talking about the importance of the school as the center for teacher education I do not mean to say that university teacher education programs have no important responsibility in this matter. They do. Universities ought to initiate prospective teachers into the leading ideas of the field of education and into the particular specialty in which they work. Universities ought to provide prospective teachers with cutting-edge visions of educational possibilities; they ought to help them imagine what is not now, but what might be. In addition, they ought to provide the initiating conditions through which prospective teachers could gain at least rudimentary skills to function in a classroom.

However, as important as the university is, it is my view that its role is secondary. Universities provide the initiating conditions, but it is the school that can and ought to provide the long-term context for the development of teaching competence and the intellectual climate for teachers to grow as reflective professionals.

I turn now to the third topic relevant to the preparation of teachers for the century before us: the ecological character of schools.

We have a tendency, those of us who specialize in some aspect of education, to see the improvement of education as belonging primarily to our specialization. If we are teacher educators, we ground the improvement of education in the improvement of teacher education. If we are curriculum specialists, we tend to argue for the importance of improved curricula as a major condition for the improvement of learning. If we are educational psychologists, we study cognitive processes and argue for the importance of understanding cognition in order to improve instruction. If we are school administrators, we talk about the importance of educational leadership. If we are evaluation specialists, we see the improvement of education as being closely tied to the sorts of assessment devices that are used in schools. In short, we think about school improvement as if our specialty were the key.

One of the things that we have learned in the past two decades is that schools are *ecological* institutions (Eisner 1988). By ecological institutions I mean that just as the heart within the body is influenced by the health of the lungs, the pancreas, and the liver, so too is teaching influenced by a complex of factors that collectively constitute schooling: time, space, work-load, expectation, and the like. Furthermore, just as the organs of the body are influenced by the environment that the human inhabits, so too is the school influenced by its environment: the community and the culture in which it resides. Put as simply as possible, school improvement—and there-fore the improvement of education for students—requires attention to a complex interacting set of living relationships. Ecology is perhaps the best metaphor that I can use to characterize these living, interacting relationships. Just what are the relationships within the school that need attention if teachers in the twenty-first century are to be able to do the kind of job that we would want to have done?

I would like to identify five dimensions that I believe to be criti-cally important. I will speak of each very briefly. These five dimensions are called the *intentional,* the *structural,* the *curricular,* the *pedagogical,* and the *evaluative.*

The intentional pertains to the aims to which the institution is directed. Just what is the core mission of this school? Is it to get youngsters to ingest cultural content? Is it primarily to develop an inclination or proclivity toward problem solving? Is it to nurture individual talents? Is it to socialize students into cultural norms? Is it to engender beliefs that will lead to a socially homogenous culture? Is it to enable youngsters to learn how to take responsibility for the creation of their own educational journey?

I will not specify what I believe to be most important, but what I will do is indicate that questions such as these are non-trivial and that the way they are answered has implications for the kind of educational culture that is developed within schools. Hence, the first dimension that needs attention has to do with the question: What are the major intentions of the institution or, more precisely, what are the major intentions of those who work in or support the school? In different schools there may be different intentions.

Second, intentions alone are inadequate. Schools are structures. They are organizations of time, space, and people guided by intentions. We need to understand something about the way in which schools are organized and the extent to which that organization facilitates or interferes with the realization of our intentions. For example, in most secondary schools in the United States, the subject matters students study are divided into separate courses taught by different specialists. As a result, we have a secondary school curriculum that in many ways has no sense of intellectual integration. Students study history with one teacher and then, fifty minutes later, move on to another teacher who might be teaching mathematics. Fifty minutes later the student moves on to take a class in literature. That literature class—say in American literature—may be taught in a way that makes it difficult for the student to see any relationship between his or her course in literature and his or her course in American history. In short, by isolating teachers and dividing content into disciplinary categories, curricular integration is made more efficient. In addition, the teacher is assigned to a room with twenty-eight or thirty students and is the only adult present. As a result, seldom do teachers have an opportunity to get feedback or to work cooperatively with other teachers. Ironically, teachers adjust to the physical insolation, assume it to be in the nature of things, making it even more difficult to develop a critical consciousness of their own teaching.

But structure does not pertain to time and space alone. It also includes our conception of what the role of the teacher is in a school. Our customary view of the teacher is of an adult who has responsibility for twenty-five to thirty students and who remains with those students from 8:00 or so in the morning until 2:30 to 3:00 in the afternoon. The classroom in which the teacher works becomes, for all practical purposes, the world in which the teacher lives his or her professional life. It is almost as if this conception of the teacher's responsibility in a school were God given. In fact, in virtually all schools there are essentially only two professional roles: teacher or school administrator.

I believe it is important to redefine the scope of professional work for a teacher: to diversify the sorts of responsibilities that a teacher can have in the course of a career, to make available to teachers opportunities to perform services, and to pursue professional visions within the school that would enhance the quality of education for the students who attend. This will mean making it possible for experienced teachers, for example: to devote one year out of five serving as mentors to beginning teachers; to work on curriculum development projects with one or two of their colleagues; and, to function as liaisons between the school and other community agencies such as nursing homes, cultural centers, museums, and hospitals. It means giving teachers the time needed to work together to plan evaluation projects and to be in touch with families who need assistance helping their own children in school. My point here is that what it means to be a teacher needs to be reconceived so that it includes far more than working alone in a classroom from 8:00 in the morning until 3:00 in the afternoon for twenty-five years.

In the United States, about 50 percent of those who enter the teaching profession leave after five years of teaching experience. About half of those who leave return at one time or another during the course of their professional lives. I believe that much of this attrition is due to the lack of opportunities teachers experience; the job as it is now defined is too constrained. Expanding our conception of what the work of teaching consists of is one way to keep the best and the brightest within the profession while at the same time enhancing the quality of education within the school.

In discussing the ecological character of schools, I have thus far addressed the importance of intentions and the impact of school structure on how teachers work and how students learn. What we aim to achieve and how we organize the work place are extraordinarily important factors affecting the life of school. What also needs attention, however, is the curriculum that is offered and the way in which what students have learned is evaluated.

I have already indicated that the fragmentation of learning is a problematic consequence of how we define the school curriculum. If we want to help students see the relationship between ideas within various disciplines and their application or relevance to some problem, then curricula need to be fostered upon problems that students and teachers can address, and disciplinary structures—such as biology and history, art, and mathematics—need in some way to be related to the resolution of problems they care about.

Disciplinary structures are essentially conceptual devices that amplify our cognitive abilities. They are technologies of mind, as Jerome Bruner (1990) calls them, for conceptualizing, storing, and retrieving what we have learned. These tools can be related and, I would argue, need to be related to almost all complex practical problems. Each discipline provides its own perspective that can enable students to appreciate the richness of the situation and the alternative courses of action that are almost always possible in the practical domain.

Rethinking curriculum relationships among fields has important implications for the way in which teachers are prepared and for the conditions in school within which they have to work. Isolation and integration are hardly compatible. If integrated forms of learning are to be fostered among students then teachers will need to have opportunities to work collaboratively. This will require reorganizing the structure of the school day and redefining the teacher's responsibility.

Evaluation, the fifth and last dimension I will address, also matters. In the United States we have at long last begun to realize that much of the evaluation practices that we have employed from the early part of the century to the present have depended upon a testing methodology that has trivialized education. Objective tests have been employed which had very little predictive validity in the real world. Hence, we are now developing what we call "authentic evaluation," implying that so much of what we have done before in evaluation, largely through standardized, norm-referenced, objective tests, was educationally inauthentic.

To the extent to which these new forms of assessment address forms of student performance that are directly related to the ongoing tasks within the school day or to complex projects that require them to apply and integrate disciplinary ideas, they will also make new demands on the teacher's skills. This, in turn, will require the preparation of teachers who understand the educational purposes of authentic evaluation and who have the skills needed to employ such forms of evaluation in their own classroom.

In addition, such approaches to evaluation place a greater premium on the assessment of individual outcomes than the standardized conception of outcomes that are inherently embedded in standardized measurement practices. When the major aim of the educational process is to cultivate what is personally idiosyncratic about students, teachers will need to be able to identify such uniqueness in those they teach. This will require a kind of educational connoisseurship that is sensitive to what is subtle and significant in the student's work. It will also make it difficult to make comparisons across students; when uniqueness is valued and when both teaching and curriculum are designed to make uniqueness not only possible but probable, assessment criteria other than comparing a student to other students or comparing a student's performance to a known criterion becomes necessary. Neither norm-referenced nor criterion-referenced evaluation will have the kind of significance that they now possess. Whether a tax-paying public will accept non-comparative descriptions of student performance remains to be seen.

I wish to conclude by recapitulating the major points I have tried to make. First and primary among these is that any justified conception of teacher education must be rooted in a justified conception of the kind of education that students are to receive. Second, that the major location of teacher education is not the year and a half that a nineteen- or twenty-one-year-old spends in a university teacher education program, but the twenty to twenty-five years that a teacher spends in a school; it is the school and the conditions that it makes available to its professional staff that ought to constitute the major resource for the professional development of teachers. Third, I have tried to make the case that the improvement of schools and hence the improvement of teaching and learning requires attention to what I have called the ecology of schooling.

Schools, we have learned in our largely failed effort at school reform, are robust institutions that are difficult to change. Piecemeal approaches to change are usually rendered feckless by virtue of those other powerful forces within the school that are not altered. Thus, educational reformers will need to understand how five major dimensions of schools interact. These dimensions are the intentional, the structural, the pedagogical, the curricular, and the evaluative. We need to formulate intentions we sincerely believe in, redesign school structures so they are consistent with the spirit of those intentions, address matters of pedagogy by creating an environment in which teachers get helpful feedback concerning their work, redesign curricula so that there is some sense of integration and problem-centeredness to what students study, and design evaluation practices that do not trivialize what we are trying to accomplish.

The agenda for *genuine* educational reform and significant teacher preparation for the twenty-first century is awesome. There is much work to be done. Now is not the time for pessimism. What is pessimistic concerning school improvement is an unwillingness or inability to appreciate the complexity that actually exists. What is optimistic is the ability to face up to this complexity and to begin to work together to address the challenging future before us. To do this will require us to give up old habits and traditional expectations, but in the end it might open new vistas before us. It might give us some new seas on which to sail. Isn't that what education is about, not arriving at a destination but traveling with a new view (Peters 1960)?

Notes

1. America 2000 represents a national effort to develop within a set of core subject fields a common array of goals and standards. Although these goals and standards are described as "voluntary," it will be difficult for many school districts to resist embracing these as long as they want public legitimacy for their educational efforts.

2. From my perspective a major shift has taken place in the views of many researchers concerning the sources of human understanding. Twenty years ago theory derived from the social sciences was seen as the sine qua non of intelligent action. Good teachers were expected to understand theories out of the social sciences as a way of directing their practice. At present, there is a growing realization that theoretical structures have their own inherent limitations and that matters of representation count in the way in which understanding is generated. This is opening up a broad and fresh conception of both cognition and action.

3. The ancient roots of the distinction between the sources of knowledge and the limits of

theory are found in Aristotle's distinction between the theoretical, the practical, and the productive. Theoretical knowledge was based upon relationships that existed by necessity. The practical and the productive rested upon relationships that were contingent and contextual. The modern-day exposition of this view is most acutely displayed in the important work of Joseph Schwab, particularly his work on "the practical" in curriculum.

4. The use of videotapes of classroom teaching is predicated on the ability of those viewing such tapes to be able to critically describe, interpret, and appraise what they see. Such skills depend upon educational connoisseurship. It is, in my view, both possible and desirable to develop within school districts the capacity to train teachers to effectively use such tapes.

Works Cited

Apple, M. 1982. *Education and Power.* London: Routledge & Kegan Paul.

Applebee, A. 1981. "Writing on the Secondary School: English and the Content Area." Research Report no. 21. Urbana, IL: National Council of Teachers of English.

Arnheim, R. 1990. *Notes on Art Education.* Los Angeles: J. Paul Getty Center for Education in the Arts.

————. 1985. "The Double-edged Mind: Intuition and Intellect." In *Learning and Teaching the Ways of Knowing,* edited by E. W. Eisner, 77–96. Chicago: University of Chicago Press.

————. 1969. *Visual Thinking.* Berkeley: University of California Press.

————. 1957. *Art and Visual Perception.* Berkeley: University of California Press.

Atkin, J. M. 1989. "Can Educational Research Keep Pace with Educational Reform?" *Phi Delta Kappan* 71 (3): 200–205.

Atkin, M. 1989. Curriculum Action Research: An American Perspective. American Educational Research conference, San Francisco, CA, March.

Ayer, A. J. n.d. *Language, Truth, and Logic.* New York: Dover.

Barone, T. 1983. "Things of Use and Things of Beauty: The Story of Swain County High School's Art Program." *Daedalus* 112 (3): 1–28.

Barth, R. 1985. *The Responsibility of Forms.* New York: Hill & Wang.

Bell, C. 1958. *Art.* New York: Capricorn Books.

Berlin, I. 1986. "The Concept of Scientific History." In *Philosophical Analysis and History,* edited by W. H. Dray. New York: Harper & Row.

Berliner, D. C. 1986. "In Pursuit of the Expert Pedagogue." *Educational Researcher* 15 (7): 5–13.

Bernstein, B. 1971. "On the Classification and Framing of Educational Knowledge." In *Knowledge and Control,* edited by M. Young. London: Collier-Macmillan.

Bloom, A. 1987. *The Closing of the American Mind.* New York: Simon and Schuster.

Bourdieu, P. 1977. *Reproduction in Education's Society and Culture.* London: Sage.

Broudy, H. S. 1987. "The Role of Imagery in Learning." Occasional paper no. 1, Getty Center for Education in the Arts, Los Angeles, CA.

————. 1979. "The Arts Education: Necessary or Just Nice." *Phi Delta Kappan* 60 (5): 324–50.

————. 1976. "The Search for a Science of Education." *Phi Delta Kappan* 58 (1): 104–11.

Bruner, J. 1990. *Acts of Meaning*. Cambridge, MA: Harvard University Press.

————. 1985. "Paradigmatic and Narrative Modes of Knowing." In *Teaching and Learning the Ways of Knowing*. 84th Yearbook of the National Society for the Study of Education, edited by E. W. Eisner. Chicago: University of Chicago Press.

————. 1961. *The Process of Education*. Cambridge, MA: Harvard University Press.

Callahan, R. 1962. *Education and the Cult of Efficiency*. Chicago: University of Chicago Press.

Case, R. In press. "Neo-Piagetian Theories of Child Development." In *Intellectual Development*, edited by R. J. Steinberg and C. A. Berg. New York: Cambridge University Press.

Cassirer, E. 1961. *The Philosophy of Symbolic Forms*. New Haven: Yale University Press.

Clark, C. 1990. "What You Can Learn from Applesauce: A Case of Qualitative Inquiry in Use." In *Qualitative Inquiry in Education: The Continuing Debate*, edited by E. W. Eisner and A. Peshkin. New York: Teachers College Press.

Cole, M. 1985. "Mind as a Cultural Achievement: Implications for I.Q. Testing." In *Learning and Teaching the Ways of Knowing*, edited by E. W. Eisner, 218–49. Chicago: University of Chicago Press.

Cole, R. 1989. *The Call of Stories*. Boston: Houghton Mifflin.

Collingwood, R. G. 1958. *The Principles of Art*. New York: Oxford University Press.

Connolly, M., and J. Clandinen. 1988. *Teachers as Curriculum Planners*. New York: Teachers College Press.

Cronbach, L. 1975. "Beyond the Two Disciplines of Scientific Psychology." *The American Psychologist* 30 (2): 116–27.

Cuban, L. 1990. "Reforming Again, Again, and Again." *Educational Researcher* 19 (1): 3–13.

Dewey, J. 1938. *Experience and Education*. New York: Macmillan.

————. 1934. *Art as Experience*. New York: Minton, Balch and Co.

Dreeben, R. 1968. *On What Is Learned in School*. Reading, MA: Addison-Wesley.

Du Pont, S. 1992. "The Effectiveness of Creative Drama as an Instructional Strategy to Enhance the Reading Skills of Fifth Grade Readers." *Reading Research and Instruction* 31 (3): 41–52.

Eisner, E. W. 1994. *Cognition and Curriculum Reconsidered*. New York: Teachers College Press.

————. 1991. *The Enlightened Eye: Qualitative Inquiry and the Enhancement of Educational Practice*. New York: Macmillan.

————. 1988a. "The Ecology of School Improvement." *Educational Leadership* 45 (5).

————. 1988b. "The Primacy of Experience and the Politics of Method." *Educational Researcher* 17 (5): 15–20.

————. 1986. *What High Schools Are Like: Views from the Inside*. Stanford, CA: Stanford University School of Education.

————. 1985. *The Educational Imagination: On the Design and Evaluation of Education Programs*. 2d ed. New York: Macmillan.

————. 1983. "The Art and Craft of Teaching." *Educational Leadership* 40 (4): 4–13.

————. 1982. *Cognition and Curriculum: A Basis for Deciding What to Teach*. New York: Longman.

————. 1969. "Instructional and Expressive Educational Objectives: Their Formulation and the Use of Curriculum." In *Instructional Objectives*, AERA Monograph Series on Curriculum Evaluation by W. J. Popham et al. Chicago: Rand McNally.

Elkind, D. 1981. *The Hurried Child: Growing Up Too Fast Too Soon*. Reading, MA: Addison-Wesley.

Elliott, J. 1986. *Action Research in Classrooms and Schools.* London: Allen and Unwin.

Epstein, T. 1989. An Aesthetic Approach to the Study of Teaching and Learning in the Social Studies. Doctoral dissertation, Harvard University, Cambridge, MA.

Erickson, F. 1982. *The Counselor as Gatekeeper.* New York: Academic Press.

Flinders, D. 1987. What Teachers Learn from Teaching: Educational Outcomes of Instructional Adaptation. Doctoral dissertation, Stanford University, Stanford, CA.

Forseth, S. 1980. "Art Activities, Attitudes, and Achievement in Elementary Mathematics." *Studies in Art Education* 21 (2): 22–27.

Fry, R. 1947. *Vision and Design.* New York: P. Smith.

Gage, N. 1978. *The Scientific Basis of the Art of Teaching.* New York: Teachers College Press.

Gardner, H. 1989. *To Open Minds.* New York: Basic Books.

———. 1983. *Frames of Mind: The Theory of Multiple Intelligence.* New York: Basic Books.

Gavin, W. 1986. William James and the Need to Preserve "the Vague." Speech given at the University of Southern Maine, Portland, ME.

Geertz, C. 1988. *Works and Lives: The Anthropologist as Author.* Stanford, CA: Stanford University Press.

———. 1973. *The Interpretation of Cultures.* New York: Basic Books.

Giroux, H. A. 1989. *Critical Pedagogy, the State, and Cultural Struggle.* Albany: State University of New York Press.

———. 1983. *Theory and Resistance in Education.* South Hadley, MA: Bergin & Garvey.

———. 1981. *Ideology, Culture, and the Process of Schooling.* Philadelphia: Temple University Press.

Glaser, B. G., and A. Strauss. 1967. *The Discovery of Grounded Theory.* Chicago: Aldine.

Goodlad, J. I. 1984. *A Place Called School: Prospects for the Future.* New York: McGraw-Hill.

Goodlad, J. I., and R. Anderson. 1987. *The Non-graded Elementary School.* Rev. ed. New York: Teachers College Press.

Goodman, N. 1978. *Ways of Worldmaking.* Indianapolis: Hackett.

———. 1976. *The Languages of Art: An Approach to a Theory of Symbols.* 2d ed. Indianapolis: Hackett.

Greene, M. 1988. *The Dialectic of Freedom.* New York: Teachers College Press.

———. 1978. *Landscapes of Learning.* New York: Teachers College Press.

Greeno, J. 1989. "Perspectives on Thinking." *American Psychologist* 44 (2): 134–41.

Hadamard, J. 1945. *An Essay on the Psychology of Invention in the Mathematical Field.* Princeton, NJ: Princeton University Press.

Hamblen, K. 1993. "Theories and Research That Support Art Instruction for Instrumental Outcomes." *Theory into Practice* 32 (4): 191–98.

Hanson, N. R. 1971. *Observation and Explanation: A Guide to Philosophy of Science.* New York: Harper & Row.

Harding, S. 1991. *Whose Science? Whose Knowledge?* Ithaca, NY: Cornell University Press.

Harnischfeger, A., and D. Wiley. 1975. *Achievement Test Scores Decline: Do We Need to Worry?* Chicago: CEMREL.

Henderson, J. In press. *Transformative Curriculum.* New York: Macmillan.

Hirsch, E. D., Jr. 1989. *Dictionary of Cultural Literacy.* Boston: Houghton Mifflin.

———. 1987. *Cultural Literacy: What Every American Needs to Know.* Boston: Houghton Mifflin.

Holton, G. J. 1982. *Albert Einstein: Historical and Cultural Perspectives.* Princeton, NJ: Princeton University Press.

Hughes, L. 1958. *The Langston Hughes Reader.* New York: Braziller.

Hunter, M. 1982. *Mastery Teaching*. El Segundo, CA: TIP Publications.

Jackson, P. 1992. *Untaught Lessons*. New York: Teachers College Press.

———. 1986. *The Practice of Teaching*. New York: Teachers College Press.

———. 1968. *Life in Classrooms*. New York: Holt, Rinehart & Winston.

James, W. 1980. *The Principles of Psychology*. New York: Holt.

Jensen, A. R. 1969. "How Much Can We Boost IQ and Scholastic Achievement?" *Harvard Educational Review* 39 (1): 1–123.

Johnson, M. 1987. *The Body in the Mind*. Chicago: University of Chicago Press.

Jončich, G. 1968. *The Sane Positivist*. Middletown, CT: Wesleyan University Press.

Judd, C. H. 1915. *Psychology of High School Subjects*. Boston: Ginn.

Kagan, D. M. 1985. "The Heuristic Value of Regarding Classroom Instruction as an Aesthetic Medium." *Educational Researcher* 2 (6): 11–17.

Keller, E. F. 1983. *A Feeling for the Organism*. San Francisco: Freedman.

Kentucky Alliance for Arts Education. 1990. "Building a Case for Art Education: An Annotated Bibliography of Major Research."

Kozol, J. 1992. *Savage Inequalities*. New York: Crown.

———. 1968. *Death at an Early Age*. New York: Bantam.

Kubie, L. 1961. *Neurotic Distortion of the Creative Process*. New York: Noonday Press.

Langer, S. 1976, 1957. *Problems of Art*. New York: Charles Scribner's Sons.

———. 1960, 1942. *Philosophy in a New Key*. Cambridge, MA: Harvard University Press.

Lave, J., and E. Wegner. 1991. *Situated Cognition: Legitimate Peripheral Participation*. New York: Cambridge University Press.

Lewis, O. 1961. *The Children of Sanchez: The Autobiography of a Mexican Family*. New York: Random House.

Lightfoot, S. 1983. *The Good High School: Portraits of Character and Culture*. New York: Basic Books.

Lincoln, Y., and E. Guba. 1985. *Naturalistic Inquiry*. Beverly Hills: Sage.

Lortie, D. C. 1975. *School Teacher: A Psychological Study*. Chicago: University of Chicago Press.

Luftig, R. 1995. *The Schooled Mind: Do the Arts Make a Difference? Year 2*. Oxford, OH: Center for Human Development, Learning, and Teaching, Miami University.

———. 1993. *The Schooled Mind: Do the Arts Make a Difference?* Oxford, OH: Center for Human Development, Learning, and Teaching, Miami University.

Madsen, C. 1981. "Music Lessons and Books as Reinforcement Alternatives for an Academic Task." *Journal of Research in Music Education* 29 (2): 103–10.

Mager, R. 1962. *Preparing Instructional Objectives*. Palo Alto, CA: Fearon.

Maryland Alliance for Arts Education. 1995. *The Arts and Children: A Success Story*.

McKeon, R., ed. 1941. *The Basic Works of Aristotle*. New York: Random House.

Merleau-Ponty, M. 1962. *Phenomenology of Perception*. New York: Humanities Press.

Moore, B., and H. Caldwell. 1993. "Drama and Drawing for Narrative Writing in the Primary Grades." *Journal of Educational Research* 87 (2): 100–10.

Murfee, E. 1995. Eloquent Evidence: Arts at the Core of Learning. President's Committee on the Arts and Humanities.

Neisser, U. 1976. *Cognition and Reality*. Ithaca, NY: Cornell University Press.

Nisbett, R. 1976. *Sociology as an Art Form*. London: Oxford University Press.

Oliver, D. 1990. "Grounded Knowing: A Postmodern Perspective on Teaching and Learning." *Educational Leadership* 48 (1): 644–67.

Parlett, M., and D. Hamilton. 1977. *Introduction to Illuminative Evaluation*. Cardiff-by-the-Sea, CA: Pacific Soundings.

Peirce, C. S. 1960. *Collected Papers.* Edited by C. Hartshorn and P. Weiss. Cambridge, MA: Harvard University Press.

Peshkin, A. 1986. *God's Choice: The Total World of a Fundamentalist Christian School.* Chicago: University of Chicago Press.

Peters, R. 1960. *Authority, Responsibility, and Education.* London: George Allen and Unwin.

Phillips, D. C. 1987. "Validity in Qualitative Research, or Why the Worry About Warrant Will Not Wane." *Education and Urban Society* 20 (1): 9–24.

———. 1983. "After the Wake: Postpositivistic Educational Thought." *Educational Researcher* (May).

Plato. 1941. *Republic.* Translated by B. Jowett. New York: Modern Library.

Polanyi, M. 1967. *The Tacit Dimension.* London: Routledge and Kegan Paul.

———. 1962, 1958. *Personal Knowledge: Toward a Post-critical Philosophy.* Chicago: University of Chicago Press.

Popham, W. J. 1972. "Must All Objectives Be Behavioral?" Educational Leadership (April): 605–608.

Popper, K. 1968. *The Logic of Scientific Discovery.* New York: Harper & Row.

Powell, A. G., E. Farrar, and D. K. Cohen. 1985. *The Shopping Mall High School: Winners and Losers in the Educational Marketplace.* Boston: Houghton Mifflin.

Read, H. 1944, 1958. *Education Through Art.* London: Pantheon.

Reimer, B. 1989. *A Philosophy of Music Education.* 2d ed. Englewood Cliffs, NJ: Prentice-Hall.

Resnick, L. 1989. *Toward the Thinking Curriculum: Current Cognitive Research.* Alexandria, VA: Association for Supervision and Curriculum Development.

"Restructuring California Education: A Design for Public Education in the Twenty-first Century." Recommendations to the California Business Round Table. 1988. Berkeley, CA: B. W. Associates.

Rico, G. L. 1983. *Writing the Natural Way.* Los Angeles: J. P. Tarcher.

Ricoeur, P. 1981. *Hermeneutics and the Human Sciences.* New York: Cambridge University Press.

Rist, R. 1972. *The Invisible Children.* Cambridge, MA: Harvard University Press.

Rorty, R. 1979. *Philosophy and the Mirror of Nature.* Princeton, NJ: Princeton University Press.

Rosenshine, B. 1976. "Classroom Instruction." In *The Psychology of Teaching Methods: Seventy-fifth Yearbook of the Natural Society for the Study of Education,* edited by N. Gage. Chicago: University of Chicago Press.

Ryle, G. 1949. *The Concept of Mind.* London: Hutchinson's University Library.

Schaff, A. 1973. *Language and Cognition.* Edited by R. S. Cohen. New York: McGraw-Hill.

Schoen, D. A. 1983. *The Reflective Practitioner: How Professionals Think in Action.* New York: Basic Books.

Schwab, J. J. 1969. "The Practical: A Language for Curriculum." *School Review* 78 (4): 1–24.

Scriven, M. 1967. *The Methodology of Evaluation.* AERA Monograph Series, Perspectives on Curriculum Evaluation. Chicago: Rand McNally.

Sergiovanni, T. J. 1983. *Supervision.* 3d ed. New York: McGraw-Hill.

Shepard, R. 1990. *Mind Sights.* New York: Freeman.

———. 1982. *Mental Images and Their Transformation.* Cambridge, MA: MIT Press.

Shulman, L. S. 1987. "Knowledge and Teaching: Foundations of the New Reform." *Harvard Educational Review* 57 (1): 1–22.

Singer, M. 1991. Sound, Image, and Word in the Curriculum: The Making of Historical Sense. Doctoral dissertation, Stanford University.

Sizer, T. 1984. *Horace's Compromise: The Dilemma of the American High School*. Boston: Houghton Mifflin.

Smith, L., and W. Geoffrey. 1968. *The Complexities of an Urban Classroom*. New York: Holt, Rinehart & Winston.

Snow, R. 1997. "Aptitudes and Symbol Systems in Adaptive Classrooms." *Phi Delta Kappan* 78 (5): 354–60.

———. 1996. "Individual Differences and the Design of Educational Programs." *American Psychologist* 41 (10): 1029–39.

Stake, R. 1975. *Evaluating the Arts in Education: A Responsive Approach*. Columbus, OH: Merrill.

Statt, D. A. 1981. *Dictionary of Psychology*. New York. Barnes and Noble.

Stodolsky, S. S. 1988. *The Subject Matters: Classroom Activity in Math and Social Studies*. Chicago: University of Chicago Press.

Tennyson, A. 1870. *The Poetical Works of Alfred Tennyson*. New York: Harper.

Thorndike, E. L. 1914. *Educational Psychology*. New York: Teachers College Press.

———. 1910. "The Contribution of Psychology to Education." *Journal of Educational Psychology* 1: 5–12.

Tolstoy, L. 1899. *What Is Art?* New York: Crowell.

Tom, A. 1984. *Teaching as a Moral Craft*. New York: Longman.

Toulmin, S. 1990. *Cosmopolis: The Hidden Agenda of Modernity*. New York: Free Press.

Tyack, D. 1974. *The One Best System*. Cambridge, MA: Harvard University Press.

USA Research. 1984. *A Nation at Risk: The Full Account*. Cambridge, MA: USA Research.

United States Department of Education. 1986. *What Works: Research About Teaching and Learning*. Washington, DC: U. S. Department of Education.

———. 1991. *America 2000*. Washington, DC: U. S. Department of Education.

von Wright, H. 1971. *Explanation and Understanding*. Ithaca, NY: Cornell University Press.

Waller, W. W. 1932. *The Sociology of Teaching*. New York: Wiley.

Welch, N., and A. Greene. 1995. *Schools, Communities, and the Arts: A Research Compendium*. Tempe, AZ: Morrison Institute for Public Policy, Arizona State University.

Wiesel, E. 1969. *Night*. New York: Avon.

Wiggens, G. 1989. "A True Test: Toward Authentic and Equitable Assessment." *Phi Delta Kappan* 71 (9): 703–13.

Willis, P. 1977. *Learning to Labor*. Lexington, MA: D. C. Heath.

Wittrock, M., ed. 1986. *Third Handbook on Research on Teaching*. New York: Macmillan.

Wolcott, H. 1984. *The Man in the Principal's Office*. Prospect Heights, IL: Waveland Press.

Yerkes, R. 1929. *Army Mental Tests*. New York: Henry Holt.

Index

abstraction
  cognitive functions of, 74–75
  intelligence and, 39
  language and, 63–64
academic achievement
  arts experience and, 87–100
  effect of rewards on, 90
  motivation and, 94
  research on, 88–94
academic institutions, schools as, 160
accountability movement, 138, 155
acculturation, 3, 26. *See also* culture
action research, 112
  teacher empowerment and, 164
adaptation, by teachers, 203–4
aesthetic
  common function of, 34
  comprehension of, 96
  consummatory function of, 42–43
  form and, 36–38
  function of, 36
  lack of attention to, 39–42
  modes of knowing, 32–33, 32–43
  order, 37–39
  referential function of, 42–43
  relation to larger intellectual community, 142
  student awareness of, 97–98
aesthetic literacy, 37
affective subjects
  arts as, 1
  marginalization of, 115n
alternative paradigms, 103–15
  conceptual implications, 103–6
  defined, 103–4
  diversity and, 113–14
  educational aims and, 112–14
  educational policy and, 110–12
  educational research and, 108–9
  evaluative methods, 108–9
  policy implications, 109–12

practice implications, 106–9
resistances to change and, 114–15
scientific method and, 104
ambiguity
  tolerance for, 99
  truth and, 122
  value of, 126
America 2000, 70, 77, 175, 217
Ancillary Outcomes of Art Education, 95–97
Apple, Michael, 115n., 172
Aristotle, 83, 108–9, 135
Arnheim, Rudolf, 61, 63, 71, 79
art forms. *See* forms of representation
artistry
  attention to, 5
  in educational research, 153–54
  in research, 149–54
  role of, 110–11
  in social sciences, 152–54
  theory and, 6
artistry in art, 149–52
  awareness of particularity, 152
  coherence, 152
  defined, 150
  features, 150–51
artistry in teaching
  developing, 209–12
  features, 65–67
  importance of, 197–98
artists
  creation of, 35
  motivation of, 36
arts
  as affective activities, 1
  artistry in, 149–52
  coherence in, 37
  contributions of, 56, 81–85
  defined, 88
  devaluation of, 59–60
  differences among, 64–65

arts *(continued)*
  educational role, 55–56
  facilitating learning through, 76
  form created through, 34–35
  functions of, 152
  human development role, 77–86
  literacy in, 16–17
  marginalization of, 70, 75–76, 81
  meaning of, 149
  mental engagement and, 2
  misunderstanding of role of, 77, 85
  neglect of, 28
  order in, 37–39
  perception through, 82
  science *vs.,* 154
  as source of pleasure, 58
  task assessment, 146–47
  value of, 2, 95
Arts Bases Outcomes of Art Education, 95–97
arts education, 1
  academic achievement as justification for, 88–89,
    94–95
  ancillary outcomes, 95–97
  arts based outcomes, 95–97
  arts related outcomes, 95–97
  contributions of, 95–99, 97–99
  justification for, 97
  marginalization of, 107, 115n
  value of, 99–100
arts experience. *See also* experience
  academic achievement and, 87–100
  attitudes promoted by, 94
  defined, 88
  effects of, 91–94
  motivational effects, 94
  research design, 92–94
  transfer of learning through, 92, 96
  value for children, 116–17
Arts Related Outcomes of Arts Education, 95–97
art works
  context of, 96
  features of, 150–51
  as noncognitive, 48
  responding to, 96
  understanding personal side of, 96
  "wide-awakeness in," 150–51
assessment, 132–48. *See also* evaluation
  allowing multiple solutions, 144–45
  art experience research design and, 93
  authentic, 137, 216
  defined, 132
  diversity and, 148
  features of, 140–48
  forms of representation and, 147–48
  functions of, 138–40
  of group performance, 143–44
  historical influences, 132–38, 137–38
  intellectual community values and, 142–43
  of reasoning process, 141–42
  relevance to nonschool tasks, 140–41
  standardization in, 30
  transfer of learning, 145–46
  of understanding of relations between ideas, 142
  of understanding of whole, 146–47
Atkin, Mike, 112
authentic assessment, 127, 137, 216

"back to basics," 138, 162
bees, as architects, 25
behavioral objectives movement, 155, 177
Berliner, D. C., 200
Bernstein, Basil, 107, 117–18, 170
Bloom, Alan, 21
body knowledge, 110
Bourdieu, Pierre, 159
brain, mind *vs.,* 23–24, 45, 78
Bronowsky, Jacob, 14
Broudy, H., 201
Bruner, Jerome, 11, 125, 142, 208
Building a Case for Art Education: An Annotated
  Bibliography of Major Research, 89–90

cadence of language, 33
Caldwell, H., 90
canonical images, 71
Cassirer, Ernst, 6, 18
categorization, perception *vs.,* 82
celebration, 21
celebration of thinking, 21–31
  efficiency and, 22
  value of, 30–31
change, resistance to, 114–15
charts, as forms of representation, 71, 120
children at risk, 58–59
Civil War, teaching about, 107–8
Clark, C., 200
classification, language and, 14
"classification code," 107
classrooms
  cohesiveness of, 194
  culture of, 191
  diversity in, 191
  ethnographic studies, 136–37
  rule-governed activities, 191
  self-regulation in, 191
  standardized management procedures, 136
  teacher perception and interpretation of events in,
    199
coaches, for teachers, 211
cognition. *See also* thinking
  activity types, 79
  alternative paradigms and, 106
  broadening the definition of, 62–63
  connative aspects of, 98
  defined, 106
  perception as, 130n
  sensory system functions, 12–13
  visual learning functions, 74–75
cognitive artifacts, 45–46
cognitive development
  forms of representation and, 7–8, 47–48, 50
  influence of curriculum on, 51
  potential, 16
  sensory system and, 12–15
cognitive hooks, 50
cognitive pluralism, 104–5
cognitive psychology, 62
coherence
  in artistically crafted works, 152
  in classroom culture, 191
  creation of, 37
  need for, 38
cohesiveness, classroom, 194

collection-type curriculums, 170, 172
computer technology, forms of representation and, 120
conation, 5
concepts
  defined, 71
  formation of, 120
  intentions and, 120
concrete poets, 10
concrete universals, 81
connative aspects of cognition, 98
constituency, fallacy of, 201
constructive neglect, 153
consummatory function of the aesthetic, 42–43
content
  connecting form to, 82
  defined, 82
content validity, of evaluation, 145–46
conventions
  forms of representation, 130n
  standards and, 181–82
creative drama, 90
criteria, *vs.* standards, 182–83
criterion-referenced evaluation, 127, 130n, 143–44
Cronbach, L., 112
cultural literacy, 19
  alternative paradigms and, 113
culturally referenced curricular balance, 107, 113
"cultural reproduction," 159
culture
  anthropological sense of, 52
  art forms and content and, 97–98
  assumptions of, 3
  biological sense of, 52
  classroom ethnography and, 136–37
  cognitive artifacts, 45–46
  defined, 52
  forms of representation and, 52, 120–21
  imagination and, 25–26
  intelligence and, 119
  role of, 105
  schools, 4–5, 77–78, 168, 191
  teacher-created, 191
cummings, e. e., 10
curricular balance
  culturally referenced, 107, 113
  individually referenced, 113
  personally referenced, 107
curricular dimension of educational reform, 171–72, 215
curriculum
  aesthetic values of, 40–41
  art experience research design and, 93
  boundaries among subject fields, 107
  cognitive competency and, 51
  collection-type, 170, 172
  common, specification of, 21
  disciplinary structures, 215
  facilitating learning through the arts, 76
  fragmentation of, 41, 171–72
  functions of, 40
  hidden, 204
  integration of, 107
  intended, 172
  learning opportunities and, 16
  as a mind-altering device, 13, 23, 64, 105, 117–18

multiple forms of representation and, 29–30
  null, 171
  operational, 172
  quality of, 139
  relationships among fields, 215
  standardization of, 28
  time allocated for subjects, 77
  uniformity in, 180
curriculum development
  as educational research, 125
  rational educational planning model and, 67
curriculum reform. *See also* educational reform
  history of, 175, 177
  school reform as, 2
curriculum reform movement (1960s), 175, 177
  aims of, 134–35
  evaluation, 135
  test scores and, 138

dance, 51
de-centering perception, 130n
departmentalization, educational reform and, 169–70
detachment, reflective thought and, 80–81
developmental psychology, 61–62
development rates, variability in, 184–85
Dewey, John, 61, 63, 73, 80, 82, 105, 118–19, 130n, 136, 182, 183
differential psychology, 62
differentiation, 142–43
disciplines, artificial barriers between, 165–66
discovery, 17–18
  opportunities for, 27
  role of the arts in, 85
discursive knowledge, 73
dispositional outcome, 5
dissertations, forms of representation for, 127
distance, reflective thought and, 80–81
distillation, 74–75
diversity
  alternative paradigms and, 113–14
  assessment and, 148
  classroom, 191
  need for, 206
  in teaching, 209
doctoral students, forms of representation used by, 127
drama, 90–91
Dreeben, R., 204
Duchamp, Marcel, 151
Du Pont, S., 90

earning how to learn, 142
ecology of schools, 155–56, 168–69, 212–13
"edification," 123
editing, 17, 27
education
  aims of, 35, 44–45
  artistry in, 5
  defined, 7
  outcomes of, 67–68
  problem resolution in, 5
  purpose of, 141
  scientific method and, 134
  strategic aspirations of, 182
educational connoisseurship, 67, 168, 189, 197, 211, 216

educational criticism, 168, 189, 211–12
educational equity, 18
  diversity and, 113–14
  forms of representation and, 50, 52
educational parity, alternative paradigms and, 106–7
educational policy
  alternative paradigms, 110–12
  effects on education, 109–10
educational reform. *See also* curriculum reform
  conservative expectations and, 162–63
  constraints, 203–5
  curricular dimension, 171–72
  defining, 1, 2
  dimensions of, 169–74
  ecology of schools and, 168–69, 213
  evaluative dimension, 172–73, 216
  factors limiting, 157–67
  failures of, 217
  familiar teaching routine and, 158–59
  history, 155, 157
  images of teacher roles and, 158
  inservice education and, 161–62
  intentional dimension, 169–70, 213
  pedagogical dimension, 172–73, 216
  piecemeal efforts, 166–67
  potential for, 155–56, 217
  school norms and, 159–60
  standardized achievement testing and, 167
  structural dimension, 170–71, 213–15
  structural fragmentation and, 165–66
  teacher commitment to, 163
  teacher implementation of, 163–65
  teacher isolation and, 160–61
  top-down, 163
educational research. *See also* research methods
  action research, 112
  aims of, 151–52
  alternative paradigms, 108–9, 111
  artistically crafted, 149–54, 153–54
  arts experience and academic achievement, 88–94
  conventional role of, 111
  curriculum development and, 125
  educational significance, 94
  effects on teachers, 201–2
  expectations for, 195–203
  experimental and control groups, 93
  forms of understanding and, 125
  future of, 116–31
  limitations of, 207–9
  qualitative, 102, 168–69
  recommended design features, 92–94
  scientific experimentation *vs.*, 101
  student diversity and evaluation, 127
  teacher interest in conducting, 164
  use of, 112
  value of, 129
educational theory. *See* theory
efficiency, in learning, 22
efficiency movement, 133, 136, 177–78
Eisner, Elliot
  experience influencing, 188–89
  influence of visual arts on, 57–61
  influences on, 4–6, 116–17
Elliott, John, 112
empirical studies of teaching, 135–36
Enlightenment, 132, 133

environment, expressive features, 96
equity, forms of representation and, 50, 52
Ethics (Aristotle), 108–9
ethnography, 66–67, 136–37
evaluation. *See also* assessment
  aims of, 135
  alternative paradigms, 108–9
  artistic perspective on, 68
  assessment *vs.*, 137–38
  authentic forms of, 216
  content validity, 145–46
  criterion-referenced, 127, 130n
  defined, 132
  development of, 135
  educational content and, 172
  history of, 132–38
  norm-referenced, 130n
  of teachers, 201–2
evaluative dimension of educational reform, 172–73, 216
"excellence movement," 175
experience. *See also* arts experience
  concept formation and, 120
  construction of meaning and, 117
  culture and, 120–21
  forms of representation and, 123–24
  meaning and, 120–22
  perception and, 34, 188
  value of, 190–91
expert perception, 201
expressiveness
  forms of representation, 130n
  role of the arts, 84–85
externalization, 27

fallacy of constituency, 201
feedback, for teachers, 139, 162, 203, 211, 212, 214
feeling
  knowledge *vs.*, 115n
  language forms and, 11
  reflective thought and, 80–81
fiction, 81
flexibility, value of, 83–84
form
  aesthetic properties of, 36–38
  connecting to content, 82
  defined, 82
forming, 35–36
formmaking
  through scientific inquiry, 34–35
  through the arts, 34–35
forms of meaning, 122–25
forms of representation, 44–53
  access to, 16
  with ambiguous referents, 121–22
  artistic treatment of, 149
  assessment methods and, 147–48
  cognitive development and, 7–8, 47–48, 50
  combining, 48–49
  competency in use of, 51–52
  contributions of, 2
  culture and, 97–98, 120–21
  curriculum and, 29–30
  defined, 44, 96
  for doctoral students, 127
  educational equity and, 50, 52

expectations for, 109
experience and, 123–24
functions of, 18, 26–29
influence of, 2, 34, 46–47, 48
integration of, 127–28
making sense of, 7
marginalizing, 16
meaning and, 119–20, 121, 130n
student creation of, 98–99
student skills in, 126–27
syntax, 28–29
understanding and, 126, 127–28
use of, 51
using wide array of, 126–27
value of, 106
forms of understanding
educational research and, 125
forms of meaning and, 124–25
forms of representation and, 127–28
poetic, 123–24
fragmentation
of curriculum, 41, 171–72
resolving problems of, 215
structural, educational reform and, 165–66
Frankenthaler, Helen, 151
Freud, Sigmund, 133–34

Gage, N., 197
gain scores, 93
Gardner, Howard, 24, 62, 105, 107, 118–19
gate-keeping function, of assessment, 139
Geertz, Clifford, 66–67, 136
Geisteswissenschaften, 208
generalizations, 63
about teaching effectiveness, 196–97
methods, 81
partitioning, 198
from qualitative research, 101–2
teacher artistry and, 197
uses of, 196–97, 201
Geoffrey, William, 136
"getting in touch," 117
goals
alternative paradigms and, 112–14
flexible, 83–84
Goals 2000, 155, 175
Gombrich, E. H., 2, 48
Goodlad, John I., 172
Goodman, Nelson, 16, 17, 18, 63, 96, 120, 146, 188
graphics, as forms of representation, 71, 120
Greene, Maxine, 150
grounded knowing, 141
group performance, assessment of, 143–44

Hamblen, Karen, 92
hearing, 118
hidden curriculum, 204
hierarchies of knowledge, 38
higher-order thinking, standards and, 183
Hirsch, E. D., 19, 21
history
forms of representation and, 125–26
as the past, 126
as text, 125–26
Hubbard, Charles, 197
Hughes, Langston, 124

human development. *See also* cognitive development
individual differences in, 184–85
role of the arts in, 77–86
use and development of the mind, 117–18

ideas, understanding relationships between, 142
ignorance
primary, 161
secondary, 161
imagination
as arts education outcome, 99
extrapolation, 153
importance of, 24–26
role of, 118
role of the arts in, 85
individual accomplishment, group performance and,
143–44
individual differences
development rates, 184–85
generalizations and, 196–97
national standards and, 180
observing, 190–91
proclivities, 107
promoting, 113–14
individually referenced curricular balance, 113
individuation, 63
innovation, standards and, 181–82
inquiry, joy of, 36
inservice education, 115n, 161–62, 203, 210
"insider" knowledge, 209
institutions
milieu created by, 4–5
norms, educational reform and, 159–60
instructional cues, 193
intellectual community, understanding ideas as part
of, 142
intellectual functioning, Plato's hierarchy of, 79
intellectual institutions, schools as, 160
intelligence
knowledge and, 38–39
language and, 22–23
logic and, 79–80
multiple, 24, 62, 105, 119
myths about, 78–81
sensory experience as, 79
talent *vs.,* 39–40
intelligible world, Plato's analysis of, 79
intended curriculum, 172
intentional dimension of educational reform, 169–70,
213
intentions, concept formation and, 120
intuition, role of, 110–11
inventive work, standards and, 184
isolation of teachers, 160–61, 166, 203, 211, 212
iterative forms of learning, 49

Jackson, Philip, 136, 200
James, Henry, 123
James, William, 126

Kaplan, Stanley, 22
knowledge
aesthetic modes of knowing, 32–43
cultural beliefs about, 40
differentiated, 142–43
discursive, 73

knowledge *(continued)*
feeling *vs.,* 115n
grounded, 141
hierarchies of, 38
"insider," 209
intelligence and, 38–39, 39–40
language and, 22–23
myths about, 78–81
nondiscursive, 73
paradigmatic, 208
positivist view, 60
practical, 135
situated, 65
tacit, 208
through rationality, 38–39
through sensory information, 38
transmission of, alternative paradigms and, 113
Kollwitz, Käthe, 51
Kubie, Lawrence, 153

Lang, Dorothea, 151
Langer, Susanne, 18, 24, 42–43, 61, 73, 123
language
aesthetic values of, 41
complexity of, *vs.* visual images, 72
as cues to referents, 15
forms of, 10
homogenizing effect of, 14
inadequacy of, 45
knowledge and, 22–23
literary, 33–34, 123
propositional, 10, 73
as a symbolic device, 78–79
thought and, 22, 78–79, 106
language forms
functions of, 10–12
narrative, 11–12
paradigmatic, 11–12
Lave, J., 92
learning
biological basis for, 23–24
facilitating through the arts, 76
iterative forms of, 49
multiple forms of, 15–17
situated, 141
life-drawing class, assessment in, 146–47
literacy, 9–19
acquisition of, 11
aesthetic, 37
in the arts, 16–17
cognitive functions of, 9
defined, 9, 52
encoding and decoding meaning as, 7
language forms and, 11–12
meaning and, 12
multiple forms of, 9–10, 15–17, 19, 29–30
literary meaning, language and, 10
literature
as alternative paradigm, 105
artistry in, 151
literary features of, 33–34
value of, 122–23
Luftig, Richard, 91

Madsen, C., 90
Mager, Robert, 177

mathematics
arts experience and, 91–92
core beliefs, 133
inadequacy of, 45
intelligence and, 39–40
language of, 10
rewards and, 90
meaning
construction of, 7, 117
encoding and decoding, 7, 9
experience and, 117, 120–22
forms of representation and, 119–20, 121
language and, 121–22
literacy and, 12
of meaning, 121
modes of treatment and, 119
rationality and, 122
through visual learning, 73, 75
variety in, 73
visual qualities and, 71
memory, cognitive process, 24–25
metaphor, 72–73, 109
mimesis, 130n
mind
as a cultural achievement, 105
influence of experience on, 45–51
myths about, 78–81
use and development of, 117–18
vs. brain, 23–24, 45, 78
minding, 24
modes of treatment, meaning and, 119
Monet, Claude, 74
Moore, B., 90
motivation, academic achievement and, 94
multiple-choice tests
limitations of, 147
objectivity and, 144
multiple intelligences, 24, 62
alternative paradigms and, 105
culture and, 119
musical cognition, 16–17

narrative language, 11–12
narrative understanding, 208
National Endowment for the Arts, 90
national outcomes, 207
national standards
concerns about, 179–87
emphasis on, 206–7
individual differences and, 180
Naturwissenschaften, 208
negative reinforcement, 194
neologisms, 10–11
Nevelson, Louise, 96
nondiscursive knowledge, 73
norm-referenced evaluation, 130n
norms
constraints of, 204
persistence of, 159–60
null curriculum, 171

objective tests, limitations of, 141
objectivity
ontological, 144
procedural, 144
ontological objectivity, 144

operational curriculum, 172
order, need for, 37–39
organicism, 2

painting, 59
    cognition and, 60–61
    learning process, 118
    watercolor, 47–48
paradigmatic knowledge, 208
paradigmatic language, 11–12
parity of subject fields, 106–7
particularity, awareness of, 152
patterns in visual learning, 73
pedagogical dimension of educational reform,
        172–73, 216
pedagogical routines
    attachment to, 158–59
    automatic, 193–94
Peircian triadic relationship, 121
perception
    categorization and, 82
    cognitive character of, 130n
    cognitive development and, 13–14
    de-centering, 130n
    emotion and, 80–81
    experience and, 34, 188
    expert, 201
    forms of representation and, 48
    lack of attention to, 63–64
    selectivity of, 74
Perot, Ross, 71, 120
personal interpretation, 82
personally referenced curriculum balance,
        107
philosopher king, 74
phronesis, 135
Piaget, Jean, 13, 60
Plato, 23, 38, 39, 60, 74, 79
pluralism. See also diversity
    assessment and, 140
poetry
    as alternative paradigm, 105
    concrete, 10
    experiencing, 119–20
    extra-logical features of, 80
    as form of understanding, 123–24
    intelligence and, 79
    language and, 10
Polanyi, Michael, 61, 64, 106, 201
policy, 109. See also educational policy
Popham, James, 177
positive reinforcement, 194
positivism, 60
practical knowledge, 62, 135
preactive, interactive teaching, 200
pre-conscious, 153
primary ignorance, 161
problem solving
    assessment of, 141, 146
    lessons from the arts, 82, 84
    preparation for nonschool tasks, 141
    standards and, 184
procedural objectivity, 144
productive diversity, evaluation and, 68
professional vision, for teachers, 214–15
propositional language, 10, 73

propositions, knowledge and, 22
psychology
    cognitive, 62
    core beliefs, 133
    development, 61–62
    development of, 133
    differential, 62

qualitative research, 115n
qualitative standards, 180–81
qualitative thinking, 110–11, 117

rational educational planning model, 67
rationality
    broad concept of, 83
    intelligence and, 80
    knowledge through, 38–39
    meaning and, 122
Read, Sir Herbert, 34–35, 115n
reading scores
    arts experience and, 91–92
    creative drama on, 90
reasoning
    assessment of, 141–42
    as measure of intelligence, 79–80
recognition, 63
referential function of the aesthetic, 42–43
referents
    ambiguous, 121–22
    for schemata, 200–201
reflective teaching, 166–67
reflectivity, 110
reinforcement
    negative, 194
    positive, 194
relationships
    of aesthetic to larger intellectual community,
        142
    among subject fields, 215
    between ideas, 142
    in visual learning, 73
representation
    as cognitive function of abstraction, 74
    defined, 118
    discovery through, 18
    stabilization through, 17
    symbolic, 74
representation, forms of. See forms of representation
research methods. See also educational research
    improving, 3
    issues in, 93
    results and, 1, 2
resource-rich environments, 49
responsive evaluation, 130n
responsive outcomes, 130n
restructuring, 165
rewards, 90
rightness, sense of, 38
rightness of fit, 96, 145–46
Rorty, Richard, 123
routines
    classroom culture, 191
    pedagogical, 193–94
rule-abiding activities, 28
rule-governed activities, 191
Ryle, Gilbert, 118

scaffolding, 50
schemata
    creation of, 201
    referents for, 200–201
    in teaching, 199–200
Schoen, D. A., 200
Scholastic Aptitude Test (SAT), 39, 139
school-based management, 155
school restructuring, 165
schools
    conservative expectations for, 162–63
    constraints to change, 203–5
    culture of, 4–5, 77–78, 121, 168, 191
    ecology of, 155–56, 168–69, 212–13
    as intellectual *vs.* academic institutions, 160
    as living systems, 167–69
    norms of, 159–60
    as robust institutions, 157–67
    structural dimensions of reform, 213–15
    structural fragmentation of, 165–66
Schwab, Joseph, 5–6, 134, 136
science
    aesthetic features of, 83
    artistry in, 5–6, 152–54
    art *vs.*, 154
    creation of coherence in, 37
    joy of inquiry in, 36
    language of, 10
    meaning in, art *vs.*, 105
    overemphasis on, 81
    teaching as, 195–96
scientific inquiry, form created through, 34–35
scientific management, 133, 136, 137, 177–78
scientific method, 132
    alternative paradigms and, 104
    influence of, 134
    as only means of generalization, 81
secondary ignorance, 161
self-esteem, 194
self-realization, 115n
self-regulation, 191
sense-making, 38
sensory experience
    as *cognitio inferior*, 70
    cognitive functions of, 12–15
    intelligence and, 23–24, 79
    knowledge derived from, 38
    learning and, 76
    value of, 49
sharing, communication as, 17–18
Shulman, L. S., 198
Singer, Marcy, 126
situated knowledge, 65
situated learning, 141
slang, 10–11
Smith, Eva, 58
Smith, Louis, 136
Snow, R., 51, 62
socialization, to norms, 204
social sciences
    artistry in, 152–54
    core beliefs, 133
    development of, 132–33, 137
    structures of appropriation in, 188
Spectra, 91–92
Sputnik, curriculum reform and, 157, 175

Stake, Robert, 130n
standardization
    assessment and, 30
    of curriculum, 28
    problems of, 21–22
standardized achievement tests
    appeal of, 134
    educational reform based on, 167
    practices, 55
    relevance of, 169–70
    remoteness from nonschool tasks, 140–41
standards, 175–87
    of appropriate behavior, 159–60
    arguments in favor of, 178–79
    characteristics of, 182–83
    concerns about, 179–87
    criteria *vs.*, 182–83
    definitions of, 176–77
    emphasis on, 206–7
    individual variability and, 184–85
    national, 179
    preoccupation with, 186–87
    qualitative, 180–81
    quantitative, 181
    teachers and, 179
stimulation, need for, 37
Stodolsky, S. S., 168, 198
strategic aspirations of education, 182
structural dimension of educational reform, 170–71, 213–15
structural fragmentation, 165–66
structure-seeking activities, 28
structures of appropriation, in social sciences, 188
subject fields
    boundaries among, 107, 170
    educational uses of, 179–80
    intellectual community and, 142
    parity of, 106–7
    plurality of approaches to, 198
    rethinking relationships among, 215
surrealist art, 65
symbolic representation. *See also* forms of representation
    abstraction and, 74
    invention of symbols for, 74
syntax, of forms of representation, 28–29

tacit knowledge
    theory *vs.*, 208
talent, intelligence *vs.*, 39–40
Taylor, Frederick, 133, 177–78
Taylorism, 110
teacher education, 206–18
    inservice education, 210
    theory and, 207–9
    university education programs, 210, 212
teachers
    adaptation by, 203–4
    artificial barriers between, 165–66
    attachment to pedagogical routine, 158–59
    coaches for, 211
    common culture created by, 191
    competence of, 206
    educational reform and, 158, 163–65
    educational research and, 164, 201–2
    empowerment of, 164–65

teachers *(continued)*
  evaluation of, 110, 201–2
  feedback, 162, 203, 211, 212, 214
  flexible roles for, 170–71
  instructional cues provided by, 193
  interaction with colleagues, 211
  internalized images of, 158
  isolation of, 160–61, 166, 203, 211, 212
  pedagogical thinking by, 193–94
  perception and interpretation of classroom events
    by, 199
  professional vision for, 214–15
  standards and, 179
  temperaments of, 193
teaching
  as art, 65–67, 197–98, 209–12
  art experience research design and, 93
  context of, 203–5
  context of action, 200
  context of planning, 200
  diversity in, 209
  educational policy and, 110
  empirical studies of, 135–36
  generalizations about effectiveness, 196–97
  intentionality, 110
  as lifelong professional activity, 210–11
  limitations of theory, 207–9
  objectives, 110
  preactive, interactive, 200
  reflective, 166–67
  research expectations, 195–203
  research-proven behaviors, 201–2
  role of intuition in, 110–11
  schemata in, 199–200
  science of, 195–96
  secondary ignorance of, 161
  standards and, 184
  turnover in, 215
temperaments, of teachers, 193
temperature-taking function of assessment, 139
tempo of language, 33
testing. *See also* assessment; evaluation
  accountability defined by, 138
  alternative paradigms, 109
  limitations of, 141–47
  multiple-choice, 144, 147
textbooks, student views of, 126
theory
  aesthetic features of, 83
  artistry and, 6
  limitations of, 207–9
  vs. tacit knowledge, 208
thinking. *See also* cognition
  biological basis for, 23–24
  celebration of, 21–31
  form of representation and, 46–47
  language and, 22, 78–79, 106

writing and, 57
third-grade classes, observational research, 189–95
Third Handbook of Research and Teaching, 65
Thorndike, Edward L., 92, 133–34, 195–96
time allocation, subject important and, 77
time off task, 199
time on task, 199
transfer of learning
  assessment of, 145–46
  through arts education, 92, 96
truth
  ambiguity and, 122
  language forms and, 11
Tuchman, Barbara, 32–34

university admission requirements, 55–56
U.S. National Assessment of Educational Progress, 139

values
  educational reform and, 160
  school support of, 4–5
verbal skills, intelligence and, 39–40
vernacular poetics, 10–11
visible world, Plato's analysis of, 79
visual arts
  artistry in, 151
  cognitive skills, 17
  differences among, 65
  effect on Eisner, 57–61
  information presented through, 73
  language *vs.,* 72
  as representational, 71–72
  simplification through, 72
  uses of, 75
visual learning, 70–76
  abstraction and, 74
  cognitive functions of, 74–75
  creating meaning through, 71–72, 73
  defined, 71
  example, 72
  meaning through, 71
  patterns and relationships in, 73
visual literacy, 75–76

wait time, 199
Waller, Willard, 135–36
watercolor painting, 47–48
Whitehead, Alfred North, 36, 142
"wide-awakeness," 150–51
Wiesel, Elie, 122–23
words, meaning and, 15
writing
  cognitive skills, 17
  improving, 90–91
  thought process and, 57

Yerkes, Robert, 134

"Rethinking Literacy" originally printed in *Educational Horizons* 69 (3), Spring 1991. "The Celebration of Thinking" originally printed in *Educational Horizons* 66 (1), Fall 1987. "Cognition and Representation: A Way to Pursue the American Dream?" originally printed in *Phi Delta Kappan* 78 (5), January 1997. "What the Arts Taught Me About Education" originally printed in *Reflections from the Heart of Educational Inquiry,* edited by George Willis and William Schubert. New York: State University of New Yori Press, 1991. "The Education of Vision" originally printed in *Educational Horizons* 71 (2), Winter 1993. "The Misunderstood Role of the Arts in Human Development" originally printed in *Phi Delta Kappan* 73 (8), April 1992. "Does Experience in the Arts Boost Academic Achievement?" originally printed in *Art Education* 51 (1), January 1998. "Reshaping Assessment in Education: Some Criteria in Search of Practice" originally printed in *Journal of Curriculum Studies* 25 (3), 1993. "What Artistically Crafted Research Can Help Us Understand About Schools" originally printed in *Educational Theory* 45 (1), Winter 1995. "Educational Reform and the Ecology of Schooling" originally printed in *Teachers College Record* 93 (4), Summer 1992. "Standards for American Schools: Help or Hindrance?" originally printed in *Phi Delta Kappan* 76 (10), June 1995. "Preparing Teachers for Schools of the 21st Century" originally printed in *Peabody Journal of Education* 70 (3), Spring 1995.